ONE WEEK LOAN

Crime Prevention and Security Management

Series Editor: **Martin Gill**

Titles include:

Mark Button
DOING SECURITY
Critical Reflections and an Agenda for Change

Paul Ekblom
CRIME PREVENTION, SECURITY AND COMMUNITY SAFETY USING THE 5IS
FRAMEWORK

Janice Goldstraw-White
WHITE-COLLAR CRIME
Accounts of Offending Behaviour

Bob Hoogenboom
THE GOVERNANCE OF POLICING AND SECURITY
Ironies, Myths and Paradoxes

Kate Moss
BALANCING LIBERTY AND SECURITY
Human Rights, Human Wrongs

Kate Moss
SECURITY AND LIBERTY
Restriction by Stealth

Adam White
THE POLITICS OF PRIVATE SECURITY
Regulation, Reform and Re-Legitimation

Forthcoming:

Joshua Bamfield
SHOPPING AND CRIME

Crime Prevention and Security Management
Series Standing Order ISBN 978–0–230–01355–1 (hardback) 978–0–230–01356–8 (paperback)
(outside North America only)

You can receive future titles in this series as they are published by placing a standing order.
Please contact your bookseller or, in case of difficulty, write to us at the address below with
your name and address, the title of the series and one of the ISBNs quoted above.

Customer Services Department, Macmillan Distribution Ltd, Houndmills, Basingstoke,
Hampshire RG21 6XS, England

White-Collar Crime

Accounts of Offending Behaviour

Janice Goldstraw-White
Goldstraw-White Associates, UK

First published 2012 by
PALGRAVE MACMILLAN

Palgrave Macmillan in the UK is an imprint of Macmillan Publishers Limited, registered in England, company number 785998, of Houndmills, Basingstoke, Hampshire RG21 6XS.

Palgrave Macmillan in the US is a division of St Martin's Press LLC, 175 Fifth Avenue, New York, NY 10010.

Palgrave Macmillan is the global academic imprint of the above companies and has companies and representatives throughout the world.

Palgrave® and Macmillan® are registered trademarks in the United States, the United Kingdom, Europe and other countries

ISBN 978-0-230-58185-2

This book is printed on paper suitable for recycling and made from fully managed and sustained forest sources. Logging, pulping and manufacturing processes are expected to conform to the environmental regulations of the country of origin.

A catalogue record for this book is available from the British Library.

A catalogue record for this book is available from the Library of Congress.

10   9   8   7   6   5   4   3   2   1
21 20 19 18 17 16 15 14 13 12

Printed and bound in Great Britain by
CPI Antony Rowe, Chippenham and Eastbourne

To my late father – Derrick Warham

Contents

List of Tables and Figures

Tables

Figures

Acknowledgements

So many people have helped me to undertake the research for and the writing of this book, that it is impossible for me to acknowledge them all. Their names may be missing here, but I wish to thank those who have provided such guidance and support throughout this project.

I owe a particular debt of gratitude to Professor Martin Gill, for his faith and encouragement from the inception of this book, and to the helpful and patient staff at Palgrave Macmillan.

Special thanks also go to those scholars who have commented on my research for the book over the past few years, at conferences and elsewhere. In particular, I would like to thank Professor Susanne Karstedt, Professor Richard Sparks, Professor Tim Hope, Professor John Braithwaite, Professor Peter Grabosky and Dr Russell Smith, as well as former colleagues, including the late Professor Ellie Scrivens and Dr Katherine Birch.

I would also like to extend my thanks to family and friends for their moral and practical support throughout this research, especially Kerry Bush, Ludovica Campus, Laura Fletcher, Marlee Fletcher, Jon Godfrey, Aidan Goldstraw, Clare Kerr, Margaret Warham and John White. I am also grateful to Peter Barnes for copy-editing my text.

I am forever indebted to my husband Lee White for his unfailing love and support, and for the many ways he has helped me to complete this book by making sure the conditions were right for doing so.

Finally, I would like to thank the staff of the prisons I visited, for organising interviews, and the prisoners who gave their time to take part in the research – without them, this book would not of course have been possible.

Series Editor's Introduction

In this book Dr Janice Goldstraw-White discusses fraud from the perspective of different types of fraudster. Indeed, she devotes considerable space to identifying and evaluating types, based on motivation for and approaches to fraud as well as whether they are low-level or high-level fraudsters. Her sample includes men and, women (a much neglected group), who have committed a range of white-collar offences. As her findings highlight, there are gender differences in approaches to taking money dishonestly. This includes not just the reason for committing fraud, but also the way they perceive the offences and reflect on them afterwards and when in prison. Her hope, I am sure shared by many, is that her research will provide a platform on which others will build.

Her critique of offenders' scripts is important. There are a host of reasons why we should be cautious about what offenders tell researchers in interviews. Indeed, one of the questions I am most asked by audiences after a presentation about my own work with offenders is, 'but how do you know they are telling the truth?' Janice presents her own account of the role of the script in offender research, outlining benefits and drawbacks; documenting the opportunities for learning on the one hand and the need for caution on what is said on the other.

She charts the various ways in which fraudsters reflect on their offences, for example with a discourse on 'excuses' versus 'justifications'; on the levels of acceptability of their behaviour (which includes the notion of the 'good criminal'); develops a typology on the degree to which different interviewees accept the label of criminal to their actions (and noting that some don't agree that what they did was criminal); the level of rationality they show noting how some offenders are 'pressurised' and some 'seduced' into their crimes; and the impact of their offences on their victims, families and themselves.

Janice's work offers an important insight into the 'invisible' offences of the fraudster, including many vivid vignettes. Her book builds on previous studies in this area and will hopefully generate further interest in this type of work from both scholars and practitioners.

Martin Gill

'The differing reasons men give for their actions are not themselves without reasons.'

Mills (1940: 904)

1
Introduction

Why focus on accounts of white-collar criminals?

Whereas the stereotypical image of criminal activity in our society is street crime – visible, public and threatening – white-collar crime tends to be hidden, committed in the workplace or a private sphere, and does not usually involve physical danger. Yet this does not mean that it is any less damaging or costly to society. In fact, the National Fraud Authority (NFA) (2010) estimated the cost to the UK of fraud in 2008 at some £30.5 billion, or an average of £621 per adult in the population.

Although criminologists have attempted to explore the motivations of offenders in general, and of white-collar criminals in particular, Wikstrom argues that explanations and causations in this latter area have not been fully addressed; reasons given for this include problems related to interviewing white-collar criminals and to the reliability of their accounts (2006: 61). Bernasco, however, considers that white-collar offenders are a good source of information, showing little reluctance to talk about their behaviour because they often do not see it as wrong – though he cautions those who interview such offenders to alter their vocabulary to avoid words that relate directly to crime and offending (2010: 10). It would therefore seem that accounts by white-collar criminals could be useful in providing further information about motivations and causations, as long as such accounts are treated with suitable caution.

Typically, accounts are normally used by individuals who want to, or feel they must, explain their behaviour in order to save face and restore the equilibrium of a situation where they have violated a social norm. Scott and Lyman define accounts as '[s]tatements made by a social actor to explain unanticipated or untoward behaviour' (1968: 56).

Accounts are therefore typically produced when individuals perceive that their criminal activity has been at odds with the normal, accepted behaviour of the social group to which they belong. Scott and Lyman also say that accounts are used to '... bridge the gap between actions and expectations when subjected to a valuative enquiry' (ibid: 46). In other words, an account will only be seen as plausible if it is seen and accepted as such by the audience hearing or reading it. Accounts may be 'intra', detailing how individuals explain their behaviour to themselves, or 'inter', how they do so to another person or group. There are two main types of accounts: excuses and justifications. Excuses tend towards defending criminal activity, whereas justifications are more positive statements, seeking to explain why it was undertaken.

A number of scholars have developed theories of accounting since C. Wright Mill's celebrated essay, *'Situated Actions and Vocabularies of Motive'*, was published in 1940. The most important criminological work is probably that of Sykes and Matza (1957), which considers a master set of 'neutralisation techniques' which the individual offender may employ, and Scott and Lyman (1968) have developed a similar set of accounts which draws heavily on this earlier categorisation. Whereas many researchers have added various types of excuses and justifications to this 'master set' of accounts, very little changed until Schönbach (1980) produced a category system for account phases, adding two general types of account, which he termed 'concessions' and 'refusals'. Further refinements and additions have been made since, notably by Fritsche (2002).

Accounts are affected by a number of variables. These include the social situations and environments in which they are produced; the status of the person or persons constituting the audience for them; the author's expectations in producing the account; and his/her vocabulary of motives used in doing so (Mills, 1940; Scott and Lyman, 1968). Such factors will influence whether the account is 'honoured', i.e. successfully – accepted by those responsible for the valuative enquiry. Accounts are particularly important when an individual needs to 'save face' (Ting-Toomey, 1994) because a norm violation has occurred. These violations have also variously been termed 'incidents' (Goffman, 1959; 1971), 'predicaments' (Schlenker, 1980), 'face-threatening acts' (Brown and Levinson, 1987) and 'account episodes' (Schönbach, 1980). By succeeding in having their accounts honoured, individuals may be able to exempt themselves from the consequences of behaving in a way which goes against the expectations of their normal social group (Sykes and Matza, 1957; Fritsche, 2002).

Of their very nature, accounts will always be of interest to criminologists; and this applies in particular to those researching white-collar crime. Because such offenders frequently belong to higher social strata compared with other types of criminal, it is not always easy to understand why such individuals would get involved with offending in the first place, and this question has attracted a certain amount of research attention. Indeed, the background, status and experience of white-collar offenders often make them more fluent and more capable of explaining their behaviour than lower-level offenders, and one could thus argue that white-collar criminals' accounts are more interesting to study. As Hobbs states: 'This arena of criminality sets a range of unique conundrums before the researcher that are not apparent in the relatively simple world of theft, violence, and vice' (2000: 168).

This book will therefore hopefully add to the existing body of academic knowledge on white-collar crime and accounting theory. However, it also aims to give valuable information to accountants and auditors in businesses about white-collar crime. It provides fresh and up-to-date accounts of white-collar offenders, incorporating modern working practices and arrangements, including the use of information technology to perpetrate crime. By reviewing this research, managers will be better informed when making decisions about implementing crime-control procedures and policies in their organisations.

Defining white-collar crime

Any discussion of white-collar crime will tend to start with a debate about defining what is actually meant by this term, even where definitions of it are to be found. The Fraud Act 2006 in the UK made some headway towards legal definitions, but still the area remains fragmented, covering a variety of activities (see Doig, 2006; Levi et al, 2007; Croall, 2010, for relevant discussion), often with little resemblance to each other (Gill and Goldstraw-White, 2010). Attempting a precise definition is thus problematic (see Croall, 2010). It has also been argued that the media tend to glamourise such offending (Croall, 1992: 5), highlighting cases involving well-known characters and celebrities who are generally atypical of most white-collar criminals (Gottfredson and Hirschi, 1990: 183).

Additionally, definitions can become confused and blurred even in academic writing, especially with respect to the distinction between corporate and individual white-collar crime; in more populist media, the two are frequently used as synonyms. Clinard and Quinney define corporate crime as: '... offences committed by corporate officials for the corporation and the offences of the corporation itself', whereas they define individual crime as: '... offences committed by individuals for themselves in the course of their occupations and the offences of employees against their employers' (1973: 188).

Sutherland was the first to introduce the concept of white-collar crime. He defined it as: '... crime committed by a person of respectability and high social status in the course of his occupation' (Sutherland, 1947: 9). His definition not only distinguishes white-collar crime from 'upper-class crime', which can be any type of criminal activity, but also from crimes committed by the less 'respectable' and those of 'low social status'. This of course does not describe the reality – individuals of all occupations and social classes may commit white-collar crime (Levi, 1987; Gill and Goldstraw-White, 2010). As a result, Sutherland's initial definition has been heavily criticised because it concentrates too much on the social status of the offender, thereby excluding others of a lower social status. However, Sutherland used this definition as a way of drawing attention to a deficiency in criminological theories, which did not extend to higher-status individuals, as well as of highlighting a bias in the criminal-justice system, which tends to concentrate on the lower social strata. However, it should be added that the inclusion of all social levels in the definition has created research and analysis problems (Croall, 1992: 10). Sutherland's definition was also criticised because it included activities that were not legally defined as criminal and this in turn led to a more legalistic approach to white-collar crime such as that put forward by Tappan (1947).

Moving on now to consider the area of accounts, in 1953 Donald Cressey published *Other People's Money*, which was the first piece of criminological research to employ the concept of accounts, and concentrated on embezzlers. Cressey considers how different individuals, in positions of financial trust, violate that trust when they find themselves faced with what he terms a 'non-shareable' problem. This is a situation which they cannot share with others, and can see no way out of but by committing an illegal act. From his research, Cressey develops a general statement about embezzlement, concluding that three conditions, all of which must be present, are necessary if embezzlement is to occur. First, that the potential embezzler has financial problems which he/she sees as non-shareable; secondly, that the opportunity to violate trust placed upon him/her must be available, and finally that the offender must be able to rationalise the act. Dorothy Zietz (1981) conducted a similar study, considering female offenders convicted of embezzlement, and replicating the work of Cressey (1953). Both these studies will be discussed in further detail later in this book (see Chapters 3 and 8).

In contrast to Cressey and Zietz, Michael Benson, in *The Fall from Grace* (1984) and *Denying the Guilty Mind* (1985), considers offenders' accounts according to the type of offence; he concludes that these accounts are indeed influenced by the type of crimes committed, the acts themselves and the organisational context in which they take place. Benson believes that accounts need to be constructed so as to avoid the conditions required for a successful 'degradation ceremony' (1985: 585).

Structure of the book

This book takes a slightly different approach to the usual research undertaken on white-collar crime, the primary aim of which is to establish the causes of such offending. Instead, it examines offenders' accounts and the meanings behind them, thus allowing for an analysis of the reasons each gives for committing his/her crime. In order to undertake this it was felt necessary at the outset to determine the level of guilt to which each had admitted, not only in court, but also to themselves. It was hoped that this would show both their moral position towards their crimes and also how much importance they attached to avoiding the stigmatisation of their previous characters. Because each individual plays a number of roles in society, it is acknowledged that white-collar crime offenders may find themselves in a number of social situations, each of which might lead them to account for their criminality differently. It is also felt that gender differences might be relevant to accounts. Finally, in concluding whether or not the crimes are thought to have been worth committing, the afterthoughts of offenders in prison are analysed in terms of costs and benefits. To achieve answers to these areas the following broad questions will be explored in the forthcoming chapters:

1. How do offenders account for their criminal acts, both in terms of legal pleas and to themselves?
2. How do offenders account morally for their behaviour?
3. How do offenders account for their behaviour as actors in different social situations?
4. Does gender affect the accounts of white-collar offenders?
5. How do offenders view the gains and losses they have experienced?

The book is divided into three parts. Part I provides an overview of the research carried out by myself and others, on accounts and white-collar crime. Chapter 2 defines and charts the development of the theory of accounting, from the perspectives of both social psychology and criminology. In doing so, it distinguishes between excuses and justifications, and details the various account types to be addressed later in the book. These include more contemporary additions to accounts theory, such as those detailed by Schönbach (1980; 1990) and Fritsche (2002).

In Chapter 3, the methodology underlying the research project is discussed. It opens with an overview of different methodologies which can be used for researching white-collar crime, assessing the advantages and disadvantages of each. Following that, methodologies which have been utilised for researching white-collar crime are discussed. In particular, attention is paid to the methodology of in-depth interviewing.

In detailing the approach taken in this book, the target population is identified via the definition of white-collar crime given by Edelhertz (1970). The steps undertaken to obtain a suitable sample consistent with this definition are then outlined; these include discussing issues of access to prisons in order to undertake the interviews, and of selecting appropriate offenders. The interview process, including recognised problems in using this kind of methodology, is then considered. This includes data-recording methods and their assessment. The chapter ends with a brief overview of the general characteristics of the sample, including the backgrounds of the offenders, their socio-demographic characteristics, their crimes and alleged resulting gains, as well as convictions and sentences imposed.

Part II of the book explores the accounts of the white-collar criminals in detail. The analysis starts with Chapter 4, which explores how the offenders account for their criminal acts in both legal and moral terms. A typology is developed which considers different levels of individuals' acceptance of their criminality, and the tension created in their accounts by presenting both their outer, legal self and their inner, moral self. This is undertaken by comparing the pleas given in court with the levels of acceptance of guilt by individuals in non-judicial situations. The typology consists of four main categories: total rejectors, who deny their criminality totally; tactical acceptors, who deny their criminality to their inner self but present an acceptance of guilt by pleading guilty; tactical rejectors, who admit their guilt to themselves but deny this in a formal judicial setting; and acceptors, who accept their criminality totally, both legally and to their inner self.

Individuals often find themselves affected by multiple factors, which can be considered from a number of perspectives. In Chapter 5, therefore, how offenders see themselves as actors in these situations is discussed. The three main ways in which individuals present themselves is as rational, pressurised or seduced actors. Rational actors are considered on a scale of rationality, ranging from accidental or opportunist through to fully-planned actions. Actors at the latter end of this spectrum commit sophisticated, complex and organised crimes, having set out to identify a suitable opportunity in which to undertake them, whereas at the other end opportunist actors are likely to have come across a set of circumstances or opportunities of which they can take immediate advantage. Pressurised actors are influenced by different types of forces, ranging from the self-imposed pressure of demanding aspirations, to more critical situations involving a degree of desperation, and finally to pressure imposed by others, in the form of threats. The final category of actors considered in this chapter is seduced actors, who are individuals subjected to the persuasive influence of other people, mainly close others such as spouses, partners or intimate business associates.

Many of the offenders interviewed, not unnaturally, sought to stress the good and moral side of their characters, and to play down the negative (Chambliss, 1964). In Chapter 6, how offenders accounted for their acts as moral individuals is discussed. They gave, from their perspective, reasons which they viewed as either 'acceptable' or 'unacceptable'. The latter related to acts committed out of greed or due to an addiction, and the former to acts committed, for instance, out of altruistic motives, or where the actors had tried to 'make good' their crimes. Additionally, some individuals felt justified in committing their crimes because of the situations they had found themselves in; such justifications included feelings of revenge, often towards employers, and particularly where blocked opportunities had been encountered. To stress their morality further, individuals were keen to point out how 'normal' they were. This included using a number of distancing techniques, stressing the out-of-character and one-off nature of their crime, as well as pointing out that they had no previous convictions. Finally, the chapter concludes with accounts from individuals who, even when in prison, were still fighting to retain their good moral profile by claiming that they were 'good criminals' and 'good prisoners', that their crimes had been victimless and that no-one had been hurt. They also tended to stress how they had been 'good' individuals in having restrained themselves from taking further advantage of the situation. Even when caught and incarcerated, they were still pleading their morality by pointing to their co-operation with investigating agencies, and to how in prison they were morally superior to other, non-white-collar prisoners.

One area that has been severely neglected in the study of white-collar crime is the issue of losses. Whereas losses relating to the victims of such offending have been considered – for example, by Moore and Mills, 1990; Levi, 1991; Levi and Pithouse, 1992; 2000; Shover et al, 1994; Spalek, 1999; Buttons et al, 2010 – how losses have affected the offenders themselves has hardly been researched at all (but see Payne, 2003, an exception to this). In Chapter 7, the costs and benefits of the crimes offenders examined are discussed. The loss of liberty is considered, as well that of status, reputation and professional recognition. How offenders feel about the losses they have caused their close others and victims is also questioned and explored. Finally, in putting these factors together, offenders were asked to consider their afterthoughts in order to assess whether their criminal activities and resulting outcomes had been worth it.

The sample consisted of both male and female white-collar offenders, so in Chapter 8 the differences in accounts between the genders are identified in an attempt to add to the existing body of knowledge and to challenge previous theories and assumptions about female white-collar criminality.

Finally, Part III of the book includes the conclusions drawn from the research, and points to the implications these might have for the academic community, and for policy-makers in business and government.

Part I

Overview and Background to the Research

2
Accounting for Behaviour – Theoretical Approaches

Introduction

Throughout life, we find that our actions can have an undesirable effect on others (or groups of others), either directly through our behaviour – careless, stupid, offensive and so on – or indirectly, through confounding their social expectations (Gonzales et al, 1992: 958). These situations may have considerable implications for individuals, and can range from a hurtful remark directed at another person through to deliberate, deviant behaviour of an illegal nature. It is for these types of situations that individuals normally feel that they need to account for their actions.

Scott and Lyman have defined accounts as 'statements made by a social actor to explain unanticipated or untoward behaviour' (1968: 56). They note that one of the features of such statements is '... its ability to shore up the timbers of fractured sociation, its ability to throw bridges between the promised and the performed, its ability to repair the broken and restore the estranged' (ibid: 46). An account may therefore be seen as a linguistic device '... to bridge the gap between actions and expectations' (ibid) which is employed when an act is subject to a valuative enquiry from others. Accounts are usually presented as conversations, but they can be made via other mediums, such as written prose or recorded monologues. Whatever the medium used, the account still involves making oneself understood by another or others. These exchanges are governed by the rules of social interaction, where the verb 'explain' is used in the context of someone explaining 'something' to 'someone' (Hilton, 1990: 65). These verbalisations should make behaviour more intelligible to others through a common set of symbols shared by the social group to which the individual belongs. It follows therefore that when relying on accounts to be used successfully, the persons giving their account need to address both their behaviour and the social expectations of others observing that behaviour. Accounts also need to be 'situated' (Scott and Lyman, 1968) in the context where they are being used. This means that they will differ according to a number of variables, including the status of interactants, expectations, and the vocabulary of motives utilised (as defined by Mills, 1940). In addition, accounts may depend on the social setting of the act of accounting, including features of the environment and who is included in the audience.

Accounts may be classified as inter- or intra-individual (Fritsche, 2002) – i.e. they may be given to others or made to oneself. Inter-individual accounts may be adapted by the individual for their acceptability to the person making the valuative enquiry (Cohen, 2001: 59). The level and the importance of this acceptability will be determined by the individual's perception of the subjective, cost-benefit appraisal of the situation (Baumeister and Newman, 1994). In other words, if people wish to maintain or restore the status quo ante of the situation – what it was before their untoward behaviour or norm violation – they will give an account that looks to minimise the costs to themselves and exaggerate the benefits of the situation to others (Heatherton and Nichols, 1994: 665). The account therefore becomes situated in both social and historical contexts (Benson, 1985: 588). It is these situations that determine the types and range of plausible accounts which a person can produce.

However, social interaction when these norm violations are being explained may not always go smoothly – in some instances 'disruptions' may occur (Gonzales et al, 1990: 610). Disruptions have also been termed 'incidents' (Goffman, 1959 and 1971), 'predicaments' (Schlenker, 1980), 'face-threatening acts' (Brown and Levinson, 1987) and 'account episodes' (Schönbach, 1980). Those wishing to maintain or salvage their identity and to 'save face' (Ting-Toomey, 1994) need to identify anything that threatens their favourable 'social identity' (Hudson, 2005: 16). To achieve this offenders have to acknowledge that they do not exist in a void, but in a dynamic society (some of) whose members may show disapproval towards them. In an attempt to restore the situation to its original state, a number of strategies may be employed, including attempting to explain the undesirable act. Where accounts are formulated before the act, this may allow individuals to behave in a way which goes against what might be regarded as the pre-determined, acceptable behaviour of their normal reference group (Sykes and Matza, 1957; Fritsche, 2002).

In seeking to restore the situation, or 'status quo' (Baumeister and Newman, 1994), between interactants and to 'save face' (Ting-Toomey, 1994), a situational equilibrium may be achieved through a number of techniques. Gonzales et al (1990: 612) refer to these as 'saving face concerns', which they believe involve having one's self-image acknowledged, honoured and accepted in a positive way. The need for justification, to oneself but especially to others, has a special bearing on account construction, and individuals need to tailor their narratives in a way which makes sense and justifies their actions to others. For offenders in particular, this can be crucial, as they may need to try and salvage their prior non-criminal identity and to address any potential threats to it. Clearly, then, the process of presenting themselves in a more favourable light to preserve their previous identity is pertinent to this group of individuals (Goffman, 1959). Though as Minor points out (1981: 311), some offenders have little moral inhibition, and therefore not all criminals use accounts to defend their behaviour.

Because individuals may present themselves differently to others, depending on the particular audience, situation and environment, accounts may vary in linguistic styles (Scott and Lyman, 1968: 55). Benson (1985: 585) notes how white-collar-criminals' accounts often vary between, for example, those given to a judge and those given to their probation officer. However, he cautions that how individuals account for their activity in a non-judicial setting is to a large extent an unknown quantity. In relation to giving accounts to researchers (such as in the present study), it has been suggested that offenders may wish themselves to be seen in as favourable a light as possible (Ross, 1989: 352). However, not all agree that individuals go out of their way deliberately to manage their accounts. Greenwald and Breckler (1985), for example, defend many individuals by pointing out that not all self-presentations are deliberate falsifications.

Accounts may also be used for a number of other motives besides saving face. These reasons include guilt-defence, managing self-image and self-presentation, self-esteem, exerting personal control, avoiding or minimising punishment or the effects thereof, settling conflicts, and finally as a means of justifying a departure from the social norms of the group to which an actor currently belongs. Besides criminological research, accounting theory is also used in social psychology. Both these areas will be explored in this chapter.

Types of accounts and theories

Any discussion of account types needs to consider the theory and development of such accounts. Scott and Lyman (1968) developed a typology, drawing heavily upon Mill's (1940) vocabulary of motives and Sykes and Matza's (1957) neutralisation theory. Other typologies include those developed by Schönbach (1980; 1990), Minor (1981), Coleman (1987) and Fritsche (2002). These are detailed in Table 2.1. This is not how-ever an exhaustive list of all accounts in use, but does include some developments and refinements that have been introduced to the ori-ginal categories. These typologies all have a common feature in that they fall into two distinct categories: 'excuses' or 'justifications'. Excuses may be seen as more defensive in nature, and justifications as more positive.

Scott and Lyman (1968) define 'excuses' as 'socially approved vocab-ularies for mitigating or relieving responsibility when conduct is ques-tioned' (1968: 47). They found that people generally admit that deviant

Table 2.1   Summary of the development of accounts theory

Author/Year	Excuse	Author/Year	Justification
Sykes and Matza, 1957	Denial of responsibility	Sykes and Matza, 1957	Denial of injury Denial of the victim Condemnation of those who condemn Appeal to higher loyalties
Scott and Lyman, 1968	Appeal to accidents Appeal to defeasibility Appeal to biological drives Scapegoating		Denial of injury Denial of the victim Condemnation of those who condemn Appeal to loyalties Sad tales Self-fulfilment
Minor, 1981	Defence of necessity Metaphor of the ledger		
Coleman, 1987	Denial that a law is necessary Claim of normality Claim of entitlement		

Notes: 1. Schönbach (1980) adds two further account category types: 'refusals' and 'concessions'.
2. Fritsche (2002) introduces a meta-category of 'referentialisation', situated between 'excuses' and 'justifications'.

acts are wrong, but usually decline in some way to accept full responsibility for them. Individuals may do this by claiming that factors were beyond their control, or they never intended to cause any harm, or the consequences of their actions were not foreseeable, or they 'couldn't help it'. Snyder and Higgins (1988: 24) believe that 'excuses occur because people *perceive* the benefits associated with them' (emphasis as in original), and that they work because they attempt to shift the focus away from the individual – though these authors doubt that this can be successfully and totally accomplished without the help of outside influences. They also detail how the literature on excuses suggests that '... excuses are designed to protect the individual from self-esteem threats' (ibid), and point out that 'excuse-making' is a highly adaptive mechanism for coping with stress, relieving anxiety, maintaining self-esteem and even enhancing retrospective control over past mistakes (Wortman, 1976).

In their model of accounts, Scott and Lyman (1968) outline four typical areas which are used as excuses, as detailed in Table 2.1 above. These are appeals to accidents, to defeasibility, to biological drives and to scapegoating.

First, accidents are seen as mistakes where individuals rely on deficiencies in others, or in other things, to mitigate responsibility, such as environmental hazards or uncontrollable human behaviour. Whether these acts are accepted as accidents or not is based on the premise that they are unpredictable, irregular and do not happen all the time or to the same person. Secondly, excuses which appeal to defeasibility rely on the fact that not all actions are totally based on 'free will'; individuals putting forward such excuses may claim that they lacked information which might have changed their behaviour, were under duress or undue influence, or had insufficient knowledge of the consequences of the acts – Scott and Lyman's example is: 'I did not know that I would make her cry by what I did' (1968: 48). Thirdly, appeals to biological drives are included in what Scott and Lyman (ibid: 49) term 'fatalistic forces'. They suggest that such drives are commonly sexual in nature, which may be influenced for example by the individual's culture, race or body type. Finally, they use the term 'scapegoating' as a final technique for self-exculpation, seeking to blame the victim by shifting the burden of responsibility elsewhere, in other words, that the actions of another or others are the 'real' cause of the deviance.

For Scott and Lyman, justifications, like excuses, are also '... socially approved vocabularies for mitigating or relieving responsibility when conduct is questioned' (ibid: 47); they take the view that the difference between justifications and excuses is that in the former case individuals accept responsibility for their act, but deny '... the pejorative quality associated with it' (ibid). This leads to the act being viewed as legitimate under some (though not all) circumstances – i.e. the individual tries to claim that the act is not as bad as, in another context, it might be judged. Scott and Lyman assert that: '[T]o justify an act is to assert its positive value in the face of a claim to the contrary.' Justifications therefore recognise the wrongfulness of the act; however, unlike in the case of excuses, the perpetrator claims that it was permissible, or even necessary, under the circumstances pertaining at the time (ibid: 51).

In formulating their typology of justifications, Scott and Lyman (1968) drew upon four of Sykes and Matza's (1957) techniques of neutralisation; the latter's fifth neutralisation – denial of responsibility – is subsumed under Scott and Lyman's excuses as 'appeal to defeasibility'. Sykes and Matza proposed five such techniques: denial of responsibility, denial of injury, denial of the victim, condemnation of those who condemn, and appeal to higher loyalties. In addition to these, Scott and Lyman added two other categories of justifications: sad tales and self-fulfilment.

One of the most salient approaches to accounts in criminological theory is Sykes and Matza's (1957) work on neutralisation, which, it may be argued, is one of the most important and visionary pieces of work so far to emerge in the field (Maruna and Copes, 2004: 222–3). Developed from Sutherland's (1947) theory of differential association, Sykes and Matza attempt to explain through the study of juvenile delinquents how people are able to move between law-abiding and delinquent behaviour. Neutralisation theory – or 'drift theory', as it is also known (Matza, 1964) – explains how a person's sense of moral obligation, normally bounded by the law and by group norms, may be temporarily suspended. During such a period, individuals find themselves 'freed' from these moral boundaries, allowing them to drift into deviant behaviour. Matza does not claim that drift causes delinquency, but instead that it creates the conditions where social controls are loosened, and which may in turn permit deviant behaviour (ibid: 29).

Sykes and Matza's theoretical model is based on the following four observations: first, delinquents express guilt over their illegal acts. Secondly, they frequently respect and admire honest, law-abiding individuals. Thirdly, a line is drawn between those whom they can victimise and those whom they cannot. Fourthly, delinquents are not immune to the demands of social conformity (1957: 665). The authors propose that delinquents, in order to justify their behaviour, learn techniques which allow them to neutralise it, thereby creating a move or 'drift' from unacceptable to acceptable behaviour. Rather than the delinquents accounting for their behaviour in a way that might suggest they do not sign up to their group norms, Sykes and Matza propose that the delinquents are able to neutralise their violation of social norms through different accounting techniques, which justify this behaviour. This results in allowing them to temporarily suspend their commitment to societal values, thereby giving them the opportunity and freedom to engage in delinquent behaviour. They point out that the original five techniques of neutralisation are not available only to delinquents, but also to society in general. Neutralisation theory has also been used to explain participation in many less serious activities, for example playing bingo (King, 1990; Chapple and Nofziger, 2000) and appearing in pre-teen beauty pageants (Heltsley and Calhoun, 2003).

Returning to the original five neutralisation techniques, denial of responsibility is clearly the 'master account' (Maruna and Copes, 2004: 231), where delinquents will claim that certain factors were outside their control and that they were pushed or pulled into the behaviour in question. Offenders often try to excuse their behaviour by using the phrase 'it was not my fault'. As Box points out: 'They may plead "momentary insanity", "ignorance", "accident", or "acting under orders" or try and shift the blame to a higher authority' (1983: 540–5). Other factors which may be blamed in denying responsibility include family, peers, schooling and environment.

Those offenders who use the neutralisation technique of denying injury do not claim that the act did not take place, but rather define the situation on the basis that no real harm (none or minimal) was caused through their behaviour (Sykes and Matza, 1957: 667). Coleman cites an example from the responses in the 1961 trials of those executives accused of fixing the prices of heavy electrical equipment: 'I assumed that a criminal action meant hurting someone, we did not hurt anyone' (1987: 411). This exemplifies the widespread belief among white-collar criminals that their activities have not harmed anyone, and therefore they do not see their action as in any way criminal. Friedrichs notes that sometimes offenders even claim their victim may benefit economically through their actions, and therefore good rather than harm has been done (1996: 231). For example, as a result of their crime, older goods may be replaced by newer ones through insurance claims. Such justifications serve to solicit further support from society, which in turn may reinforce the offenders' denial of injury. White-collar offenders, particularly embezzlers, may use this technique, claiming they were 'merely borrowing' someone else's funds, with the intention of repaying the purloined money. Therefore, they would argue, the act should not be viewed as delinquent, since the victim had not been injured. However, the reality of most of these situations is that the money does not get paid back, and therefore the offender has taken it without permission, and caused injury to the victim through its loss. Using the denial-of-injury technique relies heavily on the definitions and interpretations of exactly what an injury is, which may or may not be reaffirmed by society's reaction to the offences. This is of course particularly critical in white-collar crime, when the line between legal and illegal is often difficult to draw.

To consider now denial of the victim as a neutralisation technique: the offender does not deny that an act took place, that it caused harm or that it was wrong, but believes victims brought it on themselves, thereby excusing, in the offender's eyes, the criminal behaviour (Goldstraw, 2003). This may be because the offender believes that the victims deserve the crime committed against them, i.e. sees it as an act of revenge or retaliation (Thurman, 1984: 292). The offender attempts to deprive the victims of their status as such, and to turn them into the wrong-doers (Cohen, 2001: 61). Additionally, offenders may try to deny that there were any victims at all (Sykes and Matza, 1957: 665), hence denying that any harm has in fact been inflicted.

By contrast, those offenders using the technique of 'condemning those who condemn' (or 'rejection of the rejectors', the term used by McCorkle and Korn, 1954), try to shift the blame to someone else by claiming that the circumstances surrounding their act were unfair or that they are being picked upon, or singled out for opprobrium. In addition, they often attempt to put a negative label on the condemners by claiming that they are 'no better' than or 'were just as bad in their day' as themselves, or that they are corrupt, hypocritical or spiteful in their behaviour. Such feelings can intensify towards those enforcing the rules (Sykes and Matza, 1957: 668), leading offenders to project blame for their actions onto law-makers and law-enforcers in particular.

Finally, by appealing to higher loyalties, offenders try to justify their behaviour by claiming it was necessary in the interests of the community or group to which they belong. They try to achieve this by arguing that their behaviour is consistent with the moral code of their own social group (Maruna and Copes, 2004: 233), and that it is this code which has caused them to break the law (Sykes and Matza, 1957: 669). Such a reaction does not imply total rejection of the norms being violated, rather that at particular times other norms are seen to be more deserving or pressing. For example, they may claim that their friends, colleagues or associates needed them, so that morally they had no choice but to act as they have.

Scott and Lyman (1968) added a further two justifications to those detailed by Sykes and Matza (1957), being 'sad tales' and 'self-fulfilment'. Sad tales are defined as those alleged facts in their past which individuals may use, often selectively and distortedly, to explain their present situation. Frequently, they may focus on a dismal past to 'explain' their present situation; examples of such narratives may for instance include claiming to have been denied a full education, as a consequence of having to work to help support the family, or having to look after a sick relative. Self-fulfilment, meanwhile, may be seen in activities which provide a justification for aberrant behaviour, in that they may be perceived as self-development and a furtherance of the offender's chances in life (Scott and Lyman, 1968: 52). Deviant behaviour at work, possibly to achieve recognition or promotion, would be an example of this.

The model proposed by Scott and Lyman in 1968 for a theory of account remained relatively unchanged until Schönbach in 1980 added two more to the main categories of excuses and justifications – these being 'concessions' and 'refusals'. Concessions, as defined by Schönbach, are what others, such as Goffman (1971) and Scher (1989), term elaborate apologies. In these, the offender acknowledges the action and its outcome, and accepts responsibility for both. This may involve regret, embarrassment and possibly, in some cases, restitution. An example of this would be where a white-collar offender shows remorse and voluntarily repays the amount stolen, in part or in full.

Gonzales et al (1990: 611) define refusals as strategies which involve actors denying responsibility for an offence or its consequences; this may be denial of the act itself or of their own involvement in it. Technically, refusals may not constitute accounts because there is no face to save, due to the denial. What this means is that the actor, through these refusals, is either directly or indirectly refusing to acknowledge any reproach from witnesses or others. Individuals may deny the existence of the act or deny their involvement in it and its consequences. This may include denial of guilt, of the crime, of the facts or of their awareness or knowledge.

Schönbach (1990) considered that accounts can be ranked at escalating levels of defensiveness, from concessions through to justifications, excuses and finally refusals, as demonstrated in Figure 2.1.

In 1981 Minor, having undertaking further research into neutralisation, added two categories of accounts specifically relating white-collar crime to the framework of accounting theory. These categories were 'defence of necessity' and the 'metaphor of the ledger'. He defined defence of necessity as utilising a technique to reduce an individual's

Figure 2.1   Escalation of defensiveness in accounts

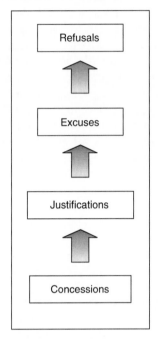

Note: Based on Schönbach (1980; 1990).

guilt by claiming that an action was necessary, whilst at the same time acknowledging that it was morally wrong. Minor developed this category of account especially for white-collar criminals, where business individuals argued the necessity of bending the rules to achieve the economic goals essential to the survival of the business, or simply to provide for their families. Metaphor of the ledger was first coined by Klockars (1974) as a means of balancing good and bad behaviour. Through this neutralisation technique, offenders believe that previous 'good' behaviour gives them 'credit' and in some way cancels out and justifies any 'bad' behaviour in which they may indulge later, leaving them guiltless.

The remaining three techniques of neutralisation – denial of the necessity of the law, claims of normality and claims of entitlement, were introduced by Coleman in 1987, through his research with white-collar criminals. The technique of denying the necessity of the law is used by offenders who claim the law they are accused of breaking is unfair or unjust. This may be the case with some taxation-related offences, where individuals feel they are paying unnecessary taxes or higher rates than they judge to be fair.

In claims of normality, however – that 'everyone is doing it' – individuals do not see why they should be punished when others indulge in the same activities without penalty. White-collar criminals often feel this when they see or hear of others committing the same criminal behaviour, which they regard as giving them licence to act in the same way.

Claims of entitlement, meanwhile, describe those situations where offenders believe they have a moral right to their illicit gains. It is often difficult to separate white-collar criminal activity from custom and practice – such illegal activities may be seen by many staff as perks or entitlements of the job. The purloining of stationery, or the use of computers, telephones or photo-copiers for private purposes, would be examples of such behaviour. These acts are commonly seen as an entitlement by employees, and frequently committed in office environments, whereas they are legally a matter of theft or embezzlement from their employers.

Fritsche further expanded the four main categories of accounts (refusals, excuses, justifications and concessions) put forward previously by Scott and Lyman (1968) and Schönbach (1980), by adding what he termed a fifth 'meta-category', referred to as 'referentialisation' (2002: 381). He considers that this category is required when individuals add further information not known to the person responsible for reproaching them, in an attempt to lessen their guilt further. He believes that this omission is a weakness in previous typologies, particularly in respect of applicability to specific social-norm behaviour and to what he regarded as a poorly-defined, grey area located between justifications and excuses. (Figure 2.2 above shows where accounts of referentialisation fit with the categories described previously). In cases of referentialisation, Schönbach believes individuals use such information to lessen their own culpability by reference to their previous behaviour, as well as to that of others, at the same time acknowledging the violation of norms.

Factors affecting accounts

Most empirical research based on accounting theory has emanated from the realm of social psychology rather than criminology, and thus does not necessarily relate to offenders or even to deviant behaviour. Much of what is described here therefore derives from more generalist studies. Accounts may be verbal, handwritten or emerge from the analysis of

Figure 2.2   Referentialisation situated in the escalation of defensiveness in accounts

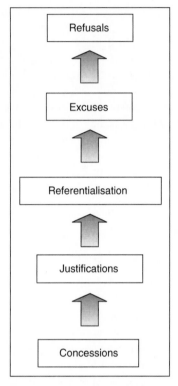

Note: Based on Schönbach (1980; 1990) and Fritsche (2002).

questionnaires. With regard to offenders, it has been suggested that the style, nature and even length of an account may be affected by a number of variables, including the severity of the offence, the status of the offender and additionally, gender (Gonzales et al, 1990: 612).

In relation to the severity of the offence, Gonzales et al (ibid) conclude that there is no consensus on the correlation between it and the deployment of accounts. However, Schlenker suggests that accounting strategies may be used more in an 'extreme way' in such circumstances, i.e. using more aggravating than mitigating strategies (1980: 147). Aggravating accounts may also be called refusals, and may be perceived as aggressive and challenging. However, they may threaten a loss of face and make the situation worse. Unlike mitigating accounts, they show a lack of respect for others' need to save face. Mitigating accounts (or concessions) are more conciliatory in nature in that they attempt to minimise face threats (Cupach and Metts, 1994). Schönbach (1985) regards the use of accounts by offenders as a more defensive tactic, whereas McLaughlin et al (1983) believe that because an account is more likely to be accepted if offenders take a conciliatory approach, they commonly avoid an aggravating strategy in favour of a mitigating one. These assertions were also supported by McLaughlin et al (ibid), who report that higher-status offenders are likely to employ more aggravating strategies (such as the justification of refusals) compared to lower-status offenders, who probably use more mitigating ones (such as concessions or excuses).

Account-giving in criminology

The use of accounting theory in criminology has to date predominantly focused on neutralisation theory (Sykes and Matza, 1957). Others, such as Potter and Wetherell (1987), Billig et al (1988), Krambia-Kapardis (2001) and Willott et al (2001), have also considered the importance of present-ing accounts to justify offences, in other words to remove the criminality from the act and the perpetrators via these 'vocabularies of adjustment' (Cressey, 1953).

In *Other People's Money*, Cressey (ibid: 12) conducted his research through interviews, with the intention of explaining why some people in positions of financial trust violate that trust, whereas others in sim-ilar or identical positions do not. The results of his research included the development of a general statement about embezzlement, demon-strating that for an offence to take place, the individual must first define their financial problems as non-shareable, because they are either too ashamed and have too much pride to ask for help from others. Secondly, individuals must have the opportunity to violate the trust placed in them if they are to commit the crime successfully. Finally, they must be able to rationalise their actions, whether before, during or after the crime, possibly by viewing the theft as an act merely of 'bor-rowing'. Cressey argues that when all these three factors occur together, they provide the environment for embezzlement to take place. His theory led to the development of what many have termed the 'fraud triangle' (portrayed in Figure 2.3), where the three elements of motive, oppor-tunity and rationalisation all come together, allowing the subject to com-mit the offence. This model has since been further developed by Wolfe and Hermanson as a 'fraud diamond' (2004: 40). This adds a fourth ele-ment to the model, termed 'capability', which adds further components

Figure 2.3　Fraud triangle

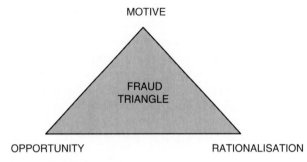

Note: Based on Cressey (1953).

such as position, function, brainpower, confidence, ego, coercion skills, effective lying and immunity to stress, showing that the capability to commit a crime is as important as motive and opportunity. This supports Pearce's (1976) assertion that fraud was no longer a crime of the powerful, but more of people 'in the know'. Although Cressey's conception of fraud is still widely used today, other refinements by those researching fraud and white-collar crime have been put forward.

In criminology, offenders have been seen as using accounts to avoid stigmatisation and to minimise shame and perceived harm, by making the deviant act more acceptable in the eyes of the social group to which they belong, or to society as a whole. Some individuals may also use accounts to try to neutralise their criminality in a way that may lessen or even avoid sentences. Accounts have also been used by researchers into white-collar crime such as Weisburd et al (2001), Lewis (2002), Hunter (2004) and Gill (2005; 2007), who have considered the areas of motivation, re-offending and desistance.

Accounts have also been used in victimology research on the area of white-collar crime, including Moore and Mills (1990), Levi (1991), Levi and Pithouse (1992, 2000), Shover et al (1994), Spalek (1999; 2001a; 2001b) and Button et al (2010). Findings have shown that victims are rarely asked about victimisation, and when they are, do not always answer; indeed, many may be unaware they have been victimised, and when they are, may choose to keep their experiences to themselves (Levi and Pithouse, 2000). Although victims may go through the same psychological, emotional, physical and financial traumas as those victimised by non-white-collar, 'street' criminals, some may feel foolish in coming forward and admitting what has happened to them, and possibly partly blaming themselves for entering into risky activities in the first place (Spalek, 1999; Button et al, 2010).

As Maruna and Copes note, however (2004: 230), neutralisation should not be confused with outright deceit, and verbal explanations may be interpreted in a number of ways (Mills, 1940: 907). In addition, one of the routine assumptions of past criminological research in this area has been that offenders will try to 'manage' their guilt and their being labelled a criminal, rather than simply admitting their crime and accepting any associated stigma attached to it. Minor, however, points out that some offenders have little moral inhibition, and therefore do not use accounts to defend their behaviour (1981: 311).

In 1981, Dorothy Zietz attempted to replicate the work of Cressey, this time with convicted female embezzlers, in order to compare and contrast typologies with those identified by Cressey. In terms of accounts given, she found that women embezzlers generally did not make use of the 'just borrowing' rationalisation, especially when they found they could not repay what they had taken. However, she did conclude that Cressey's hypothesis was in the main applicable to women, though only if modified to account for female violators of their employer's trust, in particular where there was an urgent need for funds, in situations, possibly involving family needs, perceived as desperate.

The use of accounts in white-collar crime has also been seen in studies of neutralisation, especially where this involves attempts to reduce shame and to avoid any associated stigma attaching to the offending behaviour (Benson, 1984; Braithwaite, 1989; Levi, 2002). The investigatory procedures to which an alleged white-collar offender may be subject tend to magnify this stigmatisation. Some theorists believe that white-collar offenders are particularly vulnerable to this, especially given the positions of trust, power and authority held by many of them and the perceived harm such stigma might inflict. Benson shows how the stigmatisation process is based on the assumption that the embarrassment of conviction and the psychological trauma of the actual trial are, in themselves, sufficient punishment (1984: 576). Rothman and Gandossy (1982) have also suggested that it might be advantageous for white-collar criminals to offer 'elaborate accounts' to minimise stigmatisation.

Accounts are also used in interior narratives as well as in public, and they have different functions for each. In public, exposure is at the heart of the stigmatisation process for white-collar (as for other) offenders, confirming the significance of non-legal consequences for this group of offenders. Therefore it is in the self-interest of individuals to manage this process as much as effectively possible through the giving of accounts, specifically where this involves neutralising their guilt through a series of rationalisations. As Sutherland notes: 'Businessmen develop rationalizations which conceal the fact of crime ... Even when they violate the law, they do not conceive of themselves as criminal ... Businessmen fight whenever words that tend to break down this rationalization are used' (Sutherland, 1947: 222, 225, cited in Benson, 1985: 584).

Punch (1996: 226) believes that deviant practices can be perceived as normal and routine, which can act to diffuse any moral opprobrium and criminal labelling, and be seen as acceptable to individuals and society. He believes that this is achieved through rationalisation – that is, statements concerning motives for the offending behaviour (Matza, 1964) which counter offenders' 'consciences', or justify the behaviour. He gives such examples of this as managers claiming that it is part of their job, that they were following the rules of the game, or that they were only doing as they are told.

Benson, in *Denying the Guilty Mind: Accounting for Involvement in White Collar Crime* examined the accounts of a number of convicted white-collar criminals (30 via interview and 50 via judicial files) in order to see how they attempted to '... account for their adjudication as criminals'. He concluded that their accounting is tied into the type of offence they have committed, the detail of that offence and the organisational environment in which it occurred. His belief is that these accounts '... must be constructed so as to defeat the conditions required for a successful degradation ceremony' (1985: 585). His focus, therefore, is on how offenders attempt to avoid the success of this 'ceremony' and deny their own criminality through the use of accounts.

From his research, Benson (ibid: 598–9) identifies three main areas of accounting strategies used to minimise the effect of a potential degradation ceremony on an offender. These three areas concern the event (the offence), the perpetrator (the offender) and the denouncer (the prosecutor). If one or more of these can be undermined, the impact of the ceremony may be reduced. Where the event is concerned, the offender needs to present it in such a way that it can be perceived and accepted as routine practice. Benson (1985: 599) found that tax violators and those who had broken the trust placed in them were generally able to achieve this, and although they suffered convictions had minimised social opprobrium by claiming that the offence could not be separated from the environment in which it had taken place – that such acts were 'not out of the ordinary' and were a widespread practice, for example because of organisational loyalty and the complexity of the business environment (ibid). Embezzlers in Benson's sample, however, had more difficulty in using this strategy, as they needed to show that their offence had been a one-off rather than part of everyday, routine activity (ibid).

Offenders also needed to demonstrate that the offence with which they were charged was not indicative of their usual character and behaviour – in other words, to distance themselves from the offence. Not only would the perpetrators have to show that the event was out of the ordinary, but also understandable in the circumstances and not part of a pattern of usual behaviour (ibid: 601). Finally, 'The denouncer should not be seen as personally involved in the case but instead represent the group values and act in their interests' (ibid). Although Benson does establish that trust violators convicted of fraud condemned the condemners, his study shows (he concluded) that whether offenders avoided the effect of a successful degradation ceremony depended upon the seriousness of the offence and the extent of the offender's blameworthiness.

Coleman believes that neutralisation is fundamental in explaining why those involved in white-collar crime are able to justify their acts (1987: 411). In particular, he believes this ability stems from Sykes and Matza's (1957) techniques of neutralisation, specifically that of 'denial of harm' – the offender involved in such activities rarely believes they hurt anyone. In addition, he finds in the accounts numerous examples of justifications which he believes present a number of ways in which criminals account for and seek to neutralise their behaviour.

The use of accounts in more recent studies on victimology in white-collar crime cannot be overlooked. Maruna and Copes describe the finding that victims (in a similar way to offenders) rely on techniques of neutralisation in seeking to preserve their self-identity (2004: 286). For white-collar crime Spalek, through her in-depth interviews with individuals defrauded by the Robert Maxwell pension-scheme scandal, examines the issue of financial trust (1999; 2001a). In addition, Levi and Pithouse, continuing their interest in victims of fraud, examine the accounts of victims, the general public and business executives to ascertain how the victims feel about different white-collar criminals and their offences (1992; 2000). Such research has been particularly important in criminology studies, as victims are often ashamed to come forward when they have been offended against. In addition, Button et al (2010) use victim accounts (both written and verbal) in accessing the support for victims in England and Wales for provided by the National Fraud Authority (2010).

Accounting theory, however, is not without its critics. In particular, the original five techniques of neutralisation have been criticised in that some of the categories are not conceptually distinct, and at times overlap. Maruna and Copes (2004) argue that categories formulated by, inter alia, Sykes and Matza (1957), Scott and Lyman (1968) and Schönbach (1980; 1990) might be more theoretically precise and useful for research purposes if they were clearer and more distinct. They note also that the theory has not substantially evolved (ibid: 226), though as already noted some other refinements (detailed in Table 2.1 above) have been made in recent years.

Hirschi (1969) and Levi (2008) have also criticised neutralisation theory, on the basis that it is not always clear whether the neutralisation takes place prior to the criminal act or afterwards. Sykes and Matza suggest the possibility of a specific chronological sequence when using neutralisation techniques, although they emphasise that this order is not meant to imply a deterministic or causal relationship. In other words, neutralisations do no more than make deviant behaviour possible (1957: 666). Neutralisations may precede the act, so as to counter in advance the potential harm to the individual's image, or they may simply be post-event rationalisations.

Hindelang (1970) on the other hand, views neutralisations as purely 'after-the-fact rationalisations', and therefore not part of the causation of the crime. However, Coleman (1987: 406) and Benson (1985: 587) both acknowledge that techniques of neutralisation are not simply *ex post facto* rationalisations, and therefore may indeed form part of the motivation itself. Hirschi suggests that both schools of thought could be correct, hypothesising that neutralisations may start off as such rationalisations but later could facilitate offending in the future. He termed this the 'hardening process' (1969: 208), possibly enabling offenders to continue with their criminal behaviour into the future – with the aid of their rationalisations – even after their initial prosecution. In addition, Hirschi believes that if neutralisation takes place after the act, then the theory loses its credibility, since it merely describes how people react to their delinquency, as opposed to explaining their misdeeds.

One of the most important questions for someone giving an account of events or of their behaviour, particularly in court or other legal settings, is knowing whether their account will be 'honoured' or not. As Scott and Lyman state: 'If an account is honoured, we may say that it was efficacious and equilibrium is thereby restored in a relationship' (1968: 52). For neutralisations to be used successfully, they must be at least partially believed (Maruna and Copes, 2004: 230). Whether an account is honoured or not may depend on a number of circumstances, including the background of the offender, the expectations of interacting partners, and the social milieu in which the account is situated. Accounts which are not honoured may be termed illegitimate or unreasonable. This usually occurs when the account does not match the seriousness of the event, or when the 'vocabulary of motives' is not accepted. As a result, the equilibrium of the situation cannot be restored, as the actors' stated reason for their behaviour does not adequately account for their norm violation, and is thus not accepted.

Summary

The theory of accounting, from the perspectives of both social psychology and criminology, is undeniably useful for analysing the accounts of white-collar criminals. Scott and Lyman define accounts as 'statements made by a social actor to explain unanticipated or untoward behaviour' (1968: 56), and base much of their theory on earlier research by Sykes and Matza (1957), placing their account types into two main categories, of excuses and justifications. Since then, very few structural changes to these two main categories have occurred; however, many others have contributed to the account types, including for example Coleman (1987), who addressed accounts specifically of white-collar crimes. Work in more recent times has included research by such as Schönbach (1990) and Fritsche (2002), who have suggested additions to the two main account categories.

Scott and Lyman (1968) regard an account as a linguistic device '... to bridge the gap between actions and expectations' (1968: 46). This is crucial for social interaction. When offenders commit an act which is regarded as untoward or unacceptable by the rest of their social group, they may seek to use an account of their behaviour to save face and to restore the situation back to the *status quo ante*. However, the acceptance of such an account is not just dependent on the account given by the actor, but also on the expectations of the group to which the actor is giving the account. Accepting the account is described as 'honouring' it.

This social interaction is particularly applicable to white-collar criminals, who – compared to other, lower-status offenders – may feel a more pressing need to preserve their quasi-elite identity and status within society. They may have further to fall than most, and wish to avoid or minimise the damage liable to ensue from a degradation ceremony.

Applying accounting theory to white-collar criminals is also important to researchers, as this group of offenders are generally more able to give more detailed and fluent accounts than other offenders traditionally the subject of research. The accounting theories outlined in this chapter will be used as guiding frameworks, throughout the book, for the analysis to be undertaken.

3
Undertaking the Research

Introduction

This chapter outlines my approach to the study, detailing the method-ological strengths and weaknesses of the research. The chapter starts by considering the characteristics of the samples in other, similar studies of white-collar crime, then moves onto examine the various methodo-logies that can be used to undertake such research, paying particular attention to interviewing as a technique for collecting data. Finally, the data collection for the present study is detailed – outlining all the processes gone through, from selecting the target population to the finalisation of the sample, the characteristics of the latter are then described in detail. Throughout this book, the offences for which indi-viduals were convicted are described both in their legal terminology and in the more general terminology found in criminological and socio-logical texts. For example 'theft from employer' may also be referred to at times, as 'embezzlement'.

Researching white-collar crime

White-collar crime, as many criminologists would agree, is a much under-researched area (Levi, 2008), for many well-documented reasons. As Croall (1992: 17) notes, researchers are far more likely to turn their attentions to more visible, less complex offences, where offenders are more readily accessible and (a significant factor) where funding is more forthcoming. She argues that these factors might explain the typical approach to much white-collar crime research, typified by the prevalence of in-depth case-analyses or of media accounts (which she notes may or may not accurately represent the facts). Nevertheless, Friedrichs (1996) warns that such 'journalist research' is often biased, aimed at producing a 'good story' rather than a factual report, and tends to highlight particular types of offenders, such as those regarded as 'famous', 'victimised' or particularly 'evil' (1996: 40).

In his book *Trusted Criminals: White-collar Criminals in Contemporary Society*, Friedrichs provides what is probably the most comprehensive account to date of the main research methodologies used to study white-collar crime, although he acknowledges that much of this research employs a number of these methodologies (1996: 41). These methods include: surveys; interviews; in-depth case-analysis; historical accounts; media analysis; statistical analysis; experiments; participant observation; and biographical or autobiographical accounts.

Surveys are one of the most common means of gathering research data, being relatively easy to administer compared to other methods. They can be conducted face-to-face, over the telephone, or by mail (including email). One of the greatest difficulties in using surveys, however, is obtaining a representative sample and ensuring questions are appropriately formulated for the research being undertaken. For white-collar crime, surveys have been used in a number of areas, such as the extent of crime (e.g. Uniform Crime Reporting (UCR) data), fear of crime, victims (e.g. Blum, 1972; Vaughan and Carlo, 1975; Spalek, 2001b), and attitudes and responses to criminal behaviour (e.g. Benson, 1984; Braithwaite and Makkai, 1991).

Interviews remain a popular means of obtaining research data, and qualitative researchers may argue that the richness of the data garnered in this way can only be obtained through gathering this primary information directly. However, as with other methods, similar methodological problems exist in relation to obtaining representative samples and formulating appropriate research questions. Issues such as access to subjects, accuracy of accounts and interviewer interpretations are also pertinent. A number of white-collar crime studies have successfully been carried out via interviewing, for example those conducted by Cressey (1953), Spencer (1959), Zietz (1981), Benson (1984; 1985) and Gill (2005; 2007).

Given the difficulties of obtaining support for the research, then identifying participants and gaining access to the subjects, in-depth case-analysis is also a popular method of research (Croall, 1992). Researchers such as Geis (1967), Vaughan (1983), Cullen et al (1987) and Dodge (2009) all employ this methodology, though frequently such studies are tightly focused on topical or political issues. Historical accounts may also be used to examine particular crime features; one example is that conducted by Scott (1989) in his analysis of policing corporate collusion. Other types of in-depth subject analysis may include biographical or autobiographical accounts, such as those written by Nick Leeson, Jeffery Archer, Jonathan Aitken, Ernest Saunders and Frank Abagnale. It must be acknowledged, however, that few offenders have the ability or opportunity to publish their accounts (Maruna, 1997; Hunter, 2004) and this may remain the privilege of 'celebrities'. It has also been suggested that these accounts (as their authors frequently claim in titles or forewords) are the only true and accurate depiction of events (Hunter, 2004: 42).

Of course, the use of secondary data (in other words, that not generated by the research itself) through statistical analysis overcomes some of the problems outlined in the previous examples, and is therefore a popular method used for research into white-collar crime. Researchers are obviously reliant on the quality of the primary data collected and in using this methodology, the issue of interpretation becomes key to effective research outcomes. That aside, a number of studies, such as those by Clinard and Yeager (1980) and Wheeler et al (1982) have utilised secondary data in their research and analysis of white-collar crime.

Although not traditionally used to research white-collar offending, observation and experiments have been employed in a number of relevant studies. Such social science investigations have focused almost entirely on field (as opposed to laboratory) experiments, though Milgram's (1963) study of authority and obedience must be considered relevant here. Field experiments have included Schwartz and Scholnick's (1964) work relating to the legal stigma attaching to lower-class assaulters and to doctors, as well as Fox and Tracy's (1989) on fraudulent claims for car repairs. Obviously, one of the biggest drawbacks of such methodology, as for any research involving experiments, is controlling for the number of variables within any particular scenario.

Finally, observation may be used as a research methodology, i.e. direct observation of individuals, groups or organisations over a period of time (Friedrichs, 1996: 45). Jackall's (1988) study of corporate morality and Blumberg's (1989) study of students, involving misdemeanours in retail businesses, are examples of this type of methodology employed for research into white-collar crime. Not all scholars in this field are supportive of such an approach, with Shapiro (1980; 1990) arguing that observational practices are more successful in street-crime situations than for white-collar crime.

Target population

Before selecting the target population for the research or making approaches to organisations and institutions, it is important to ensure that terminology is clearly defined. The definition of white-collar crime offered by Sutherland has not stood the test of time, has caused confusion and has been applied inconsistently (Rosenmerkel, 2001: 313). Definitions are often 'more colourful than precise', sometimes focused on the crime, at other times on the criminal (Gibbons, 1994: 49). The definition of white-collar crime utilised for this study is that proposed by Edelhertz (1970): 'an illegal act or series of illegal acts committed by non-physical means and by concealment or guile, to obtain money or property, to avoid the payment or loss of money or property, or to obtain business or personal advantage' (1970: 3). The offenders referred to in the present study thus include individuals from any social and occupational background who had committed white-collar crimes, as defined by Edelhertz. In the introductory letter sent to prison governors, the types of offences which fit this definition – such as false accounting, conspiracy to defraud, deception, tax offences and fraudulent trading – were detailed.

Gaining access to the prisons

The methodology used in this study involved face-to-face interviewing of offenders, carried out during some 14 visits to five prisons between 1997 and 2002. Opportunities for access varied between prisons, and changed very quickly over short periods of time. As a result, such opportunities had to be seized as they presented themselves. From previous research I had undertaken, contacts had been established in HMP Sudbury and with a former governor of HMP Ford, and this helped me to gain access to their current institutions. The other prisons visited for this research were identified after sending out letters to the governors of all open prisons in England (whether housing male or female offenders), outlining my research intentions and the type of offenders suitable for interview.

Open prisons were selected after advice by the Home Office Research and Statistics Department that, at the time, most white-collar crime offenders were likely to be located in this category of institution. Although immediately after sentencing offenders would be sent to local or dispersal prisons, white-collar criminals are usually risk-assessed as posing very little threat to others, and are generally considered non-troublesome; they therefore normally serve the majority of their sentences in open prisons. Of the replies to my letters (all of which later were answered), about half showed some interest in my research, with various levels of enthusiasm about taking part in the research. The majority of outright refusals listed practical and resource problems, mainly related to staffing levels or to preparations for forthcoming inspections. Four institutions, though willing to participate, simply wished to send out questionnaires on my behalf; but as the core theme of the research was how individuals accounted verbally for their criminality, this method of data collection could not be pursued.

A provisional list of establishments willing to accommodate my research was drawn up. However prisons are, as King points out, 'volatile' places and ones where arrangements can change from day to day (2000: 291). Indeed, some institutions that had originally agreed to grant access withdrew this at a later date for various reasons, often with little notice. As Arksey and Knight warn, although a timetable may initially show a research programme is running to schedule, the interview stage often takes longer than anticipated (1999: 63); this was certainly the case for the present study.

Finally, the five institutions identified as suitable and as permitting the visits – from each of which data was eventually obtained for use in the research – were the following HMPs: Drake Hall; Guys Marsh (including a Young Offenders Institution); Morton Hall; Spring Hill; and Sudbury.

At the time of the interviews, HMP Guys Marsh was a closed prison, while the remainder were open. However, by the time of the second visit to HMP Drake Hall, it had been reclassified as semi-open (and is now a closed prison).

Selection of individual offenders

Once the list of establishments identified for visits had been finalised, the next stage was to decide which offenders would be in the sample. At this point, the help of individual prison personnel was needed in the selection of suitable offenders to interview. As a result, I had no direct contact with any of the prisoners prior to my visits, and in some instances, no details of which prisoners I would be seeing on any particular day, nor details of the exact nature and type of offences they had committed. The recruitment of offenders differed widely between individual establishments, but basically two methods were used. First, the identification of suitable offenders (following the criteria mentioned in my earlier letter to the prison governor) from the inmate database, followed by individual approaches made to these inmates through their personal prison officers. Secondly, individual departments, such as Education, Training or Psychology, were given the responsibility of identifying and approaching individuals.

By leaving the selection process to the prisons, this added a 'gate-keeping' role to the research. It would be naïve to think that offender participation was not affected by how and by whom the proposal was 'sold' to inmates, let alone the different approaches taken at each prison. As mentioned above, prisons were generally unable to provide in advance any specific details of the backgrounds of the individuals who had volunteered to take part in the study. The main reason for this was confidentiality, but a subsidiary factor was high prisoner turnover – as there was always the possibility of offenders being moved to different establishments prior to the time arranged for the interviews.

On the days I visited, therefore, no prison could be totally certain who would actually be available for interview. By the end of the fieldwork, only one offender had not been seen as arranged, but a number of additional prisoners were added to the interview schedule during this period. As Martin states, 'prisons are like goldfish bowls – everything that happens is seen and talked about by large numbers of other people' (2000: 225), and this was certainly true of each of my visits, especially those to open prisons. Although I initially blended in with the usual day-visitors, word soon circulated about what exactly I was doing. As a result, some people who had previously been approached by members of the prison staff to take part in my study, and who had declined at the time, subsequently came forward to be added to the list of interviewees, either having seen me or (more frequently) having spoken to someone who had been through the interview process. This 'snowballing' effect was evident at all the open prisons visited.

Although it was not possible to quantify precisely how many had not agreed to take part in the sessions, conversations with prison officers, other staff and inmates themselves revealed that participation varied between institutions. This may have been influenced by the promotion of the research, or by the willingness of prisoners to take part in the study. A low level of participation by higher-tariff 'city type' criminals (for example lawyers, accountants and bankers) was noted. At some institutions these higher-tariff prisoners did volunteer for interview, while at others further discussions with prison personnel and inmates revealed a degree of resistance to participating. As Slapper and Tombs (1999) note, it is much easier for the 'powerful' to avoid or even resist research than the 'powerless'. This observation cannot be dismissed: if the composition of the sample had consisted of more higher-tariff offenders, or could have been drawn from institutions (such as HMP Ford) known for holding a larger proportion of such people, the eventual research findings might have been somewhat different. Additionally, the high

number of self-employed offenders, especially among the male subjects, may have had an impact on the accounts given to explain their
offences. Finally, it was difficult to determine whether offenders' accounts
were truly genuine and accurate ones, or those which had been formulated prior to or during the commission of the crimes, or since the
arrest, sentence or incarceration of their perpetrators. It is likely that
the accounts given consisted of a mixture of these.

Interviewing

For my research, both positivist and inter-actionist data was collected
from offenders – positivist in respect of basic facts such as gender, age
and sentence, and inter-actionist (the majority of the data in this
study) relating to the nature of accounts given by offenders. It was
crucial to have a clear understanding of the factors, circumstances and
influences which led to the commission of the offenders' crimes, as
well as the rationalisations, justifications, feelings and emotions they
had experienced since being caught and incarcerated. As Rubin and
Rubin state, 'through qualitative interviews you can understand experiences and reconstruct events in which you did not participate' (1995: 2).
Contrary to other methods of research that tend to be 'one-off' in
nature (such as questionnaires, surveys and even observation), interviewing allows both the interviewer and interviewee to delve further
into meanings, motives and feelings relating to behaviour. For my research,
this enabled me not only to explore with the subjects their primary
accounts for the crimes they had committed, but also to learn further
details of how their crime, sentence and experience in jail had affected
them and their lives. As interaction between interviewer and interviewee
allows for clarification of both questions and answers, as well as a chance
to explore meanings in-depth, this method was seen to be the most appropriate for my research. Also, it allowed me to check some of the data
verbally, which would not have been possible with other methodologies.

At all the institutions, interviews were carried out in private, in rooms
assigned for the purpose. The shortest interview lasted 30 minutes and
the longest 180, with an average time of one hour each. Before any interview, all the offenders were informed that participation was entirely voluntary, and that there would be no reward or disadvantage for them
in taking part. Anonymity was guaranteed to all participants, and they
were reassured that any output from the findings would be written up
in a way that ensured they would be non-identifiable. I did not ask
for real names, though as far as I could confirm, most gave me their

real first names willingly, and a few mentioned their surnames, either directly or indirectly, in the course of their accounts. I took a non-judgemental stance, and therefore no interviewee was challenged from a personal or ethical point of view, only questioned so as to elicit more information and understanding of the circumstances surrounding their account.

Participants were given (verbally) a general outline of the study so that each could take part on the basis of informed consent – and in any case, as Jones suggests, the interviewer will probably get more information from interviewees if they know what the research area is from the beginning (2004: 259). As the outline description was provided only when the first interview with each subject took place, this might help to explain the non-participation of some offenders prior to my arrival at the prison, and subsequent participation once they had found out what the interviews entailed.

One of the difficulties in interviewing unknown people is striking up an initial rapport which allows them (and the researcher) to feel more comfortable during the interview process. Copes and Hochstetler point out that critiques of prison interviews claim such a rapport is more difficult to establish in a prison setting, and that good relations should also maintained with staff as well as inmates (2010: 54). The establishment of such relationships was particularly crucial with this study, as time with each interviewee, and to some extent at each institution, was limited. Spradley supports the importance of establishing a good relationship with subjects, and claims that if successfully developed it will move through several stages, including apprehension, exploration, co-operation and participation (2003: 45). Such phases were observed in the interviews I undertook, where offenders were initially reluctant to enter into any conversation until I had outlined the purpose of the interview, and engaged in some general conversation with them. This included what kind of work they had undertaken before, family details and, sometimes, where their family home was. Arksey and Knight suggest that the way to gain the trust of interviewees at the outset is for the interviewer to share their experiences; however, they note that opinion is divided on this point, with some feminist researchers (such as Oakley, 1981; Finch, 1984; Measor, 1985; Ribbens, 1989), suggesting that this might be intimidating for the interviewees and compromise the safety of interviewers (1999: 103). This first phase normally lasted only a short time, and generally (though not in all instances) I soon gained the trust of the individuals, who then felt confident enough to move onto exploring the issues I wanted them to discuss and to outline the circumstances surrounding the commission of their crime(s). Those who listened and weighed up what I had said before beginning the interview proper appeared to provide more information in the end than those who tended to 'jump in' straight away with their accounts.

Use of checklist and prompt sheet

Interviews were open-ended and semi-structured, giving each interviewee a chance to account for and explore the circumstances surrounding his/ her offending behaviour, identifying motives, rationalisations and feelings associated with this and with subsequent experiences in prison. Each person was provided with a checklist consisting of questions about basic, socio-demographic information (such as nationality, age, previous occupation, educational qualifications). For additional points, which I hoped the interviewee would discuss, I used a prompt sheet for myself covering such areas as the circumstances surrounding their crimes, whether they thought they deserved any gains they might have made, their experiences in prison and what plans (if any) they had for the future. Arksey and Knight support the use of such an aide-memoire as a useful interviewing prop, which they claim provides reassurance to the interviewer that the general area of the study is being adequately covered (1999: 96).

All the prisoners selected for the study completed their interviews. One inmate did not want to go into too much detail because he was shortly due for release and intended to write a book about the circumstances surrounding his conviction (though I am not aware that he ever did this.) All planned interviews (and some additional ones) were undertaken, even if some had to be re-negotiated and re-arranged at dates other than those originally planned. Prisoners often gave up or cut into their own 'free' time or meal times to finish interviews. Some commented on the 'therapeutic' nature of the interview in being given the chance to 'give their side of the story'. Two offenders commented that it was the first time they had talked to anyone about their offending, and the first time anyone had actually asked them to give an account of it, certainly since being in prison. They said: 'Thank goodness you've come ... at long last someone will understand why I am here' (Michael), and 'You are the first person that has talked to me about why I committed the crimes' (Sheila).

Liebling received similar comments during her research with prisoners, who said that they had spent more time talking to her and her team over the 14-month period of research than they had to anyone else (staff or other inmates) in the prison (1999: 161).

The process of interviewing

Copes and Hochstetler detail the 'pitfalls and promises' involved in interviewing offenders while still incarcerated (2010: 49–67). They suggest the advantages may be that such participants can be more motivated and interested; more likely to participate because it might be seen as a break from the boredom and monotony of prison life; and better placed to interpret their lives, having had time to reflect, than active offenders. Furthermore, the sample offenders can be drawn from a wider range of geographical locations than would be possible outside prison. However, there are potentially some disadvantages to interviewing prisoners, and their motives for taking part may be suspect (ibid, 2006). Copes and Hochstetler suggest that these disadvantages may include using a sample only of unsuccessful offenders ('unsuccessful' being defined as having been caught); having individuals in the sample who take part for ulterior motives; difficulties in establishing a rapport; impression-management issues that may obscure the truth; and offenders finding it difficult to recall events (ibid, 2010: 49–67). However, they conclude that at present there is no convincing evidence to discount research involving interviews with incarcerated offenders.

However, that is not to deny that the process of interviewing has been the subject of many criticisms. Silverman (1993) notes that the interviewer may become an observer in his/her own research through the social experience of the interview, views also echoed by Punch (1996: 12), who details cases that illustrate how researchers may become part of their own research, and as a result influence the findings. Dexter also warns against allowing interviewees to define and take control of interviews, though he also mentions there may be some compensatory advantages to this, in that the interviewee may raise issues and explore areas that the interviewer would not otherwise have thought of (1970: 5). (Such instances were found during my own interviews. For example, one inmate said that he saw prison as a 'rest' or 'escape' from the business pressures outside, something I had not anticipated that a white-collar offender would admit, let alone raise of his own accord). Dexter also cautions that the interviewee should not control or use the interview to tell the interviewer what they wish to talk about (ibid: 5). Some interviewees in my study did try to do this, but the use of my prompt list usually got them back on track.

The importance of the environment, especially when interviewing, should not be under-estimated, as it is sometimes difficult to recall events accurately once in a different setting to that in which they took place. This is particularly important when considering the accounts of offenders, as they are removed from the circumstances relating to their crime and therefore have to reconstruct and reinterpret the events in new surroundings. It could be argued that this might enable them to justify their behaviour far more easily than if still faced with the same situation. As Becker and Geer (2004) note, in such circumstances it is very difficult for the interviewer to gauge what is true or untrue through this new interpretation of events, and even whether some of them actually occurred at all. In addition, I noted that some offenders' ease of recall and (possibly more important to this study) their attitudes to their criminal behaviour tended to differ depending on the stage they had reached in their sentences (see Chapter 7). Offenders just commencing their term appeared more remorseful than those who had spent longer in prison, who may arguably have had more time – as Benson (1985) points out – to consider, rationalise and justify their actions. There were also a number of offenders at the start of their sentences who remained fiercely adamant about their innocence.

Denzin (1970) outlines a number of issues which can distort responses from those being interviewed. These include the different interactional roles of interviewee and interviewer; the former's need for self-presentation (especially in the early part of the interview); the fleeting and volatile nature of the interview (especially where little commitment is offered or needed by the interviewee); and interviewees not allowing the interviewer to penetrate their real worlds. In observing all these dynamics during the course of my interviews, what I noticed most of all was what Goffman (1959) termed 'performance for the audience', where offenders gave the answers that they believed were expected of them or what I wanted to hear. This ranged from pauses in accounts while attempts were being made to align responses to the headings read off the prompt sheet, to answers based on what the offender had read in books, magazines and newspapers about white-collar crime. As Scott and Lyman note, a single account may stand for a wide collection of events, the meaning of which may depend on a set of shared background expectations (1968: 53). As most socialised persons learn a repertoire of these roles during their lifetime, it is likely they will change from one to another according to circumstances and to their interlocutor.

Using a methodology based on open-ended questions raises issues about the relationships and direction of the interview. Jones (2004) believes interviewers will always be influenced by their own research interests, beliefs and previous theories, and as a result, during the interview stage, they will be constantly (and critically) making choices about what they want the interviewee to pick up and explore further.

Finally, pertinent to this type of methodological research and to other studies of elite and powerful people is the balance of power between interviewer and interviewee. Most of the research in this area relates to interviews that take place on the interviewees' territory, by researchers perceived to wield less power. In the case of this study, however, there were two areas which were very different. First, I as the interviewer had at least equal power, coming originally from a similar or higher-level business background, not to speak of being a non-offender, to all the inmates I interviewed. Secondly, the popular view that the interviewer is the underdog in the face of his/her elite and powerful subjects fails to take account of the importance of 'territory'. For this study, because the interviews took place in prison, interviewees were potentially at a disadvantage in respect of their environment, compared with being seen in their own work or social context.

Data recording

During the interviews, I recorded the background information first and then encouraged the individuals to give an account of the circumstances that had led to the commission and continuation of their offence(s). In particular, they were asked to focus upon the reasons for their criminal behaviour, outlining any rationalisations that may have occurred during its various stages, up to and including sentencing. As tape-recorders were not allowed in prison, I made handwritten notes which covered the research area and any other additional data that I regarded as potentially useful for later research (Dilulio, 1987: 271). These notes were not of course the full and exact words used by the offenders, but represented the key points for each participant, following Braithwaite.[1] It is these notes that, throughout the book, form the basis of the quotations taken from interviews with offenders.

The research notes were written up as soon as possible after each interview – in between interviews while still on site, or if not, the same evening. This was not only to ensure the accuracy of the recording of the accounts, but also to make sure the essence of my own thoughts and feelings was captured as soon as possible, allowing time to reflect on the whole fieldwork experience. As Lofland points out, the recording of such feelings serves at least two purposes: first, being honest about one's feelings towards certain subjects, and secondly, ensuring that reading the notes later would highlight any obvious biases (2004: 235). Once all the data had been collected from the 41 offenders, I extracted the basic offender descriptors, and common themes were identified to develop the conceptual frameworks. Any categorisation of actions was based on offenders' own accounts. All names and place names were changed and anonymised to protect the identity of participants.

Using interviewing as a methodology in this way raises the issue of data reliability. The main issues were the accuracy of the interviewees' accounts, and of my own recording and interpretation of these. Studying offenders once imprisoned may lead to research which focuses on inmates and inmate behaviour, rather than on active criminals. Related to this issue, especially when considering detailed accounts of motivation and neutralisation, was the plea individual offenders had entered in court compared with what they really believed about their guilt (see Chapter 4 for more detail). This was further complicated by the fact that four offenders at the time of interviewing were in the process of appealing, against either their conviction or their sentence. There were also those who denied that what they had done was actually a crime, let alone that they were criminals; therefore, engaging with these individuals was different than with those who readily admitted their guilt.

Crucial to this study was the fact that people were able to reflect back on the offences they had committed. Because the interviews took place after the offence (sometimes considerably later), the process of recall was dependent on a number of factors, not least the interviewees' memories, and the bearing this had on the accuracy of the accounts. It was also impossible to know whether or not the offenders were entirely truthful in their accounts. Given the discussion in this chapter on the importance of giving acceptable accounts, it can be understood why some members of the sample may have seen it as in their best interests not to tell me the truth, in order to 'save face' and employ strategies to rationalise their behaviour and neutralise their guilt. Even when offenders believed they were telling the truth, their accounts may not have been reflective of actual events, for a number of reasons; therefore in talking to me they may have used various linguistic truth-value devices, including what might be termed statements, facts, assertions, beliefs and opinions. There is no current empirical evidence that the accounts of incarcerated and active offenders differ to any large extent, and the limited information that is available suggests that these differences are much smaller than might be anticipated (Copes and Hochstetler, 2010: 50).

The socio-demographics of the sample[2]

Of the total of 43 offenders interviewed, 41 were used in the analysis. Two interviewees were not included in the final research findings, one because her account did not appear complete, and in any case dealt only with a domestic issue, and the second because he did not fit the stated criteria for selection, and should not therefore have been nominated.

Of the 41 offenders at issue, 32 (78 per cent) were men and nine (22 per cent) women. The female offenders were all located at HMP Drake Hall, to which two separate visits were made, at the beginning and end of the fieldwork. The remaining male offenders were located in both open and closed prisons.

Thirty-two (78 per cent) of the offenders in the sample were born in the United Kingdom, as shown in Table 3.1 below. All the offences, however, had been committed within or from the UK, therefore falling under British jurisdiction. One of the women was originally from Italy, and had married her Italian husband there in 1992 before coming to live with him in the North East of England a year later. A further woman in the sample was a 21-year-old Nigerian girl, who had spent most of her life in rural England after being adopted by a British couple. During the period of her offence, however, she had been living in City A.

Table 3.1   Offenders' country of origin

	Men		Women		Total	
United Kingdom	25	(78%)	7	(78%)	32	(78%)
Africa	5	(16%)	1	(11%)	6	(15%)
India	2	(6%)	–	(–)	2	(5%)
Europe	–	(–)	1	(11%)	1	(2%)
Total	**32**	**(100%)**	**9**	**(100%)**	**41**	**(100%)**

Of the 32 men in the sample, all but seven were of British origin. Of these seven, two were from India and five from Africa. Both the Indian offenders had lived in the UK since they were young children, and worked in professional jobs (one an accountant, the other as a Post Office owner). Three of the seven ethnic-minority offenders raised issues of racial discrimination in their accounts. The Indian Post Office owner had suffered a number of what he described as racially-motivated robberies, causing financial and business difficulties which he believed had led to his crimes. Two of the African offenders, both from Nigeria, claimed they were innocent of their crimes and felt they had been victimised because of their race and assumptions made about it.

From the information provided by the offenders, the age when they first committed the offences in question ranged from 19 to 62 years, giving an average age of 39 years. Thirty-five (85 per cent) of the offenders in the sample had completed their secondary or some higher education, leaving six (14 per cent) who had not.

At the time of the interviews 28 of the offenders (22 men and 6 women) were married or co-habiting (Table 3.2 below). In many instances the effect of their involvement in crimes and/or imprisonment had impacted on this and several were in varying stages of separation or estrangement (see Chapter 7 for further discussion of losses).

Table 3.2   Marital status of offenders

	Men		Women		Total	
Married/ Co-habiting	22	(69%)	6	(67%)	28	(68%)
Single	10	(31%)	3	(33%)	13	(32%)
Total	**32**	**(100%)**	**9**	**(100%)**	**41**	**(100%)**

Thirty-five (85 per cent) of the offenders were either employed or self-employed at the time of their offence, with four (10 per cent) unemployed and two (5 per cent) who were students. Of the 35 in employment, 32 (91 per cent, 25 men and 7 women) had committed their offences in the course of their work. The remaining three offenders included a bar manager convicted of deception relating to housing benefit, and two convicted of conspiracy to defraud in separate, unrelated cases. One of the latter two was a property broker who had been involved in Internet credit-card fraud; the other was a legal assistant for a satellite-television company, and had been involved in conspiring to defraud high-street banks.

Occupations of offenders within the sample varied immensely, from student, transport-owner and furniture-maker to professions more traditionally regarded as white-collar, such as accountants, solicitors and a bank manager, as summarised in Table 3.3. Twenty-three of the employed offenders (22 men and 1 woman) were self-employed, either as sole proprietors or in partnerships.

Of the 41 offenders interviewed, only 26 (63 per cent, 23 men and 3 women) involved others in committing their offences. This would seem to support the findings of Coleman, who notes that men appear

Table 3.3 Occupational category

	Men		Women		Total	
Director/Owner/ Co-owner	16	(60%)	1	(12%)	17	(49%)
Licensed professions	4	(14%)	–	(–)	4	(11%)
Executive/ Management	6	(22%)	5	(63%)	11	(31%)
Administrative/ Clerical	1	(4%)	2	(25%)	3	(9%)
Total	**27**	(100%)	**8**	(100%)	**35**	(100%)

to be more task-oriented in their approach to criminal activities, and tend to work with others more than women (1994: 225). In addition, Steffensmeier and Allan found women were more likely to be solo perpetrators, and where they did work in groups did so as accomplices to men rather than as leaders (1996: 466).

Thirty-eight offenders had been involved in separate criminal activities, and three inmates, all being held at HMP Spring Hill, had been charged in the same case (which involved only these three), though all three had been charged, tried and convicted for slightly different offences, at different dates and covering different periods of time. Besides these three, I also interviewed a computer consultant at HMP Morton Hall who was part of a much larger 12-man computer scam. In this case, the other 11 offenders involved had been moved to other prisons the week before I started interviews, although for most of their sentence they had all been held together at Morton Hall.

A total of 51 offences had been committed by the 41 offenders, nine of whom had been convicted of more than one offence. The distribution of different offences is shown in Table 3.4. In overall terms, four types of offences (conspiracy-related, deception-related, false accounting and theft from employer) accounted for 70 per cent of all the offences. The next most prevalent types of offences (fraudulent trading andtaxation-related) accounted for a further 16 per cent of all offences.

The increasing use of technology, especially computers and the Internet, has been widely addressed in the literature, particularly in relation to the area of white-collar crime (for example, Grabosky and Smith, 1998; Wall, 1999; Newman and Clarke, 2003; Jewkes, 2003; Smith et al, 2004; Grabosky, 2006). Only one offender in the study,

Table 3.4   Offences committed by offenders (number of instances)

Offence	Total	%
Conspiracy-related	18	(35%)
Deception-related	8	(15%)
False accounting	5	(10%)
Theft from employer	5	(10%)
Fraudulent trading	4	(8%)
Taxation-related	4	(8%)
Forgery	2	(4%)
Credit-card offences	1	(2%)
Trades-description offences	1	(2%)
Money-laundering	1	(2%)
Attempting to pervert the course of justice	1	(2%)
Perjury	1	(2%)
Total	**51**	**(100%)**

however, had been directly involved in defrauding people by targeting services provided via the Internet. Specifically, (in the early days of the Internet when sites were not so secure as they now are) he had defrauded online credit-card companies and banks. As the use of technology has increased considerably since some of my interviews, the likelihood is that this kind of offence has now also increased. In line with this, improvements in detection procedures have also become increasingly sophisticated. The majority of offences involving technology included the use of computers. The falsification of documents ranged from tampering with paperwork to amending ledger records and forging cheques or other negotiable instruments.

Table 3.5 details the relationship between the offenders and their victim(s). Seventeen (41 per cent) of the 41 offenders committed their crimes either against their employer or the government. Most of the latter offences related to the Inland Revenue, either by knowingly evading duty payable or cheating HM Customs and Excise.[3] These were all by self-employed men who owned (or part-owned) companies, including a transport firm set up solely to import cheap tobacco from Eastern Europe and evade payment of duty, an electrician who did not pay the correct amount of VAT and income tax when the company hit financial difficulties, a builder who underestimated his corporation tax

Table 3.5   Relationship of the offender to the victim

Victim	Men		Women		Total	
Government	8	(25%)	2	(22%)	10	(24%)
Employer	2	(6%)	5	(56%)	7	(17%)
Client	1	(3%)	–	(–)	1	(2%)
Other	21	(66%)	2	(22%)	23	(57%)
Total	**32**	**(100%)**	**9**	**(100%)**	**41**	**(100%)**

to avoid payment and a market trader who tried to evade paying any taxes at all.

Speculative figures regarding the costs of crime exist for all types of offences. However, the National Fraud Authority estimated the cost of fraud in the UK in 2008 at some £30.5 billion. White-collar crime is thought to be considerably under-reported, especially to the police, with organisations often preferring to deal with the matters them-selves, in-house (Ernst & Young, 2003: 3). For my study, figures were given by the offenders during interviews relating to the amount entered at the time of trial and for which they had been imprisoned. The total amount stated in court for the 41 offenders totalled nearly £240 million (£239,520,500), ranging from £18,000 to £100 million. However, as outlined earlier, 26 in the sample had been involved in cases with one or more other co-offender(s) (the latter who may have been part of this study or not). The remaining 15 offenders, those who acted alone in the commission of their crimes, were sentenced for offences involving a total of £1,563,500.

Table 3.6   Length of sentence imposed on offenders

Months	Men		Women		Total	
<13	1	(2%)	3	(33%)	4	(10%)
13–24	4	(13%)	3	(33%)	7	(18%)
25–36	11	(34%)	1	(11%)	12	(29%)
37–48	12	(38%)	2	(23%)	14	(34%)
48+	4	(13%)	–	(–)	4	(9%)
Total	**32**	**(100%)**	**9**	**(100%)**	**41**	**(100%)**

From the accounts given by offenders at their trial, 26 (63 per cent, 19 men and 7 women) of the 41 claimed to have pleaded guilty to at least one of the charges brought against them. At the time of the study, four men who had entered a not-guilty plea at the time of their trial mentioned that they were appealing. The length of sentences imposed is detailed in Table 3.6. From the accounts given, four of the offenders (3 men and 1 woman) claimed to have had previous convictions (excluding motoring offences). Only one of these previous cases was for white-collar crime (as defined in this study), and this offender had not previously received a jail sentence.

In summary, the profile of a typical offender from the sample was male (78 per cent in total), who had originated from the UK (78 per cent) and with an average age of 39 years. Nearly all the crimes (91 per cent) were committed during the course of the offenders' occupations, and well over half (63 per cent) involved others. Four types of offences – conspiracy-related, deception-related, false accounting and theft from employer (embezzlement) – made up 70 per cent of all the offences committed by the 41 offenders in the sample, resulting in 91 per cent of them receiving sentences of four years or less.

Part II

White-Collar Crime Offenders' Accounts

4
Outer-Legal Self and Inner-Moral Self

Introduction

This chapter considers the importance of managing an individual's stigmatisation, by reviewing the pleas made in court by the offenders, compared to their own personal belief in their guilt. They may go through a number of stages in admitting their guilt over the period of their offending and incarceration. Chapters 5, 6 and 7 examine how they viewed their crime, from their original motivation through to the assessment, when imprisoned, of their gains and losses. However, the first matter considered here is how they viewed their offence when choosing to plead guilty or not guilty in court.

Within the sample of 41 offenders, 26 (63 per cent) had pleaded guilty in court. There was some variation here between the genders, with 59 per cent of men (n = 19) and 78 per cent of women (n = 7) pleading guilty. Nevertheless, as Rothman and Gandossy point out, a guilty plea is not always as clear-cut as it might first appear, and often defendants may only grudgingly acknowledge their guilt. They note that a guilty plea may not itself be an indication of admitting full personal responsibility, stating that many offenders maintain their innocence throughout their prison sentence. Furthermore, they caution that pleading guilty in court may have little relevance to the level of acceptance of guilt admitted by individuals to themselves, or other audiences outside the criminal-justice system, during the trajectory of their offending and incarceration (1982, p.455).

The importance of being able to manage the labelling process so as to avoid stigmatisation as a criminal is particularly crucial for white-collar offenders (Sykes and Matza, 1957; Benson, 1984; McBarnet, 1991). However, for many of these individuals achieving this may create personal tensions between their internal, 'inner-moral' self, and the presentation of their external, 'outer-legal' self. During the interviews, the accounts offered by the subjects – used in the first instance to measure the level of their acceptance of their guilt – gave details of their legal plea in court. Either through the accounts of their behaviour, by direct admission, or by the very nature of their accounts, a mismatch in some offenders between their outer-legal and inner-moral selves became evident. In other words, what they had pleaded in court did not always agree with what they believed to be true. By using their accounts of the formal plea entered in court, compared with those of their internal acceptance (or otherwise) of their criminality in a non-judicial setting, a typology of legal and moral acceptance of guilt was developed, as detailed in Figure 4.1 below.

The analysis highlights four distinct categories of offenders relating to their acceptance of criminality and of the preservation of their characters, which were termed 'total rejectors', 'acceptors', 'tactical acceptors' and 'tactical rejectors'. Allocating each offender to one of these categories was not a straightforward process because of the detailed nature and complexity of his/her account. In addition, data gathered during interviews was

Figure 4.1 Typology of outer-legal and inner-moral selves with respect to acceptance of guilt by white-collar offenders

LEGAL PLEA
(outer-legal)

	Not guilty	Guilty
Not guilty ACCEPTANCE (inner-moral)	TOTAL REJECTORS 14 offenders (34%)	TACTICAL ACCEPTORS 6 offenders (15%)
Guilty	TACTICAL REJECTORS 1 offender (2%)	ACCEPTORS 20 offenders (49%)

recorded at a particular point in time, and therefore could be subject to change over the duration of offenders' sentences.

Total rejectors

Of the 41 offenders interviewed, 14 (34 per cent) were classified as total rejectors. These included those offenders who claimed to have pleaded not guilty in court and who, in addition, demonstrated through their accounts, by various linguistic techniques, that they believed themselves not to be guilty. All the offenders in this category rejected the criminality of their behaviour and thus their treatment as criminals. They believed that they had been falsely imprisoned, and that the decision to label them as criminals was wrong and unjust. They fought both the legal and personal definitions of criminality.

Total rejectors were regarded as those individuals who wished, and possibly needed, to preserve their previous 'good' identity and therefore refused to accept, either legally or personally, being labelled a criminal. Given the importance to them of preserving their self-image and moral standing, it was not surprising to find that approximately a third of the total sample were in this category.

Several strategies were employed by total rejectors to demonstrate this denial. These included claims that their activities were not criminal, or that they were not personally liable for any activities that might have taken place, often displacing blame for their actions or claiming that they had merely been picked upon or victimised, thereby seeing themselves as the real victim.

Case study – Michael

Michael was a 51-year-old, single-handed solicitor who had been sentenced to 42 months for false accounting. He was accused of billing clients beyond the true value of the work undertaken on their behalf, to the extent of a quarter of a million pounds. The matter had been brought to the attention of the police when a daughter of one of his clients, for whom he held power of attorney,[1] reported her suspicions regarding over-billing. When confronted by this, Michael rejected the assertion that the bills had been costed above their true rate, and he also claimed to have had them checked by an independent, qualified person. He stated: 'The bills I originated were not inflated, in my opinion. I got a stockbroker who had been a fund manager for a firm of solicitors to advise me. He denied this in court, though.'

In his account, Michael not only denied that his actions had been criminal, or that he had been involved in any criminal behaviour, but also distanced himself from the what had taken place in his office by claiming that his input to the billing process was minimal. He explained: 'I originated these [the invoices] and my secretary typed them and posted them. The book-keeper and auditor did the accounts, VAT and control accounts. I never did my own books. My book-keeper has since died and the accountants were not helpful.'

Michael was fairly typical of other offenders classified as rejectors in his denial of his actions being anything but legitimate, and also in removing himself from the situation. In this way, he was rejecting involvement in any illegality that might have taken place, thereby attempting to preserve both his outer-legal and inner-moral self.

Unsurprisingly, because of their refusal, both moral and legal, to accept their criminality, the four offenders in the sample who were launching appeals at the time of the interviews were all located in the rejectors' category. Three were appealing against the actual conviction itself, and the fourth against the length of his sentence. Of the three appealing against the actual conviction, two – Darren and Jack – both used the argument that their particular businesses, contrary to the conclusion of the courts, had both been trading solvent,[2] and thus no criminal activity had taken place.

Case study – Jack

Jack, a self-employed accountant, had been sentenced to 60 months for fraudulent trading. He claimed that the judge and jurors did not understand the complexity of his case or of his business, and therefore no-one could comment as an expert on whether he was trading insolvent or not. He claimed: 'I was accused of fraudulent trading … it is under appeal. There was confusion in court. Someone mentioned double-entry and keeping two sets of books. The judge and jury did not understand. They thought I was keeping a false set of accounts along with the real ones.'

In a similar fashion, Darren presented an argument that the company he part-owned was trading from a solvent base.

Case study – Darren

Darren, finance director and co-owner of a motor-trade company, had been sentenced for conspiracy to defraud, along with other colleagues, totalling approximately £10 million. The issues surrounding this well-publicised case related again to whether the company was trading solvent or not, prior, in this instance, to its flotation[3] on the Stock Exchange. This was a particularly large and complex case, with the proprietors maintaining that they were trading solvent, and the prosecution arguing the reverse.

The third offender appealing against the conviction itself was Harry, an owner and manager of a jewellery business who had been convicted of conspiracy to defraud. He, like both Darren and Jack, felt that his business had been misunderstood, especially in court. He claimed: 'I'm not guilty ... they misunderstood my business. The judge and jury had no clue what it was all about.'[4]

The fourth individual whose case was under appeal did not personally believe he was guilty of conspiracy to defraud; however, he was appealing only against the length of his sentence, a course of action which, he claimed, he had only pursued on the advice of his solicitor. He commented: 'I do not accept my guilt and I am appealing against the length of sentence.'

A further strategy to mitigate their guilt used by the 14 offenders classified as total rejectors – where they acknowledged that some illegal activity had indeed taken place – was to deny responsibility for it. They attempted to do this by blaming other individuals, in a bid to preserve their own moral and legal selves. In direct contrast to Michael, for example, who denied that any illegality had taken place, a number of individuals in this category acknowledged that there had been some criminal activity, but they were at pains to deny their own involvement in it, usually by claiming that associates or colleagues were responsible.

Case study – Pam

Fifty-year-old Pam had co-owned and run a shop with her husband. She, alongside him and another person, had been sentenced to 24 months' imprisonment for conspiracy to obtain goods by deception. She had pleaded not guilty, and denied any personal involvement of these illegal activities: 'I used to have a shop selling knick-knacks. I was charged with my husband and one other at the shop. I was looking after my mother-in-law at the time through cancer, so I could not know what was going on.' She claimed her husband and his associate were responsible for the crime, and stated she did not even know where her husband was serving his sentence.

Another example of distancing himself from the criminal activity so as to deny any involvement in it was Stan, the 45-year-old owner of an electrical company.

Case study – Stan

With a partner, Stan had previously run a painting and decorating business. He had been sentenced to 36 months' imprisonment for VAT fraud, amounting to some £350,000, relating to this earlier company. He claimed that his partner had looked after all the paperwork associated with the business, and that he had only found out about the offence some time after it had commenced. Therefore he had not knowingly been involved, and as a result had pleaded not guilty: 'We had a successful business. However, around 1994 we started to hit financial difficulties and the other partner evidently never paid the VAT. He had set up an employment agency, and took people on that way as a fiddle around the tax. I only knew about it three-quarters of the way through, that he had not paid the tax. I would not knowingly get involved and was not knowingly this time at the beginning.'

Stan thus sought to deny any involvement in the criminal activity and to preserve his identity as non-criminal. He also tried to justify his innocence, and to distance himself further from the crime, by highlighting that it transpired that his business partner was also involved in other criminal activities, outside their company: 'The partner and accountant were linked to a big tax fraud in Town B.' Stan was also keen to suggest that crime was more familiar to others, and sometimes appeared to be a 'way of life' for them. He believed that those who were not criminals often got caught up in investigations, and wrongly charged by the police, merely because of their association with these more persistent offenders.

The accounts of Darren, Jack and Stan, for example, demonstrate that subjects often rely on the complexities of business situations as a defence, especially when these relate to a chain of accountability for certain tasks and areas of work. In their accounts, therefore, they attempted to stress their innocence and preserve their characters by avoiding or blurring their workplace responsibilities. Others who blamed their associates and colleagues included Matt, a 27-year-old stock accountant who had been sentenced to 54 months' imprisonment for conspiracy to defraud.

Case study – Matt

Matt claimed to have been working for individuals who ran a company which purchased stock from outside suppliers, and then sold that stock on through a number of shops which they owned themselves. In the course of their business they dealt with many companies as suppliers. When their own company hit difficult economic times, in order to be able to continue to obtain stock for distribution through their own shops, they purposely used known suppliers. These were companies which were deemed not to realise money was already owed to them. This allowed them to acquire further stock, for which they were unable to pay. Matt claimed that in his job he was not directly involved in the purchase of stock, and therefore innocent of any such crime. Like Stan, he was keen to stress that the owners and directors of the company had undertaken this kind of criminal activity before, revealing that: 'The others had done this before ... it was a way of life and the two brothers continued in our absence around Town C.'

Likewise, Tarik claimed to have been arrested for credit-card fraud only because of his association with others.

Case study – Tarik

Tarik was an unemployed 24-year-old, sentenced to 42 months for conspiracy to defraud. He said that he was merely a carer for his wife, and therefore he could not have been involved. Perceiving himself to be innocent, Tarik said that he did not believe that he would go to jail and therefore pleaded not guilty. He was keen to point out that it was his associate who was the criminal, not himself: 'A friend used my details and therefore *he* was the guilty one' (emphasis as in original).

In the same way, Alison, one of the women in this category, also blamed others for her imprisonment. Although a number of offenders in the sample gave blackmail as a factor in their getting involved in criminal activities, Alison was the only one who claimed to have been involved purely because of blackmail.

Case study – Alison

Alison, a 50-year-old credit-control assistant in a bank, pleaded not guilty in court, claiming she had been coerced into her crime by others. She did however, recognise and admit that she had committed a crime, but claimed she had no control over this. Alison viewed herself therefore as both legally and morally innocent. She claimed to have been placed in a position where she was unable to confide in anyone at her workplace because the blackmailers had told her there were others in the bank involved and they would know if she informed the company of what she was doing. She pointed out that she found her position very stressful: 'In March/April 2000 the pressure of it became too much and I phoned the Samaritans from work to talk to someone else, but they only said to do the things I had been told not to do.'

After a number of months, Alison's activities were uncovered by the bank, when they put a trace on her work computer. She was arrested and eventually brought to trial, along with a number of other offenders involved in the case. However, she was the only one of the group to plead not guilty, claiming this was on the advice of her legal team. In recalling her trial during her interview she said: 'Seven people were eventually tried at the same time ... no others from the bank. Six pleaded guilty. I pleaded not guilty, under duress; I trusted the legal people who recommended this. I had been advised by them that I would be found not guilty.'

It is suggested therefore that blackmail, which makes those subjected to it feel helpless and involved in situations beyond their control, can be used as a strategy for denying criminality.

A number of individuals in the sample felt that they had been unfairly picked upon or targeted in some way. By claiming this victimisation as a strategy for minimising their guilt is similar to that described by Sykes and Matza (1957) as 'condemnation of the condemners', or as what McCorkle and Korn (1954) term 'rejection of the rejectors'. This is where the offender seeks to shift the focus to those making the accusations, by questioning their reasons and motives for doing so. The police as the main law-enforcement agency are an obvious target for individuals to single out for such condemnation in their accounts, and this was also evident in the study. One example of an offender who accounted for his behaviour in this way was Bharat.

Case study – Bharat

Bharat, a 38-year-old management accountant, was employed by a national chain of garages. He pleaded not guilty to fraudulent trading, but with others was sentenced to 45 months. He claimed that the police made numerous visits to the motor centres he managed, and persisted with their enquiries until they found something that they classed as illegal. He complained that: 'We were hounded by the police ... lots of garages were at this time.'

Bharat told of how other staff in his organisation had also suffered as a result of this 'harassment'. He stated: 'The police went on two or three occasions to Town D to make arrests. They arrested a 17-year-old trainee who was later let go. The accountant was also let off.'

In addition to the claims of specific harassment and victimisation detailed by Bharat, a number of individuals in the sample who were of foreign origin used defences related to cultural or racial differences in accounting for their behaviour, and in refusing to accept their guilt. Two in particular, Mazi and Okeke, both natives of Nigeria, felt very strongly that Nigerians in the UK had inherited an extremely bad reputation, and that this had contributed to their being arrested and viewed as criminals. Their comments included: 'Nigerians are picked on for white-collar crime. People do not understand what it is like in Nigeria. In my eyes (and God's) I have done nothing wrong' (Okeke), and 'I was victimised because I am Nigerian' (Mazi).

Acceptors

The second category identified in the typology is acceptors. Acceptors represent those individuals who pleaded guilty in court and acknowledged, at least to some extent, that they were guilty of an offence and that their behaviour was wrong. Therefore, in contrast to total rejectors, they had acknowledged the guilt of their outer-legal self and also that of their inner-moral self, i.e. without attempting to preserve their characters either externally to others or internally to themselves. Twenty offenders (49 per cent) were originally identified in the sample as fitting this description.

By acknowledging and accepting their guilt, both to themselves and others, this group of individuals did the least to preserve their previous good characters. However, there were some accounts which, one could argue, did try to mitigate or lessen their guilt to some extent, by trying to justify some of their criminal behaviour. For this reason, the accounts of all 20 offenders were reanalysed, and this process identified two main sub-groups of acceptors – 'total' and 'reasoned'. Total acceptors were defined as those individuals who had pleaded guilty and did not put forward any mitigating factors in their accounts. Of the 20 offenders in the category of overall acceptors, there was only one participant who met these criteria, and who in her account of her criminal behaviour said nothing at all to try and mitigate or excuse it. Anne, a single, 38-year-old supermarket-garage manager, had been sentenced to 12 months (with six months suspended) for falsifying accounts and theft from her employer, amounting in total to £101,000. She had great difficulty in trying to explain her behaviour: 'I do not know why I did it ... I have no excuse or reason ... I have tried to think why ... I cannot come up with anything ... I accept that I am a criminal.'

The remaining 19 subjects in this category were defined as reasoned acceptors. The accounts of offenders in this group provided mitigating factors which they thought made their crimes seem more understandable and acceptable. Of these 19 individuals, 13 were men and six were women, representing by far the largest percentage of women in any of the four categories in the typology. As Collins and Collins noted, of their own interviews with white-collar offenders: 'The man justified committing the crime because he needed the money to keep a failing business afloat, or because "everyone did it", but only he was unlucky enough to have gotten caught. In contrast, every female interviewed acknowledged [her] crime, and was remorseful' (2000: 2).

Women in this category were thus more willing to accept a criminal label for their illegal behaviour, and generally to show remorse for what they had done. One person who was particularly remorseful was Debbie, a 42-year-old restaurant manager.

Case study – Debbie

Debbie was employed along with her husband and son by a large national chain, but acted alone in embezzling £40,000 from her employer. She claimed to have taken the money in secret to help get her daughter off drugs, before she was able to get her onto an official NHS programme. When she was caught, the thought of going to jail was just too much for her. She said: 'I sent a letter to the judge explaining why I did what I did. My barrister put over a good case. I would normally get two to three years for this amount of money, but given the circumstances, the judge overruled this.'

In the case of Debbie, such mitigating factors appear to have been taken into consideration in the final judgement and Debbie was sentenced to 12 months imprisonment, with six months suspended. Debbie thought that being open and honest, as well as possibly writing to the judge, had paid off for her. Pleading guilty though was not always met with such leniency as one offender – Jason, found.

Case study – Jason

Jason, a 29-year-old divorced furniture-maker and business owner, was sentenced for deception and for obtaining property while bankrupt. His crime did not involve others, and he claimed he was merely trying to save his company from difficult financial times. He had no prior criminal convictions, and he thought his sentence would therefore be lenient, especially as he had been honest and candid, and had pleaded guilty. He said: 'My sister said to plead guilty and I would only get six months.' However, this tactic failed, the judge sentencing Jason to 36 months in prison.

When caught, most of the offenders in this category had expressed relief that their ordeal was effectively over. Many had hidden crimes from their families (especially those crimes which could be classified as being committed out of need, rather than greed) and therefore had carried a heavy burden of guilt. Ruth, a 22-year-old single Nigerian, had been convicted of conspiracy to defraud and sentenced to 46 months in prison. She claimed that her involvement in illegal activities had been indirectly influenced by her boyfriend and by other Nigerians. Ruth accepted her guilt and expressed relief at being able to start her life afresh: 'I was relieved when caught ... I could get out of that lifestyle and the people associated with it. I accept I committed a crime.' Similarly, Jason, the furniture-maker confessed to being 'relieved when I was caught ... [that] it was all over.'

In addition, to believing their guilt and expressing relief when caught, some offenders also commented in their interviews that they deserved to be given a custodial sentence, although not all relished the prospect. As Debbie said: 'I deserve to be here. I did offer to pay costs instead of going to prison, though.'

Sally, a 33-year-old management accountant who had falsified accounts, taking £251,000 from her employer over a period of four years, expressed relief when her criminal activities were brought to an end: 'I was relieved when everything was out in the open and I was caught. I deserved a custodial sentence.'

Individuals in this category were those who accepted the fact of their crimes and their criminal labels, but also those who were able to, and did, exercise an element of choice over their outer and inner self. As such, this category consisted of those who were both totally accepting and those who put forward mitigating circumstances, who were termed reasoned acceptors.

Tactical rejectors

Tactical rejectors were defined as those in the sample who pleaded not guilty in court but who, through their accounts, believed in, acknowledged and admitted their guilt. This strategy relied on the chance of being found not guilty in court for various reasons, including poor evidence and the complexity of cases. Applying the typology to the sample, only one offender (2 per cent) fitted this description, Adrian.

Case study – Adrian

Adrian, a 30-year-old, self-employed owner of a transport business, was sentenced to 48 months for evading tobacco duty (with others), amounting to over £2.6 million. He ran a legitimate transport business alongside one specifically set up for the illegal import of large quantities of tobacco from Eastern Europe. The idea was to distribute the tobacco within the UK for profit, boosted by the evasion of import taxes. It was a highly-planned and organised operation, set up to run for a specified length of time and to import a certain quantity of tobacco.

Adrian claimed that the group's activities were discovered when one of his associates in Europe deposited a sum of money overnight in an American bank in Belgium, which the bank (because of the large sums involved) believed to be connected with drugs. The associate was arrested, turned Queen's Evidence,[5] and the company was put under surveillance for a number of weeks. Eventually, Adrian as the owner was arrested, along with others. Adrian claimed that his home computers were searched but little evidence was found. In addition, he commented that the police were not really prepared for a case of this magnitude, whereas he had claimed he had already got himself a legal team. The person in Belgium who had turned Queen's Evidence later fled to Canada and therefore was not available to give evidence in court. Adrian concluded that the police had a very weak case, and was prepared to risk pleading not guilty, as he was not sure they would be able to prove much without the fugitive's evidence. He commented: 'Only two months prior to the trial, at disclosure, did I find out about the Queen's Evidence. Without that they would have had no case. But then he [the potential witness who had turned Queen's Evidence] had fled to Canada.'

Adam, another participant in the sample, had undertaken a similarly planned and organised crime relating to online banking fraud (see Chapter 5 for further details of his offence). In contrast to Adrian, however, Adam had pleaded guilty, and was therefore classified as a tactical acceptor. He had not taken advantage of the complexity of the case and lack of understanding by the police and others, although he did comment that his barrister had said that he could consider pleading not guilty, given the nature of the case. Adam remarked that: 'The police didn't have a clue what they were dealing with.'

A tactical rejector was therefore identified as someone who liked to 'play the game', a 'wide boy' or a gambler, someone with the confidence, and perhaps even the arrogance or stubbornness, to be willing to take the chance of pleading not guilty, although they knew themselves to be guilty. In contrast to reasoned acceptors, tactical rejectors were not willing to accept their legal label as a criminal (perhaps for practical rather than psychological reasons), to preserve their 'image'. However, in comparison with reasoned acceptors, they did acknowledge their wrong-doing to themselves.

Tactical acceptors

Tactical acceptors could be seen as the opposite of tactical rejectors – individuals who pleaded guilty in court, but who, through their accounts internally to themselves and externally to others, did not accept they were guilty of a crime. Although this admission may not immediately make sense, tactical acceptors appear to be willing to accept the external legal label of being a criminal in an attempt to reduce, or even avoid, a custodial sentence. What was very apparent with this group was the effect they thought their plea would have on their sentence. In other words, if convicted, a guilty plea would in normal circumstances attract a lower sentence compared to a not-guilty plea. This strategy is well-known among this type of offender, and can sometimes inflate guilty-plea figures for white-collar criminals. In the sample, evidence of this was demonstrated by the case of Stan, discussed above in the category of total rejectors. His statement demonstrates that tactical acceptors may indeed be correct in their assumptions about pleading guilty: 'I pleaded not guilty and got three years. My partner pleaded guilty and got two years.'

Through the analysis of the outer-legal self and the inner-moral self, six individuals (15 per cent) fitted the criteria for this category. Pleading guilty in order to try and secure a lower sentence was therefore not uncommon with this group, many individuals claiming to have done so as a result of advice from their legal team or others, often including police officers – the option is commonly favoured by legal bodies such as the Crown Prosecution Service and police because of the complexity of some cases and the corresponding time and resources they can take up. An example was seen with the case of Roger, a 64-year-old garage-owner.

Case study – Roger

Roger had been sentenced to 45 months in prison for trade-description offences and conspiracy to defraud, totalling approximately £40,000. He claimed that his assistant altered the mileage of the cars he sold, thus committing the offences for which he, Roger, was charged. Roger had initially pleaded not guilty, but later claimed to have changed his plea as a result of a 'deal' with Trading Standards. He stated: 'The judge remanded me to Town E prison. While I was there, Trading Standards approached my barrister to say if I pleaded guilty they would not pursue others [cases]. So I pleaded guilty.'

Similar circumstances were also noted by three other offenders (Gareth, Patrick and Stuart), separately convicted of offences relating to a group of companies they owned and ran together. Their cases were extremely complex and time-consuming, and took a number of months to investigate. All three individuals claimed that they (the only three involved in the cases) undertook some kind of 'plea bargain' with the police to reduce bureaucracy and possibly the length of their sentences: 'I did a plea bargain for a lower sentence' (Stuart), and 'I got sentenced but did a plea bargain because of the complex nature of the case … they brought the charge down from conspiracy to defraud to fraudulent trading. I got a four-year discount for an early [guilty] plea' (Gareth).

The individuals in this tactical acceptors' category could therefore be seen as 'purposeful calculators', who had worked out the best way possible to 'play the system', and who were willing to sacrifice their external legal self for their own practical benefit. In contrast to tactical rejectors, they were not willing to take the chance of being found not guilty, and instead weighed up the most likely or even pessimistic outcome.

Summary

This chapter has highlighted that offenders are indeed to some extent sensitive to the implications of being labelled as criminal, even before conviction. Clearly, it is in their interests to maintain their social status and to be able to return to their jobs and careers at a later date, even if convicted. In order to mitigate the negative labels, a number of techniques were used to try and manage this process, through impression management (as described by Goffman, 1959). This included trying to alter their image as criminals, both to themselves and others, through inter-individual or intra-individual accounts (as defined by Fritsche, 2002). It is perhaps comforting to know that nearly half of those interviewed were willing fully to accept their labels as criminals, by pleading guilty in court and acknowledging their guilt to both themselves and others. However, there were still 34 per cent who were classified as total rejectors – those who refused to accept either an outer-legal or an inner-personal label as a criminal. Positioned between these two categories there remained seven offenders who were willing to use their legal plea as a tactic (either as tactical rejectors or tactical acceptors) to help preserve their characters internally or externally, at the same time trying to reduce, or even avoid, a custodial sentence.

Nevertheless, whether offenders accepted their guilt, either internally or externally, nearly all raised some kind of mitigating circumstances in their accounts, to try and either deny or play down their criminal involvement. These techniques ranged from claiming that no crime had been committed, through to pointing out that no one was hurt as a result of their behaviour. The fact remains that when white-collar offenders' character is threatened and attacked, they will fight in many ways to retain their status and preserve their standing to themselves, others and the community.

5
Motivation, Opportunity and Rationality

Introduction

This chapter explores various motivations given for their crimes by the offenders in the study. Braithwaite (1985) notes that while very few studies have been carried out on this aspect of white-collar crime, the literature has revealed a range of motivations, which are often interlinked (see for instance Alalehto, 2003; Friedrichs, 1996; Holtfreter, 2005; Paternoster and Simpson, 1993; Shover and Hochstetler, 2006). Levi (2008) develops a typology which distinguishes between three types of fraudsters: 'pre-planners', those who start by constructing a plan to commit their crime; 'intermediate planners', who turn from honesty to fraud because of various experiences they have encountered; and 'slippery-slope' fraudsters, who (usually through reckless behaviour) incur debts which lead them into committing crime. During their interviews, offenders in the present study detailed a multitude of motivations and reasons, some of which overlapped, for their offending. They represented themselves as 'actors' in different situations to explain their deviant behaviour (in a similar way to that postulated in Levi's typology). Individuals gave accounts describing both primary and secondary motivations, which covered a number of often multiple reasons and pressures. When these accounts were analysed, individuals presented themselves in one of three main ways – as 'rational', 'pressurised' or 'seduced' actors. However, it should be noted that individuals act in very individual ways and therefore the analysis is subjective, so considerable overlap between categories may occur.

Offenders acting rationally

From the offenders interviewed, rational actors were identified as those who were very well-organised and planned carefully in their approach

Figure 5.1   Scale of rationality shown by white-collar offenders

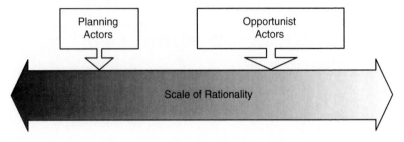

to crime, whether their opportunities were found by design or by accident. This rationality was conceived of as a scale (see Figure 5.1), at one end of which are planning actors, who behaved very rationally and who put a lot of time, effort and other resources into the planning and execution of their crimes. These offenders were likely to go looking for an opportunity to commit their crime after they had planned it. The other sub-category of rational subjects is found further along the scale – opportunist actors. Unlike the planners, these individuals had not originally set out to commit a crime as part of a wider 'life plan' and had not gone out looking for such opportunities. Instead, they took advantage of situations they had already become aware of, or when they came across unexpected opportunities they were unable to resist pursuing. In contrast to planning actors, these opportunists planned their crimes only after identifying a suitable opportunity.

The extent of rationality shown by opportunist actors in the commission of their crimes varied, depending on the circumstances – while some offenders had always been aware of the opportunities, others claimed to have stumbled upon them by chance. The important factor to note about this group is that although they found their opportunities by chance, they carried out their crimes repeatedly, mirroring some of the behaviour of planning actors. The two main opportunities described by opportunist actors in their accounts were the presence of security-system weaknesses and being able to take advantage of their position of power and authority.

Because white-collar crimes are generally intrinsically connected to everyday business environments, it is often thought that many offenders 'drift' into white-collar crime by accident (Matza, 1964). However, in most cases explanations may not be so simplistic; for example, many people will commit white-collar crime when they believe it to be economically rational to do so (Becker, 1974; Coleman, 1994; Friedrichs, 1996;

Alalehto, 2003; Holtfreter, 2005), in other words when the benefits outweigh the costs. A number of dimensions of rationality exist which are relevant to individual motivation, before and during their crimes (Paternoster and Simpson, 1993; Shover and Hochstetler, 2006).

Planning actors may be seen as those individuals who look for opportunities to advance and execute their criminal acts in an organised and planned way. On the scale, these planners are shown to exhibit a higher degree of rationality compared to the opportunists. In adopting a rational approach to their crimes, individuals are represented as reasoned, purposeful and calculating (Alalehto, 2003: 336). They will usually have investigated as many aspects of their potential criminal acts as possible, including weighing up the costs and benefits of all the factors involved (Friedrichs, 1996: 226), and assessing where known internal controls serve (or not) as sufficient deterrents to prevent them from carrying out their plans (Holtfreter, 2005: 356).

Although planning actors are not usually averse to breaking the law, should the appropriate opportunities be present (Friedrichs, 1996: 226), their rationality may be 'bounded' or 'limited' by certain constraining factors (Cornish and Clarke, 1986). In other words, individuals will only proceed to commit the crime if they have assessed the situation and made a decision to do so based on the potential risks and gains (Gill and Goldstraw-White, forthcoming). One of the most important factors for a potential offender could well be the threat of imprisonment (Ogren, 1973: 961). As Stotland puts it: '... there can be little doubt that longer times spent in prison will frighten out the less committed criminals and may handicap their scheming while they are incarcerated' (1977: 193).

In contrast to planning actors, the opportunists are located towards the other end of the scale of rationality. Individuals found here had not purposefully calculated their criminal acts in the same orderly way as the planners; instead they had identified potential opportunities and taken advantage of them. (This is not of course to say that, once identified, these situations were not then evaluated in cost/benefit terms in the same way as they were by planning actors during the latter's selection of a strategy for committing their offence).

The opportunity and ability to identify these situations are different for white-collar criminals than for other types of offenders (Benson and Simpson, 2009), yet not all individuals will pursue the opportunities once they have identified them. As Shover and Hochstetler point out, 'opportunity is in the eye of the beholder, but there is an objective and commonsense aspect to many criminal opportunities' (2006: 5). They believe that the most important factor which tempts individuals to

such opportunities is the presence of 'lure'. They define this as '...
arrangements or situations that turn heads', stressing that these need not
be concerned only with economics (ibid: 27–8). Lure may be money, ease
of exploitation or other tempting opportunities. Shover and Hochstetler
note that the presence of lure does not evoke the same response from all
individuals, and that some people may not even identify it (ibid: 28).

The question remains, therefore, why some individuals get involved
when opportunities are present while others, in the same or a similar
situation, do not. According to Becker's (1974) economic theory of
crime, if net benefits outweigh net costs, then everyone acting ratio-
nally will commit offences. Coleman (1994), however, suggests differences relate to how individuals determine the risks associated with
pursuing an opportunity, with punishment being the most influential
factor when deciding whether or not to commit a crime. The ability of
the individual to perform the contemplated act also needs consideration, as detailed in the 'fraud diamond' (see Chapter 3). Coleman
points out, in his discussion of the culture of competition, that Sutherland's (1947) claims to the effect that criminal behaviour is learned
are over-generalised; Coleman believes rather that individuals will constantly review situations, forming new ideas and definitions as the perceived situation changes (1994: 195–8). The costs and benefits identified
by the offenders in this study are considered in Chapter 7.

Planning actors

In the sample, two offenders were classified as planning actors. These
were individuals who went looking for criminal opportunities in order
to make financial gains: Adam (credit card fraud) and Adrian (evasion
of tobacco duty).

Case study – Adam

Adam was a 38-year-old who had previously been employed as
a finance manager for a well-known high-street bank. At the time
of his offending, he was a self-employed property broker. He had
been convicted of conspiracy to defraud, with others (including an ex-policeman), relating to Internet-based credit-card fraud,
and given a 30-month prison sentence. At the beginning of the
interview he commented that he believed that 'crime pays'. As
he explained: 'Since I have been in jail I have received a tax
rebate, lost weight and gained incalculable extra years on my
life compared to if I had carried on working as normal.'

Adam claimed that his offending and the resultant incarceration were part of his 'life plan'. He said that after reading an article in a national newspaper on white-collar crime, he realised that the only unknown variable to him in criminal activities was prison life: 'I knew about everything else [how to commit a crime] but prison. I researched it on the Internet and met someone to commit the crime with. I found out that prison was not as much or as bad as I had thought.'

He stated that after undertaking some further research he was able to calculate the maximum tariff he could expect to receive for committing credit-card fraud. He believed this to be between two to four years for this type of offence, and that he had expected that most of this time would be spent in an open prison. As a result of this information, he claimed that the prospect of prison, if he was caught, did not seem as bad as he had previously imagined, and that it was certainly not a major deterrent to him. His final 30-month prison sentence certainly confirmed his assessment of the likely sentence on conviction for such crimes.

Adam remarked that during his research on imprisonment, the only uncertainty he had uncovered was what type of prison he would be sent to immediately after being sentenced. He found that he might possibly have to spend time in a higher-category prison, which might mean sharing a cell in a local or dispersal institution. He stated that his army experiences in Bosnia, where he had been trapped under siege and lain next to his best friend's body for several days before rescue, had toughened him up for the prospect of this. He rationalised that he was willing to take the risk of spending some of his initial sentence time in a higher-security prison for the gains he believed that the crimes would yield. However, he did make a comment about the maximum time in prison he was willing to face: 'I would not do it if the sentence looked longer. I could handle doing two to four years, but not longer.'

During the interview, Adam was very open about having pre-planned his crimes, though he did not go into any of their technical details. While he never disclosed the full amount of money he had made, he did suggest that the amount he was sentenced for (some £1.3 million) was considerably lower than the actual total. For Adam, his plans had come to fruition, and he did not intend to work in future when he left prison (see Chapter 7).

The second offender classified as a planning actor, Adrian, also admitted to committing his crimes; like Adam, he had gone looking for an opportunity which would make him (and others) a lot of money.

Case study – Adrian

Adrian was the 30-year-old owner of a transport business. He had been sentenced, with others, to 48 months for evading payment of tobacco duty amounting to over £2.6 million. He had owned and run a number of legitimate haulage businesses before and during his crimes. Adrian claimed that after the internal border controls in Europe were relaxed, he had investigated, along with others, the possibility of importing large quantities of cheap cigarettes from Eastern Europe.

He said that prior to committing the offences, he knew that he would get a maximum of seven years' imprisonment if he was convicted of this type of crime, and had made the positive decision that he was willing to risk such a sentence for the money he could make. On the basis of this maximum tariff, Adrian calculated that in order to justify this cost, the operation needed to make a certain amount of money. With the others also involved in funding the exercise, they worked out this would equate to running the operation for seven and a half weeks, importing eight pallets[1] of tobacco per week. He stated: 'I was willing to do this for the money and rewards it would bring.'

At the beginning of the operation, Adrian and his associates imported far more goods and made far more money than they had initially imagined or budgeted for, mainly because the costs they had originally calculated had been based on shop prices, not the lower warehouse prices which they eventually paid in Eastern Europe. They sold mainly to drivers, other employees, relatives and friends. Adrian claimed: 'Once we started, more and more rolled in than we could have ever have imagined.' He admitted he carried out these activities in a calculated manner, with the aim of being able to pay for more leisure goods, cars, and so on, and to upgrade his property. He also admitted to an element of social climbing associated with this, as well as the 'buzz' he got from their activities at the time.

The activities originally planned went on for twice as long as anticipated, and the group ceased operating shortly before Christmas which, as far as he was concerned at the time, was for good. However, he claimed that over Christmas the other two involved in financing the operation approached him to start it up again. Adrian stated that he had not been bothered one way or another, because he had already made far more money than he had ever anticipated he would. However, he said that he had gone along with the others, and they had recommenced their offending. This time, however, they decided to increase the scale of the operation, and hired cargo planes as well as lorries to bring in the goods from Eastern Europe. Adrian had previously worked at Heathrow airport, and therefore had some inside knowledge of where cargo planes landed and how they were dealt with by customs personnel. He boasted that when they were finally caught they were importing around 47 pallets a week: 'At times I had so much money, mainly cash, I did not know what to do with it. I looked after the operation at my offices and remember times when I was surrounded by notes, not knowing where to put them.'

Adrian said that this second phase of the operation was first threatened in the February following the New Year after they restarted, when a lorry leaving Belgium was stopped by French Customs, who seized about £600,000 worth of cigarettes. However, he claimed, the customs officers telephoned him and asked for the equivalent of £16,000 to release the goods back into Belgium. As he explained: 'The French had their own scam going, but the amount they were asking was peanuts to us. So that was no deterrent.'

He flew to the Continent, and paid the money. In March, the same thing happened, and again the customs officers accepted a bribe. At the time, however, he claimed that the operation was succeeding to such an extent that retrieving the goods (and the resultant profit) seemed more important than the fact that their operation had been threatened through discovery by the customs authorities. As a result, however, Adrian hired a company to assess whether the lorries were under surveillance or being followed.

The operation was finally uncovered the following autumn when one of his associates in Europe (who later turned Queen's Evidence against Adrian and his associates) deposited some money overnight in an American bank in Belgium, which raised suspicions. Adrian was eventually convicted along with others (including drivers) who received sentences of between nine and 48 months. He intimated during his interview that the total gain was somewhere in the region of £300 million, despite only a total of £2.6 million in tax evasion being proved. He did acknowledge that Customs were now more sophisticated in detecting smuggling, which would put him off doing something similar again. However, prison had not been much of a deterrent for him.

What Adam and Adrian both had in common was that they had gone looking for criminal opportunities, researching them well and executing them with skill and sophistication. Both had commented that their experience of prison had not proven a major deterrent. However, Adam did suggest that the length of sentence would influence his decision whether to commit his illegal activities. The introduction of the Proceeds of Crime Act 2002 since the interviews would now be an additional factor for a potential white-collar offender to consider when weighing up the costs of criminal activity of this nature. The Act provides the Crown with powers to deprive criminals of their assets, including seizure of cash, which are reasonably considered to be the proceeds of the crime or intended for use in its commission.

In order to carry out activities at this level of sophistication, both Adam and Adrian had used their professional knowledge and skills, gained either through previous employment experience or from research. To ensure the success of their operations they had utilised all the resources available to them, whether this was via information gained from the Internet or by drawing on the expertise of others. In comparison with most other individuals interviewed, these two offenders were proud of what they had done and achieved, even boasting about their crimes and gains. One could say that there may even have been an element of exaggeration in their descriptions of the sums of money they had made from their criminal activity. For planning actors, therefore, crime was seen as highly profitable, and they actively went looking for opportunities on which to capitalise.

Opportunist actors and system weaknesses

One of the most frequent opportunities mentioned by offenders leading to crime was weaknesses in organisational systems. In the offender's eyes, organisations had 'allowed' something to happen, through poor or non-existent checks on their overall control environment. Sykes and Matza describe this type of offender-accounting as 'denial of the victim', where an individual challenges the actual nature and carrying-out of the offence, believing under such circumstances that it may be illegal, but is not wrong. In other words, in the eyes of the criminal, those offended against 'had it coming to them' (Sykes and Matza, 1957: 668). When this occurs, the actual victim is transformed by the perpetrator into the original 'wrong-doer' (Cohen, 2001: 61).

The importance of organisations having a sound and secure control environment cannot be overstated. However, these systems do not just have to be present – they need to be effective (Ghiselli and Ismail, 1998), fit for purpose and implemented appropriately (Gill and Gold-straw, 2010). There needs to be a strong culture and tone set from the top, and employees need to feel secure within a culture of openness (KPMG, 2010: 9). Nick Leeson, for example, in his autobiographical *Rogue Trader*, claims that the events leading to the eventual collapse of the 233-year-old Barings Bank, with losses of around £850 million, pointed towards weaknesses in internal control systems, and the ineffectiveness of both management and auditors in identifying these (1996: 89–94). Leeson, working as a trader in the Barings Singapore subsidiary, had been allowed to both buy and sell shares, as well as to act as trading and settlement officer within the branch. This meant that he had control of both the front office for trading and the back office for settling and reconciling accounts. When he made a number of losses by speculative trading in futures, Leeson hid his losses in an error account (no. 88888) which he claimed had originally been set up to cover mistakes from an inexperienced junior member of his team. Because no-one locally or independently checked these reconciliations, he was able to alter them and to continue hiding his losses.

A good internal control system should therefore eliminate criminal opportunities and provide good security management, including measures to tackle staff fraud (Bamfield, 2006; Hayes, 2007; 2008). If this had been the case in Barings Bank, a situation like Leeson's would never have been allowed, and the losses and the eventual collapse of the bank would have been averted. But where such situations are identified, offenders merely seize on the opportunities which present themselves, or take advantage of lax controls which they identify as weaknesses in the system, to commit their crimes. In a way, they are tempted by the environments presented to them, and often by the ease of committing the offences. Because opportunist offenders execute their crime by using knowledge and experience, they can be seen as mirroring planning actors, even though they did not set out looking for such situations in a pre-planned way.

Table 5.1 details the weaknesses in control systems which were identified by the ten offenders in the sample who raised this as an issue. It also gives an assessment of what these weaknesses resulted in, or could have led to.

Systems weaknesses were mentioned in offenders' accounts in respect both of the organisation where they worked and of external organisations with which they had dealt. For the latter case, two offenders, Jason and Marvin, described how systems weaknesses had been presented

Table 5.1   Summary of control system weaknesses identified by offenders

Weaknesses in systems identified	Possible consequences
• Poor monitoring of the use of personal information, and poor security of data removed off-site	• Data may be stolen, which could lead to identity theft and the committing of further crimes
• No independent reconciliation of subsidiaries' cash-takings with till receipts	• Cash could be embezzled from subsidiaries by staff without the group noticing
• Poor control of signed cheques	• Cheques may be altered after authorisation
• Lack of independent check or control of accounts	• Accounts may be 'doctored' to cover up financial anomalies
• Poor financial monitoring of satellite offices	• Financial irregularities may not be highlighted within a group of companies
• Lack of communication within organisations, especially sales and finance departments	• Customers who are already in debt for goods or services may be able to obtain further supplies
• Lack of surveillance equipment in postal depots	• Negotiable instruments may be removed from personal postage
• Poor monitoring of account transfers in building societies and banks	• Unauthorised transfers of stolen money may occur between accounts
• Lack of financial monitoring by management	• Financial anomalies may be covered up by more junior staff
• Poor audit assurance given to management and the board of directors	• Independent assurance from auditors may not be relied upon

to them for possible exploitation. Jason, a self-employed furniture-maker convicted of deception and of obtaining money while an undischarged bankrupt, felt that because organisations supplied him with goods without making the necessary credit checks, they deserved to be defrauded. Desperate as he was to save his company, Jason saw an opportunity to obtain extra goods in this way, and was tempted by the weakness he had identified in the suppliers' systems. He stated: 'I thought I deserved the money in a sense ... the system had allowed it to happen.'

Similar external opportunities were also noted by Marvin, the owner of a publishing company who had been sentenced for Post Office fraud, deception and forgery. He said: 'I looked to save costs and noticed an opportunity with postage.' His defrauding of the Post Office was facilitated by weaknesses in its systems. His firm was buying a certain level of postage credit for their franking machine per week. In fact, the company was using postage valued at over ten times that amount per week, by printing their own postage labels, which at the time were easy to fake. He noted: 'It was a weakness of the Post Office because they did not find this. They did not realise the amount of postage. We bought £200 a week in postage but put through £2500.' He felt that because the local Post Office had failed to notice this discrepancy, in what he described as a small community environment, it therefore deserved to be defrauded.

System weaknesses may also be present within the businesses where offenders are employed. Debbie, a restaurant manager, claimed she was able to embezzle £40,000 from the organisation she worked for because of the lack of management monitoring-procedures. She commented: 'In my job I was responsible for the wages. Once a week I took out £1,000 ... nothing was suspected as the restaurant had just moved from another chain and no one had much idea about the figures.'

The absence of management checks had aided her to embezzle money on a weekly basis for a number of months. This had been possible because the restaurant she worked for had just experienced some managerial and organisational changes. As a result, the new owners had little past information and data upon which to base the monitoring of their takings. In essence, an opportunity presented itself for exploitation, and Debbie seized it.

A similar case of ineffective management monitoring was also demonstrated in the account given by Sally, a management accountant who had embezzled £251,000 from her employer.

Case study – Sally

Sally believed that her boss had little idea what was going on in his organisation, and was unaware that at various points in the system checks were either ineffective or easily evaded. As a result, she had been able to 'teem and lade'[2] funds on the debtors account, moving money from the business's bank account direct to her own personal account. Sally was keen to stress she had not gone out of her way to hide what she was doing, and had not set up any new or falsely named account. She said: 'Basic checks were missing. The BACS[3] listing was only given a cursory check ... I moved it [the money] to my own [bank] account, not a new or specific one.'

During the period of embezzlement, Sally claimed that the company was subject to several external audits. These all passed without incident, with none of the auditors picking up any discrepancies in the accounting records.

Besides poor management-control systems within organisations, two offenders (Alison and Ruth) commented that basic security measures were either missing or ineffective in the organisations for which they had worked. Alison, a bank credit-control assistant, claimed she had been coerced into stealing personal account details from her organisation, and felt let down that security measures had not picked this up.

Case study – Alison

Alison said that she had been threatened that she or her family would come to harm if she told anyone that she had been forced to steal personal data. She claimed that her blackmailers had told her that if her employers accidentally discovered what she was doing she would not be prosecuted. Alison therefore claimed that she had relied on the company's security system to detect her illegal and out-of-character activities, which would have enabled her to get the blackmail situation out in the open in a 'safe' way. As her behaviour at work was not typical, and incommensurate with her job, she believed this would be noticed. She commented: 'I thought as time went on I would get found out. My trips to the printer past team leaders were not noticed, even though the atmosphere was one where time was monitored. I did not need many print-outs, but no-one queried it. I left sheets of print-outs on my desk and even walked out of the building with them in my hand, but I was never challenged.'

Alison stated that just to retrieve one of the print-outs required her walking quite a distance to the printer (on numerous occasions) and that she took statements out through a security cordon at the end of the day. However, she claimed she was never challenged, and was therefore never given the opportunity to reveal the situation allegedly being forced upon her. She concluded: 'Security was obviously ineffective internally.'

A similar case demonstrating poor security was highlighted by Ruth, who had been convicted of conspiracy to defraud through various postal and financial scams. She commented that she had been able to steal large amounts of money because such institutions were, in her words, 'too mean' to implement satisfactory crime-prevention measures and surveillance procedures: 'It was easy to get away with. The greed of businesses meant they did not put in costly detection equipment and controls.' Ruth believed it should not have been so easy for her to target postal items, which she looked through, opened and abstracted money and documents, as no surveillance cameras were present in the postal sorting-areas.

Two offenders found systems of control so poor in their (separate) organisations that they were literally able to alter cheques and make these payable to themselves. Sheila, a 37-year-old accounts assistant for a travel agent, embezzled £41,000 from her employer by altering cheques and credit-card refunds. One of their customers had the same surname as herself, and after the authorised cheques had been returned to her she added an 's' to the 'Mr' and paid the cheque into her own building-society account. She said: 'The first time I did it I was terrified. I took it [the cheque] to the director who was least likely to question it.' This also demonstrates that Sheila was nervous about whether her first attempt would be detected. However, because it was not, she claimed that this made it much easier on future occasions, aiding this opportunist actor to repeat her offences.

In a similar case, Dave, an assistant management accountant, embezzled £109,000 from his employer, also by altering signed cheques. Like the previous example, one customer had a similar surname to himself, which he was able to alter to his own after the cheques had been authorised by two of the directors and returned to him. This remained undetected until an occasion when he was unable to locate a second director, and forged an authorised signature.

The previous examples have demonstrated how individuals took advantage of opportunities which were presented to them through existing poor internal control systems. By contrast, two offenders claimed to have stumbled upon their opportunities by accident. What is interesting about these individuals, however, and likens them to other opportunistic actors, is that although they claimed to have committed the offence the first time following an accidental finding, they continued to repeat the offending behaviour, possibly because they found it so easy to do so.

The first of these two offenders was Tom, the owner of a building firm who was sentenced to 45 months for defrauding Customs and Excise of £106,000. He claimed to have stumbled across the opportunity by accident, after discovering a serious weakness in the Inland Revenue's systems. He commented: 'It was easy ... I did it by accident and found it was foolproof. The Inland Revenue still don't check this now.'

Tom felt particularly aggrieved because he believed that procedures surrounding his offence had not subsequently been altered by the Inland Revenue to remove the loophole. He claimed this grievance came from a concern to ensure other people could not abuse public money in the same way he had. Tom did not explain why, having found this deficiency in the system, he had continued to repeat his crimes until caught.

The second offender who claimed to have come across the opportunity by accident was Anne, a supermarket-garage manager, who had embezzled £101,000 from her employer by falsifying accounts. She said that she had spent considerable time trying to figure out why she had committed the crimes, especially since being in prison. She concluded: 'I had no debts, no worries and nothing owned that was not paid for ... I was on a good wage. I had no obvious reason for doing this.'

Anne was therefore not pressurised into criminal behaviour by any particular external factor – her offences appeared to have been prompted purely by noticing an opportunity. She claimed that her crimes commenced after she identified a weakness between the financial procedures of the garage that she managed and the main supermarket to which it was attached. Realising this, Anne started to steal more than £1,000 a week, over the following year, from the cash takings of the garage. She said: 'I felt guilt each time I did it and I was surprised when I got away with it the first time. I told myself not to do it again, but I did. I could not stop ... there was no apparent reason.'

Eventually Anne was caught, but (she claimed) only after she had asked for an audit of her department to be undertaken. Even then, she said, her employer had no single, definitive proof that Anne was the culprit and the organisation, for which she had worked for some considerable years, was reluctant to believe she was the offender. During the course of the interview with Anne, she expressed anger with her organisation for having 'let it happen'. Although she did not use this reason in any way to defend or excuse her behaviour, she did acknowledge that once she had discovered the weakness, she was to an extent 'testing' the company and never imagined she could not be caught. She felt she was loyal to her employer, and that in somebody else's hands, the crime could have been much worse. She confirmed that she blamed the organisation: 'They asked me how I had let this happen, but I felt *they* had let it happen' (emphasis hers). The nearest to a motivation therefore that Anne could identify was 'testing' the system, and she was angry at the organisation for letting it happen.

Abuse of power and authority

The question of why some individuals take advantage of system weaknesses, while others do not, may simply be whether they are in a position to exploit them. As Cressey (1953) points out, for trust violations to occur the potential offender needs to have relevant expertise, as well being in a position of trust, and often power. However, the organisational structures of many businesses make such situations impossible to avoid altogether, and although the degree of authority may vary (Friedrichs, 1996: 11), more senior staff may be able to override controls (Tilley, 1993: 23).

Those offenders in the sample who had held positions of power and authority (such as managers, accountants, bankers and lawyers) had wielded substantial influence over the running of the organisations for which they worked and on the staff who worked for them. They knew they had been placed in privileged positions, and therefore felt it unlikely that they would be suspected of committing any misdeeds; and where opportunities for offending presented themselves, this made their criminal activity even easier. Greg, a senior bank manager, confirmed this when he said: 'I was the boss, long-serving and well-respected. None of my staff were going to question me. No-one suspected ... I was in a position of power and authority.'

Sally, the management accountant mentioned earlier, said that she had worked for the same boss for a number of years, and had been left in sole charge of the accounts for his small business. This, she said, resulted in him paying very little attention to the day-to-day running of the financial side of the business. When Sally started to embezzle money from the firm, she claimed that she found it very easy and did not have to cover up anything in particular. Although Sally acknowledged that she had been placed in a position of trust, she believed that given the amount of money she embezzled from her firm, her boss should have noticed that something was wrong. She commented: 'The turnover of the company was £1.6 million … [and] a high percentage was taken. There were no management controls in place to see this.'

Additionally, where offices are separated from the main hub of the business, individuals are provided with a further opportunity to exploit their privileged positions. Anne, the supermarket-garage manager whose account was mentioned earlier, felt particularly aggrieved that the main supermarket, which was supposed to take control of the garage's finances and reconciliations, never got directly involved in her work. Her position in the garage was therefore a particularly strong and influential one. She commented: 'The manager of the garage is supposed to be attached to the store, but I had very little to do with them. Therefore, as manager, I had complete control.'

Dave, the assistant management accountant discussed earlier, said that his crimes had also been aided by the position he held. He worked in a branch office of a much larger firm and claimed that the management accountant hierarchically above him was not particularly 'hands on'. Dave had control over most of the financial activities in the office where he worked, and thus had the opportunity to alter any accounting record to tally with the amounts he embezzled. As no-one else was closely involved in these day-to-day operations, Dave was able to conceal the amounts he was taking from the company. He said: 'I thought people did not know or suspect … how could they? All accounts were well presented … timely, even "over right".'

In this way, Dave presented himself as a decent, trustworthy and reliable employee, whose work reflected those character traits.

Offenders under pressure

This section will consider those offenders who claimed to have committed their crimes as a result of being pressurised in some way. These individuals claimed to have felt compelled to behave in particular ways, driven to react when a certain set of circumstances were presented to them. The 23 individuals from the sample who were located in this category claimed that they felt overwhelmed by the issues they were facing, particularly financial ones, whether these related to their own expectations, to the business or to their family. The pressures felt by individuals appeared to produce three main types of actors: 'aspiring', 'desperate' and 'threatened', as illustrated in Figure 5.2.

Figure 5.2   Type of pressure experienced by white-collar criminals

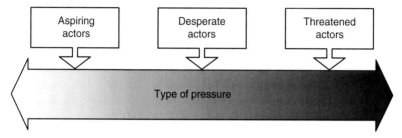

Aspiring actors appeared to be pressurised through self-imposed motives, which included increasing their status among their peers and associates and within society generally. In many cases this included being able to demonstrate their current success, which was sometimes linked to their childhood or to family pressures and expectations. Even if subjects were able to achieve the desired level of status and success, this did not necessarily put an end to these self-imposed pressures. The preservation and maintenance of such lifestyles were also seen by some offenders as exerting additional pressure on them.

Desperate actors were those individuals who appeared to be subjected to pressure associated with their businesses or families. In business, some individuals became trapped, unable to find legal solutions to worsening financial circumstances and difficult economic markets. By contrast, the final category of threatened actors represented those individuals who had, to various extents, little or no control over their offending behaviour, with others threatening them into crime.

Aspiring actors

White-collar offenders are often the product of social settings and cultural backgrounds where great importance is placed on 'material success and individual wealth' (Weisburd et al, 1991: 224; Leeson, 1996; Blickle et al, 2006: 222). Coleman describes this as 'competitive winning', where such situations may provide powerful motivations for committing white-collar crime (1994: 196). These pressures may come from various sources, including friends, peers and parents. Parental pressure may be direct, or exerted indirectly through the individual's subconscious. Where offenders are brought up in successful families, for instance, they may feel they have to live up to the example set by their parents. As Shover et al (2004: 65) note in their research on fraud by telemarketers, many of their subjects came from secure and comfortable homes where they had been exposed to entrepreneurial life very early on. They also suggested that most white-collar criminals had been imbued with similar goals of wealth and financial independence.

Cressey outlines the importance of 'status-gaining' as a motivation for committing criminal acts. He feels that the importance of recognition and acceptance as members of certain culturally-created social groups within our society is at the root of much criminality, especially where individuals are, as he puts it, 'living beyond their means and travelling with a fast crowd' (1953: 53). He states that where such ambition for status is not met, or where individuals realise they do not have the financial means to continue their association with such groups, then problems and pressures arise. They find themselves not wishing, or being unable, to renounce their membership of the group, but at the same time unable to continue to afford such membership – and to retain it, Cressey considers (ibid), an individual would often resort to illegal measures. Likewise, Spencer (1959), in his research on white-collar criminals, characterises some of their behaviour as 'reckless and ambitious', in what he sees as their desire to mix with people of higher social status and to follow similar lifestyles, even if this means taking financial risks in the process.

Nelken (1994: 368) terms this striving to gain status as 'over-investment'. By this, he means those individuals who appear to be relatively well-off financially and to exhibit the characteristics of moneyed people (with associated material goods), while in reality they are struggling to make ends meet. As Weisburd et al put it: 'Many of our offenders have the material goods associated with successful people, but may be barely holding their financial selves together' (1991: 65). Nettler provides further commentary on how theories of crime only see theft in terms of need or restricted opportunity, whereas many frauds are perpetrated merely by the desire to be richer (1982a: 80). Stotland (1977) notes that the need for additional money or goods, or the need to hold onto what one already has, may create a situation of relative economic deprivation which can be applied to both the poor and the better-off. He considers that relative wealth may be particularly important to someone if their current source of wealth or income comes under threat. This was seen by Spencer, who classifies the offenders he interviewed into a number of groups, including a category of those who appear to be driven by fear of losing what they have, rather than a desire for more (1959: 362). Coleman agrees that white-collar criminals are often driven by this fear rather than accepting the financial strain of 'keeping up with the Joneses' (1994: 195).

The importance of status

Social status is often very important to individuals – how we are viewed by our families, peers, associates and the community in general. This in turn can create pressures, often self-imposed, either through what individuals aspire to be, or what they think others expect them to be. In the offenders' accounts, the main reasons cited for this type of pressure were status, success and the preservation of a lifestyle. Two offenders directly raised the issue of status in their interviews – Geoff and Stuart.

Stuart, one of the directors sentenced along with Gareth and Patrick for illegal inter-trading, was keen to stress that: 'Image is important in business, to be perceived as professional.' He believed that to be viewed by peers, associates and senior staff as successful and important within his industry, he felt he needed to act, dress and behave in a certain way to create and maintain that image.

For some of the offenders, however, it was not just a matter of how they were perceived socially, but also having all the material goods that tend to accompany high status, such as prestigious cars and large houses. The issue becomes one of ensuring that such goods are seen by others as part of their everyday lifestyle. Geoff, who owned a manufacturing company, admitted the importance of maintaining personal effects around him that reinforced his image as a successful businessman.

Case study – Geoff

Geoff came from a traditional working-class background. He had established a successful manufacturing company, and although he had been unused to having luxury goods the success of his company had enabled him to purchase a large house and drive an expensive car. He believed that people associated his success not just with his ownership of the company, but with all the material gains which came with such status. He said that in his crime, '... self-esteem and pride played a major part. I drove a Jaguar and owned a house that was worth over quarter of a million pounds then ... it wasn't all directly about personal gain, but maintaining my status among friends and associates.'

Pressures to succeed

A further aspiring pressure which offenders cited in their accounts was the pressure to succeed exerted on them by others. Three offenders in the sample mentioned this type of pressure in their account, with the most influential factors appearing to be the expectations of their families, either directly or indirectly. Two of the offenders interviewed appeared to have felt pressurised by what their own families had previously achieved, particularly their fathers, and believed that this expectation had been placed on them, whether or not this was actually the case.

Gareth, who had been convicted along with Patrick and Stuart, claimed that he came from a long line of successful businessmen involved with large, nationally-known public companies. He said that only later in life had he found out that the man he had thought of as his father was in fact unrelated to him. He claimed that this had badly affected him.

Case study – Gareth

Gareth felt that he needed to impress and gain the respect of the 'father' who had brought him up. He said that he had been given a private education, and that the people around him had always had money and appeared to have happy and successful lives. Gareth claimed that he had started his own business in publicity and advertising very early in his working life, but had sold that company and worked for the next 15 years establishing a number of other companies (including those he owned with Patrick and Stuart). He stated: 'I needed to feel successful. I came from a line of successful businessmen in my family … it was very important. There were pressures as a child, nothing direct, more the kind of atmosphere I was brought up in.' As a result of these pressures, Gareth was determined to be seen by his family, especially his 'father', as equally successful through his own companies, even if this meant engaging in criminal behaviour.

Patrick a 32-year-old partner in one of Gareth's companies also noted in his account that his childhood upbringing, especially the involvement of his father, had influenced his thinking about business activities in later life. He stated that his father was the chairman of a number of companies and chief executive of others. Patrick had also built up his own companies, prior to working with Gareth, to prove that he could be equally successful: 'Success is important … I wanted to follow in my father's footsteps. I've read board reports since the age of 14 or 15.'

In a similar way, Sheila, an accounts assistant for a travel agency, claimed to have felt pressurised not only by personal debt, but by her parents' expectations. She claimed: 'I was pressured by my mother to get things for the house and do things. My sister was a headmistress ... the two of us were always compared. I felt I had to live up to these expectations.'

Preservation of lifestyle

Four offenders accounted for their criminality in terms of preserving and maintaining a lifestyle to which they had become accustomed, this in turn becoming a form of pressure in itself, albeit self-inflicted. Again, as Heath also notes, it is often an aversion to losing what they have, as opposed to a desire for gaining more, which motivates white-collar criminals (2008: 600).

Case study – Kevin

Kevin, a married solicitor in a single-handed practice, told how he had run into financial difficulties after leaving a large legal firm and starting up his own practice. He explained: 'Both children were now at school but my wife did not work. I took on any cases I could and did a lot of legal aid work. Anything I could do to get some money in.'

After approximately ten months, he was failing to reach the level of income to which he had previously been accustomed. He reacted to this by starting to falsify legal aid forms to an approximate value of £200,000. He continued to do this until he was caught, after suspicions were raised by the level of claims made. In real financial terms, his family was fairly well-off, but Kevin found that since working for himself he could not sustain the level of income which the family had been used to when he had been employed by the larger firm. He said: 'It became more difficult to maintain the lifestyle they [his family] had become accustomed to.'

Similar accounts to Kevin's were also noted with other self-employed offenders. Jason and Max, unlike Kevin, had achieved a new and higher standard of living as a result of their original, successful ownership of businesses. However, as economic circumstances changed for the worse and business survival became harder, they found the prospect of losing this newly-acquired standard of living very difficult to face. Jason commented: ' ... it was more lifestyle and the wife to maintain. Ordinary chances of accumulating wealth were bleak ... yes, indirectly this was greed at first, but then I was not able to carry on trading without deception.'

Jason never implied that he was under any direct pressure from his wife to maintain their lifestyle. It was more a self-imposed pressure of his own to maintain the standard of living for his family, including his wife. Similar pressure had also been experienced by Max, who said about his new-found wealth: 'We bought a new house and rented out the other ... I was able to take the wife and kids abroad, I'd never been able to do that before.'

Max had initially found a considerably higher lifestyle through co-owning his new company, confirmed by his investment in an additional house. His criminal activities might in part be explained by a fear of losing what he had gained, rather than simply a desire for even more.

The influence of family life and maintenance of a particular standard of living was a recurrent theme throughout the offenders' accounts. This lifestyle preservation was not however always influenced by current situations: in one offender's account it was due to family circumstances from the past.

Case study – Greg

Greg, a 57-year-old who had been sentenced to four years' imprisonment for conspiracy to defraud, claimed because he had recently been divorced (after a 30-year marriage), and then remarried, which together led to financial pressures within this new relationship. Although he did not admit to having been directly involved in the fraud for which he had been sentenced, he did acknowledge during his account that these financial pressures had contributed to his initial involvement in the situation which led to the criminal activity. He recalled: 'I did not really have any debt, but my first marriage finances caused tightness in money. Therefore, old family commitments affected the finances of the current relationship.'

Desperate actors

The second of the three pressurised categories identified was desperate actors. Individuals in this category appeared to have been subjected to pressures from two main sources – either business or family situations, where individuals felt propelled into criminal action by various degrees of desperation. For those self-employed individuals subject to pressures in business, pressure was encountered at various stages of trading. This was from starting up a new company with growing business pressures, through to 'saving' an established business because of economic or other changes. Offenders frequently commented about feeling 'trapped' by trying to do the correct thing for their business, even if this meant resorting to criminal behaviour. Fraud offenders may be successful, educated executives, but may also include '... struggling entrepreneurs, bad businessmen and persons caught in serious economic distress' (Ogren, 1973: 975). The common factor identified with this group of actors was the desire to save their business and to keep their family from shame or disgrace, as noted by Cressey (1953: 114).

Croall details external influences and changes in the economy which may affect the behaviour of individuals and lead to the commission of crimes through increasing pressures (1992: 69), a phenomenon also identified by Box (1983) and Passas (1990). Offenders in the present study gave accounts (especially from small-business owners and the self-employed) of this 'roller-coaster' effect. This occurred when a certain set of circumstances mutated into much larger problems, needing intervention and even criminal action by individuals in order to 'save' their business, themselves or both from failure. Such circumstances may have been due to declining demand for goods or services, rising costs or failure to meet targets. Many of the offenders who found themselves in this position became trapped, feeling unable to get out of the situation as the pressure mounted.

General business pressures

Twenty-three of the offenders in the sample consisted of individuals who owned, or part-owned, businesses. The success of these businesses, especially where the income generated was their main livelihood, was of paramount importance to these offenders and an immediate consideration in terms of economic survival for themselves, their family, their co-workers and their employees. As Levi (2002: 155) notes, individuals who turn to crime to save their businesses may not care about being shamed. Business pressure was identified as affecting both those who had just started up in business and who might be suffering from growing pressure, and those with more established businesses who may have found themselves in pressurised situations as a result of changes in economic or other circumstances.

Five of the self-employed offenders in the sample claimed their involvement in criminal activities stemmed initially from trying to start up and maintain their business. Problems had not resulted from the lack of demand for their products or services, but from higher-than-anticipated start-up costs and from resultant cash-flow difficulties. One offender who had been affected in this way was Jason.

Case study – Jason

Jason was a furniture-maker and business owner who had been sentenced for deception and obtaining property whilst bankrupt. He had previously owned and run a home-improvement business, which provided him with access to business credit, but the company, due to low demand for its products, failed to succeed. In response, Jason emptied all his bank accounts and obtained approximately £110,000 of additional credit from companies. Some of this money he spent on holidays, cars, property and other 'luxury goods', keeping the rest back for personal investment. Jason then declared his home-improvements business bankrupt, and set up the new business making pine furniture, where he employed three others. He claimed that though demand was stronger in this business than in his previous one, the main problem was that customers did not pay on time. He commented: 'I had a lot of orders. It was a well thought-of business and good quality, but not a lot of money up front.'

Jason required a good deal of initial capital investment to start up his new furniture business, and as a result he undertook large financial commitments in his early days of trading. Dependent as he was on customers for further income to invest in the firm, and many were slow to pay, the result was a poor cash-flow position. To continue trading and to obtain money to buy goods, Jason needed new credit with suppliers, and to this end he approached a number of firms, using different business names to try to obtain it. In the end, he was using 15 different false account names. One of the companies then realised he was the same person they had dealt with previously when he had run his home-improvements business before declaring himself bankrupt. They contacted a second company to confirm this, the police were informed and Jason was charged with deception and obtaining property whilst bankrupt.

Another offender who experienced similar problems over the start-up and growth of a business was Max, a 29-year-old part-owner (along with 11 others) of a computer-consultancy firm, who had been sentenced for conspiracy to defraud. He had originally been employed as a computer analyst by a large firm and had left to become a computer broker for another organisation, which he claimed to be very profitable. As a result of the success he had enjoyed while working for someone else, he decided to form his own company along with some business associates. He claimed he was good at his job, having taken a number of his old employer's accounts and clients with him. The new company was initially successful. It had a good relationship with its bank, and a number of high-earning accounts. The company soon grew further by taking on even more accounts, but although it was breaking even it had large debts – the capital invested in establishing the business. To keep pace with the growing business, Max and his associates found they needed to invest even more: 'It was breaking even, but had big debts and we needed to put a lot of money up front to get the company going and continue to expand.'

Like Jason, Max found that customers were generally slow payers, whereas at the same time costs continued at a high level. With his associates in the firm, he then conspired to defraud suppliers of a considerable amount of money.

Both Jason and Max committed their crimes to stop themselves from going bankrupt, losing their businesses and, as a result, their livelihoods. Their situation also demonstrates that pressure is present not only during the start-up phase of a business, but also when trying to keep pace with a successful and growing company.

Trapped actors through growing business and economic pressures

Jason and Max described in their accounts a set of circumstances which led to a 'roller-coaster effect'. This occurs when individuals become trapped by the pressure of their situation. Both these offenders found themselves in a position where they had no choice but to continue with an on-going course of illegal action, even if this caused further pressure. Both Jason and Max described this as like being on a fairground ride, which they wanted to get off and could not. In effect, every time they tried to break this cycle, the pressure was too great to allow them to do so, and they were forced to face the rest of the ride before they were able to 'escape'. Unfortunately, for many of the offenders in this situation, the only time this pressure ceased was when they were caught. In practice, what this meant was that in the short term individuals became trapped actors, having to carry on committing criminal acts to try to get themselves out of business difficulties. Max said: 'It was like being on a roller-coaster at times, I just couldn't get off. I didn't think about what I was doing ... I had no time ... I had to keep going.' Similarly, Jason noted about trying to save his furniture-making business: 'It felt like being on a roller-coaster ... I just ducked and dived to keep up with costs ... it was hard to stop once we had started.'

Whilst Max had slightly more professional business experience than Jason, he admitted that he had been unable to cope with the pressures of co-owning his business. He confessed: 'I was very good at my job and the business soon grew. Things moved fast, though, and I didn't fully understand or appreciate being an owner of a company.'

The lack of experience in dealing with administrative and financial matters compared with, for example, more seasoned entrepreneurs such as Adam and Adrian, was very apparent in the cases of Jason and Max. However, even those offenders with more business experience found establishing and main-taining their businesses problematic. One such offender was Gareth.

Case study – Gareth

Gareth, a managing director and co-owner of a group of companies along with Patrick and Stuart, had been sentenced to 27 months for fraudulent trading. These three individuals had originally owned a portfolio of diverse companies, including some relating to home-improvements businesses. With some of their companies struggling financially, they offset losses against the more profitable home-improvements businesses by illegal inter-trading between them. Finan-cial circumstances did not improve, however, and the levels of this inter-trading rose sharply. Gareth said that they sought to conceal the fact that some of the companies were having difficulties, and from the outside he said that everything appeared satisfactory. They felt it was important to maintain this apparent success, and meanwhile to hope that things would get better. Unfortunately they did not, and problems relating to service quality in their home-improvement businesses were highlighted several times in a consumer programme on national television. In a desperate attempt to limit damage to the successful companies which were keeping the others going financially, Gareth appeared on the programme to try and allay customers' fears. All three owners felt that the media attention had by that time adversely affected their client base, and soon the Department of Trade and Industry began investigating all their business activities. This led in the end to their conviction and prison sentences. Gareth commented how he had tried to act to try to save their companies: 'I tried to do the right thing by my [their] company ... even appearing on television.'

Certainly, business pressures are also experienced when employers feel an obligation to save their companies for the sake of their employees. Geoff, the manufacturing-company owner, claimed that his company had lost a considerable amount of money after a sharp fall in share prices on the stock market. He said: 'Pride played a major part, but I also had a duty to my employees.'

Likewise, Marvin, the owner of a publishing company, ran into difficulties paying his overheads but felt that he needed to keep the business going, not only for himself but also for his two employees and his out-workers.

Family pressures

Pressures which appear to have been exerted on offenders as a result of family circumstances also produced desperate actors. Three offenders accounted for their criminality in this way; all were women. The pressures from which they had suffered included illness, severe financial difficulties and problems with children. There was no evidence, however, that any of the three offenders interviewed had been pressurised to the extent of being forced into absolute poverty, merely evidence of changes in circumstances which had led to substantially lower levels of previous earnings and wealth. An example of pressure due to illness, in turn causing a change in financial circumstances, was experienced by Janet.

Case study – Janet

Janet had been sentenced to 15 months' imprisonment for housing-benefit fraud amounting to £18,000. She claimed to have become desperate for money after a change in personal circumstances, in this case, her husband's ill-health. He had been made redundant several years earlier after developing problems with his sight, and had undergone two cataract operations. The couple had run a pub together before his disablement. Janet claimed that she had believed she could work full-time and still receive some family credit, including housing benefit, when her husband had to stop working. The rules for housing benefit, however, only related to rented accommodation, and while they had previously rented the house, they had since bought the property. On the housing-benefit claim form Janet had indicated that the property was still rented, and altered old copies of rental agreements to support this claim. She suspected that someone in the neighbourhood had reported her to the local council, and some 18 months later she was arrested for benefit fraud. When Janet was asked if she would do it again in similar circumstances, she said: 'I don't know ... I was so desperate at the time.'

Janet's account demonstrates how, in taking charge of the family finances after her husband's ill-health, she became so desperate that she was willing to take any action to ensure that her family survived economically and kept a roof over their heads.

Likewise, Sheila also experienced personal financial difficulties, but caused in a different way to Janet's.

Case study – Sheila

Sheila was an accounts assistant who had been imprisoned for embezzlement, deception and credit-card offences. She had worked in the accounts department of a travel agent for five years, having previously been employed by a larger firm where she earned more money. When the branch where she worked closed down, she took the job with the travel agency as she wished to keep working in the same town. Her household outgoings remained the same, and she claimed that debts soon started to mount up, even though her husband had been promoted and worked long hours.

These debts started to spiral further out of control when Sheila became ill, because the statutory sick pay she received while she was off work was below her usual level of income. Sheila claimed that her husband continued his normal lifestyle, including regular and expensive visits to London to attend football matches. She admitted that communication between them deteriorated and their relationship started to drift. Worried about the debts, she started to ignore the bills, though she claimed she was chased by letter, by telephone and even at work. To try and get out of this desperate financial situation, Sheila decided to embezzle money from her firm. She remarked: 'I had a lot of figures in my head … it was a lot of pressure.' About two to three weeks later, after committing the first offence, she repeated it, finding that this was an apparently easy answer to her problems. She stated: 'At the time I did not think about it much. My main concern was the bills and the mounting debt I needed to clear.'

Over a period of 18 months she embezzled a total of £41,000, and during this time she came to rely on this extra money to pay her bills. In addition, she claimed to have become paranoid about letters demanding payment, and had started to go home at lunch times to check if any additional post had arrived. Her crimes were uncovered when one of the branches queried a customer's name on a credit-card refund.

Whereas the previous two examples demonstrate desperate financial situations for families, the third and last example in this category relates to criminal action by a mother concerned about the welfare of her daughter. Debbie, a 42-year-old restaurant manager, had been imprisoned for embezzling £40,000 from her employer. She claimed that she had used the money to buy heroin for her daughter, whom she claimed had become addicted after her boyfriend had injected her with the drug. Debbie wanted heroin for both her daughter and the boyfriend while they awaited an NHS treatment programme. She said: 'My daughter was seeing a guy who was a heroin addict ... I kept it [the addiction] from my husband ... she was the apple of his eye. But I needed £200 a day to feed the habits of both ... I needed to get him off [heroin] as well.'

Debbie worked with her husband and son at the restaurant, but she claimed that neither of them had any idea of the circumstances, or of her embezzlement. Although she claimed it had destroyed her life and she was finding life in prison very hard, her actions obviously demonstrate the lengths to which she would go to in order to 'save' her daughter and protect her family.

Threatened actors

Whereas the previous actors made conscious and voluntary decisions to get involved in their criminal activities, four offenders claimed different experiences over the trajectory of their offending. They accounted for their crime in terms of threats they had received, thereby seeing themselves as to some extent victims. It was not possible to evaluate whether the threats were genuine or, if they were, what level of threat had really existed. However, whereas all four gave accounts which included threats, only one, Alison, blamed her situation solely on those threats.

Alison had pleaded not guilty and did not accept any responsibility for her part in the criminal acts. The 50-year-old bank credit-control assistant claimed to have been targeted by a group of blackmailers because of where she worked; she recounted how she was obliged to pass on personal details relating to clients of the bank. She claimed to have been frightened of what would happen if she did not do what was demanded of her: 'At first I thought it was a sick joke, but they showed me photographs of my parent's house, the school my daughter went to, and they said they could arrange an accident for these.' Although Alison claimed her organisation's security was poor, tracing software was installed on her computer, and this uncovered her activities. She was then arrested and charged, along with others working elsewhere.

Those who did not account for their involvement in their criminal activities solely because of threats included Greg, who was a senior bank manager and who claimed to have been threatened by others and caught up in a larger blackmail case. He had worked for the bank for 32 years and believed that he might have been made a director by the year after his arrest had circumstances been different. The details of his offence related to him guaranteeing a bond, on behalf of a customer, to a Swiss bank, which he knew was not a legitimate transaction. Greg admitted that he had previously been offered a job by the same person who held the bond, and this had involved him going on a trip to Africa, which he knew was against the bank's policy. Greg then claimed that this person was able to use the information to threaten him into guaranteeing the bond. He claimed that this turned out to be just a small part of a much larger, Mafia-style, blackmail operation, involving many others.

Greg claimed that he came under suspicion in the multi-national fraud case while the police were conducting investigations into the other individuals involved. He said officers came across documents with his name in them, and a book with his details in it. Greg said that he refused to co-operate with the police, or to produce the documents they wanted. As a result he was arrested, tried alongside others involved in the larger operation, pleaded not guilty, but was convicted.

Iqbal, a married Post Office owner, also demonstrated how an ordinary situation had turned into a threatening one.

Case study – Iqbal

Iqbal claimed that he was originally approached by an associate to commit benefit fraud together, but refused. At the time, his Post Office business had suffered a number of armed robberies, and therefore he was trying to sell it. However, he was unable to find a buyer, so he eventually gave into this person's approaches and began his illegal behaviour. He confessed: 'I got sucked into it by someone else ... I had a good salary, a good life and ran the Post Office. Then I met someone who did benefit fraud ... he kept on at me to get involved. Initially I declined, but he went on and in a weak moment I said "yes".'

Iqbal claimed he regretted getting involved in the frauds in the first place, but soon the relationship between his associate and himself changed; the former put pressure on him to continue by threatening to report him to the authorities. As a result, Iqbal continued to commit the crimes. He stated: 'I wanted to get out but found it difficult ... then the threats came in for about nine months. I had suffered four armed robberies in the Post Office ... I nearly sold the business, but at the last moment it fell through, so the only way to get rid of it was to carry on with the crime.'

In a similar context, Abuu, a self-employed computer salesman, was sentenced to 18 months for deception and conspiracy to handle stolen goods. He said that the offence was supposed to be a 'one-off' to help him get out of financial problems and that he had an arrangement with the supplier. He claimed that later, when he wanted to cease criminal activity, the supplier pressured him to continue: 'A man kept coming back and making threats if I didn't continue to take the goods. Nothing or no-one were likely to have stopped me ... fear totally overcame events.'

These threatened actors felt that at some level there was a perceived level of risk to themselves and perhaps other members of their families if they did not go along with demands made on them. Unlike the previous categories of pressurised actors, these threatened individuals claimed that they had little or no choice as to their criminal involvement, often stating that they felt afraid for themselves or their families if they did not do what was being demanded of them.

Offenders as seduced actors

The final broad category of actors identified in the sample was what I termed 'seduced' actors. This referred to individuals who found themselves influenced by others which, to a lesser or greater extent, affected their criminality. Being seduced into criminal activities may take many forms, but it generally happened through personal relationships. Only three offenders in the sample were classified as seduced; this category was thus a minor one compared with most other actor groups identified.

When analysing the root cause of offences committed by those who were seduced by other people, their crimes appeared to begin as a result of the offender wishing to please, or not lose favour with, another person or persons. This situation then appeared to become the catalyst for further activities, where the individuals concerned found themselves lured into further criminal behaviour. For example, two individuals in the sample, Laura and Ruth, both claimed to have been initially involved in crime by their boyfriend.

Case study – Laura

Laura, a 38-year-old Italian who lived with her Iraqi boyfriend, had originally married another Italian in Italy and come to live in the United Kingdom with her husband in 1992. She claimed that he had treated her very badly, and she had suffered domestic violence. Due to his behaviour, she obtained a divorce in the mid-1990s. Her second partner was an Iraqi who had been granted asylum in the United Kingdom. She told me that she wanted a holiday in France with this new partner but he did not have a passport. To remedy this situation she took her ex-husband's passport, which he had left behind, and changed the photograph. She claimed that her boyfriend did not want her to do this, nor put pressure on her to do it, but she felt in need of a holiday and she personally wanted to do this for him.

While they were on holiday in France, she claimed, they met a family who were looking for an opportunity to be smuggled across the Channel into England. Although there was no direct pressure on Laura to take part in this crime, she felt that it was the right thing to do for the people involved, and, since they were also Iraqi, would show her commitment to her new partner. Laura felt that as her previous marriage had been so bad, she wanted to show her love for her new partner, fearing that she might lose him if she did not. She said: 'My boyfriend said it was my choice. We went for a drink and I decided to do it as I had no children and they [the children of the Iraqi family] looked so sad and undernourished.'

Although there was no apparent direct pressure on her from her boyfriend, the personal circumstances of her previous marriage and current relationship appeared to have seduced her into assisting in the people-smuggling offence.

When they arrived back in England with the Iraqi family, customs officers searched the car and arrested Laura and her boyfriend. He was later released without charge, but Laura was held and charged, though only with having forged the passport. She said that she had no other friends in the UK, and that her boyfriend had been the only person to visit her since she was jailed. Laura realised that she had been committing an offence, but had been scared of doing something (or not doing something) which might have meant losing her new partner.

A second offender who also appeared to have been seduced by others was Ruth, an unmarried Nigerian, who appeared to have become involved in offending through her personal and social contacts, including her boyfriend.

Case study – Ruth

Ruth had been convicted of conspiracy to defraud and sentenced to 46 months in prison. Born in Nigeria, Ruth had been adopted by a British couple and had spent several years living and working in City A around various financial institutions and Post Offices. In City A she was involved with a number of other Nigerians, including her boyfriend, who had all committed financial crimes in order to bring other Nigerians into the country. Ruth did not blame anybody directly for her involvement in this offending, but did note that because of her relationship with her boyfriend (and the social circles she moved in) this had become a way of life for her. She said: 'I was involved through my boyfriend [also Nigerian] … I was in a particular lifestyle in City A with these people.'

Ruth had feared losing her boyfriend and her shared contacts if she did not participate in the crimes and follow their way of life. During her time in jail, especially as she had previous convictions for similar offences, Ruth had realised that she needed to leave her boyfriend and break free from this lifestyle, perhaps even to move away from City A so she was not tempted to become involved again in their criminal activities. In prison she had engaged in some information-technology training and intended to apply to university to study African Studies on her release. Some of these courses were offered at City A universities, though Ruth was reluctant to go back there to live because of past influences and memories.

As well as partners or other loved ones, individuals such as associates and peer-group members also appeared to have had an influence on the behaviour of offenders. In the case of Adrian, who had committed crimes with others relating to the import of tobacco with the intention of evading payment of duty, he claimed that he had resumed the latter part of the operation after meeting up with his former associates. He said: 'I wasn't bothered one way or another whether we re-started or not ... the other two [financing the operation] questioned the success but agreed to carry on and this time to go even bigger. I had made what I set out to ... I didn't care one way or the other.'

No others in the sample mentioned the influence of colleagues or associates on their behaviour in their own accounts. Where other individuals were mentioned (such as by Matt, Pam and Stan) there was a general denial on the individual's part of being involved in anything. Their references to others (spouses, partners or associates) focused on blaming them for the crimes and disassociating themselves.

The examples in this section demonstrate how being seduced into crime differs from being pressurised into crime. Seduction, in the case of these offenders, appears to suggest the existence of some freedom of choice, resulting in a willingness to take part in offences (as demonstrated by Adrian, Laura and Ruth), whether this is direct or indirect. This shows that they may have given in to what would otherwise be seen as rational argument, or did what they thought others wished them to do. This level of involvement contrasts with that of those who were threatened, as pressurised actors who believed they had little or no control over what was happening.

Summary

Clearly, the accounts in this chapter demonstrate that there was no single, archetypical category of explanation given for the behaviour of the sample offenders, and that their accounts frequently revealed multiple reasons and motives; such reasons were often interlinked, and may to some extent help to explain the lack of research in the motivation of white-collar crime. For example, Sheila's primary motivation for her crimes was to get her family out of spiralling debt. Nevertheless, she also accounted for her illegal behaviour in terms of pressure from her parents, as well as of exploiting opportunities presented during the course of her work. By describing different motives, individuals therefore become 'actors' in different situations, depending upon the primary and secondary motivations for committing their crimes and in turn how they account and present these. Three main types of 'actors' were considered for this research – rational, pressurised and seduced. Individuals presented themselves as one of these types, or as a combination of two or all three of them.

Rational actors were classified as those individuals who either planned their crimes and went looking for opportunities to commit them, or pursued illegal activities after coming across a weakness of which they could take advantage. Only two individuals were identified in the sample as having set out in a planned and calculated way to identify a situation conducive to the commission of a crime. In terms of planning, such behaviour is in contrast to those individuals described by Matza (1964) as 'drifting' into crime. However, the majority of rational actors in the sample did appear to have 'drifted' or 'stumbled' across potential criminal opportunities, and had been tempted by what Shover and Hochstetler (2006) term the 'lure' of the situation. These opportunist situations were mostly identified by the offenders as being either system weaknesses or situations where they were able to take advantage of their positions of power and authority.

Offenders also accounted for their behaviour in terms of being pressurised actors. These were found to be of three main types – aspiring, desperate and threatened. Aspiring actors felt either self-inflicted pressure, to be successful and maintain the level of success and lifestyle they had achieved, or pressure from others, such as their parents, whether in childhood or more recently. There were, however, individuals in desperate situations, usually with financial problems, trying to extricate themselves from situations which were threatening themselves, their families or their businesses. Finally, the third type of pressurised actors identified were seduced, tempted into illegal behaviour by other individuals, such as close others.

As well as providing additional academic knowledge in the way white-collar offenders think and behave, the findings in this chapter have substantial implications for fraud prevention, by suggesting the actual reasons a white-collar criminal might commit an offence, what prompted it and what, if anything, stopped it. Cornish and Clarke (2005) developed 25 situational techniques, which they based around five key principles. These principles were: increasing the effort needed for an offender to be successful; increasing the risks offenders have to take, thereby increasing the chances of their being caught, or at the least the belief that they might be caught; making rewards less attractive to potential offenders; reducing issues that may induce people to commit offences; and changing attitudes towards workplace fraud that see it as a justified reward.

Considering the issue of workplace crime Gill and Goldstraw-White (2010) note that the most successful way of reducing fraud by employees is to eliminate the opportunities for offending and make crimes more difficult to commit. However, they consider there are other more holistic areas to be addressed within an organisational environment. These include:

1. Treating employees well and not allowing discontent to fester
2. Paying employees fairly
3. Finding out about staff problems and expectations and having done so, managing them
4. Recruiting the right people for the job at the outset
5. Fostering positive workplace cultures, by setting the tone and providing an example at the top
6. Throughout the organisation, reducing, or where possible eliminating, opportunities for committing crime
7. Setting clear guidelines as to what is acceptable behaviour and more importantly, what is not
8. Making it clear that the organisation is the victim of any white-collar crime, and that all losses have to be accounted for somewhere
9. Ensuring crime-prevention measures are effective

In conclusion therefore, when management are considering the overall control environment of an organisation, staff behaviour and welfare should be addressed as well as control systems. Where resources are not finite, it is important to have accurate and up-to-date knowledge of the risks that threaten a business in order to make the appropriate decisions as to where these resources should be targeted and where the greatest savings and gains can be made.

6
The Self as a Moral Person

Introduction

In this chapter we will examine the strategies used by the offenders, as moral individuals, when accounting for their criminal behaviour. Specifically, when they scrutinised events in hindsight, did they claim virtuousness in accounting for their behaviour, giving reasons which suggested they committed their crimes (from their perspective) for 'acceptable' reasons? While there was a wide variety of accounts, many relied on distancing techniques, explaining the offending as normal, consistent, 'everyday' behaviour, or as 'one-off', out-of-character actions.

We saw in Chapter 2 that individuals may seek to restore the 'status quo' of their character (Baumeister and Newman, 1994) when an unfavourable event takes place, and use a number of techniques in their attempt to 'save face' (Ting-Toomey, 1994) – though of course such techniques may or may not be seen positively by those hearing/reading them. As Chambliss (1964) notes, when talking about themselves individuals rarely do so in an unfavourable or negative way, and in seeking to portray themselves as moral individuals, participants in the sample tended to try and emphasise what they perceived, by their own definition, to be acceptable accounts of their offending and to play down what they considered its unacceptable facets – mainly greedy and self-centred motivation. The main categories of acceptable and unacceptable accounts identified and used for analysis are detailed in Table 6.1.

The area of morality is one branch of the philosophy of ethics. Ethics itself can be defined as the study of a set of moral values, principles or customs which may be held by an individual or a group of individuals, and has three broad categories: meta-, normative ethics and applied ethics. First, meta-ethics consists of the study of ethical values, including

Table 6.1   'Acceptable' and 'unacceptable' account types

Accounts

Acceptable	Unacceptable
Altruistic motives	Greed
Rejection of injustice	Addiction
Success and fear of failure as a motive	
Threats to self-esteem and blocked opportunities	
Distancing techniques	

the nature of ethics and of individuals' moral reasoning. Debates about whether ethics is a relative matter, or whether the individual acts only from self-interest, are pertinent to meta-ethical discussions. Psychological egoism asserts that people only act out of a belief that some benefit will thereby accrue to them. Such claims are open to debate, and other motives can be viewed as reasons for acting in a certain way. The second main area of ethics, normative ethics, addresses how morals should be determined – in other words, to which kinds of moral behaviour individuals subscribe to. Normative ethics goes beyond sociological facts and considers what is thought to be right conduct in society at that particular time, whereas meta-ethics claims that morality itself is a relative phenomenon. Finally, applied ethics is the study of the use to which a society puts ethical values.

Personal morality defines and distinguishes between right and wrong intentions or motivations – as learned, engendered or otherwise developed within each individual. However, the actual definition of right and wrong behaviour of course varies between different belief systems. In the case of group morality, the definition resides in shared concepts and beliefs, and is often used, directly or indirectly, to regulate behaviour within a particular culture, community or group. As a result, various behaviours can become defined as moral or immoral. Ethically, acceptable and unacceptable behaviours are relative judgements, and therefore two observers may view an individual's moral behaviour – for instance, addiction – in diametrically different ways. Likewise, the fear of failure as a motive for committing a crime may be seen by some as an unacceptable motive, similar to greed, but by others as totally understandable, and thus acceptable. For these reasons, using the definitions as identified by the offenders, unacceptable accounts were those in which no moral reasons for their crime were presented.

Unacceptable accounts

Accounts given by offenders which included unacceptable reasons tended to focus on the areas of greed and addiction. Each of these areas concentrated on the internal causes directly relating to the individual criminal. This contrasts directly with those offenders who gave accounts in which there figured (what they considered to be) acceptable reasons, which may have been formulated before, during or after the commission of their crimes and often focused on external reasons. Only four offenders interviewed made no attempt, or were unable, to give what they saw as acceptable moral explanations for the commission of their crimes; these subjects had committed their crimes for their own personal and selfish reasons, their primary motivation being mainly greed or addiction.

Greed

There are numerous definitions of greed. Heath (2008: 599), for instance, believes that the majority of white-collar crime is motivated by what he terms 'pecuniary incentives', where individuals commit crime for their own self-enrichment. Braithwaite (1992: 84), however, while defining needs as '… socially constructed wants that can be satisfied', sees greed as '… a want that can never be satisfied … having more leads to wanting more again'. Greed can also be regarded as making quick and easy gains, with little chance of detection (Gill, 1994: 16). Accounts of financial need from the offenders in the sample were found to focus on two main areas, sometimes interlinked – the family and business (Gill and Goldstraw-White, 2010). Some people find it surprising that white-collar offenders cite greed as a reason for involvement in criminal activity, or that they indeed actually need the money in the same way as other criminals. Nevertheless, all types of individuals may come across circumstances leading them to commit fraud, not just those in the lower social strata (Doig, 2006: 86); and many white-collar crime offenders are indeed greedy (Croall, 2001; Gill, 2005; Doig, 2006).

During the interviews, three offenders gave accounts claiming that a great deal of money could be made relatively easily, and in a short space of time, compared with other more orthodox and legal methods. Individuals found that the more money they acquired in this way, the more they wanted – possibly until their needs became 'satisfied'. One such offender – Max, a self-employed computer consultant – commented on the relative ease of earning money by committing crime, as opposed to acting legally: 'Ordinary chances of wealth were not bad, but this way was quicker and easier. I caused a lot of stress though, all for greed.'

A similar situation was that of Gerry, a market trader convicted (along with others) of being knowingly concerned in evading the payment of import duty amounting to some £1.25 million (he was sentenced to three years' imprisonment).

Case study – Gerry

Gerry had been a market-trader all his life and had also owned a shop, stating that he preferred to deal mostly in cash. He had started in a small way of business, but turnover had soon grown. He claimed: 'For 11 years I have not had to worry about money. I am not a collector, money is for spending.'

Having associated with some others through his business, Gerry became involved in the importing of goods and in evading import duty on them. He was caught, with the others, while unloading a container. He claimed that the money he had made was purely as a result of greed – 'The more money you get, the more you "need".' Now in prison, Gerry stated that he had acquired what he wanted in life and had more money than he genuinely needed. He even suggested that he appreciated money more now that he had less, especially as he was only receiving £7 a week while incarcerated.

In contrast, Peter, a 32-year-old self-employed financial consultant, admitted that the primary motivation for his crimes was simply financial gain.

Case study – Peter

Peter had been convicted of money-laundering. He had started work during what he described as the prosperous time, in the mid-1980s, dealing with finance on the Stock Exchange. Peter claimed that at one point he was earning up to £5,000 a week through his dealings on the international money markets. He claimed that he was approached to get involved in money-laundering activities (which turned out to be associated with the smuggling of drugs from Colombia). He accounted for his criminality as driven by greed – his main motive for committing his crimes was to obtain sufficient money to fund a luxurious lifestyle, and having achieved this, to maintain it. He admitted: 'The more I earned, the more I wanted. I had a cruiser on the Med … at 22 years of age that was something.'

Peter said that he had acted stupidly out of a desire for further money and for luxury goods, even though he had a more than adequate amount of both. He was well-educated, came from a good family background and had wanted for nothing. He claimed that he had no explanation other than greed for committing his crimes, and admitted his inexperience and immaturity in handling such large amounts of money: 'I put it down to a lot of spending and the middle-class boom of the 1980s.'

As such accounts illustrate, it is very difficult, once a pattern of spending is established and a certain level of lifestyle attained, to cease any associated criminality. In this sense, individuals become addicted to the money they obtain and the spending of it; in this way, greed appears to feed upon itself.

Addiction

Other accounts identified as unacceptable were related to some kind of addiction. Traditional addictive behaviours, such as those involving alcohol, drugs or gambling as motivations to commit crimes are not unknown reasons for offending given by white-collar criminals. This in part supports the hypothesis espoused by Bloch and Geis (1962), Nettler (1982b) and Sifakis (2001), in which the expressions 'babes, booze and bets' (the 'three Bs'), 'rum, redheads and racehorses' or 'wine, women and wagering' were coined to label major influences on white-collar criminals. Surprisingly, only one offender in the study (2 per cent of total subjects) claimed to have had his crimes influenced by such addictive behaviour. This relatively low figure is contrary to the findings of Sakurai and Smith (2003: 6), who, in their study of serious-fraud offenders in Australia and New Zealand, found that gambling and other addictive behaviours had a significant influence on the com-mission of white-collar crime. Sakurai and Smith (ibid) acknowledge, however, that further research is needed to confirm their hypothesis of gambling causing illegal behaviour.

Another subject, Abuu, a self-employed computer salesman, had been sentenced to 18 months' imprisonment for deception and for conspiracy to handle some £50,000-worth of stolen goods, through the creation of a bogus company. Abuu stated that his primary motivation was the need for additional money for the purchase of a new house, and that his involvement in criminal activities had been influenced by blackmail from the supplier of the goods. He also acknowledged that he had had problems at the time, stating: 'I was involved in gambling and alcohol. I wish I had sought help earlier and not hidden behind drink.'

Acceptable accounts

Acceptable accounts were viewed by offenders as those which did not contain any unacceptable elements of behaviour, such as greed and addiction. By using acceptable accounts, individuals wished to make their accounts and motives more agreeable to others and make little of the unacceptable parts. The five main areas of acceptable accounts (from the perspective of the offenders), as detailed in Table 6.1, include the following:

- Altruistic reasons – good and justified reasons
- Rejection of injustice – demonstrating elements of unfairness
- Success or fear of failure as a motive – striving to gain and maintain status
- Threats to self-esteem and blocked opportunities – the importance of progression, especially in career
- Distancing techniques – accounts which distance the offender from the crime or more traditional criminals

Each of these categories will now be explored in further detail.

Altruistic reasons

Altruistic accounts would appear to accord with what Sykes and Matza (1957) describe as 'appealing to higher loyalties'. That is, 'sacrificing the demands of the smaller social groups to which the delinquent belongs ...' (ibid: 669). Often offenders say things like 'I didn't do it for myself', or pose a rhetorical question such as 'What choice did I have?'. In this way the individual may attempt to avoid blame by claiming that the reasons behind what he did, or the people in whose interest he did it, take precedence over obedience to the law (Friedrichs, 1996: 231).

In claiming altruistic motives for their criminal behaviour, offenders were keen to stress that they committed their crimes for 'good' and 'justifiable' reasons – where someone or something else was their primary concern, not themselves. Accounts of this nature broadly resemble each other, and can thus be seen as belonging one of two broad areas. The first of these is where individuals account for their crimes due to external reasons such as needing to commit crimes for the sake of their family or business. The second of these areas involves situations where individual offenders, after committing their crimes, feel guilty about what they have done, realise that they do not deserve what their crime has gained for them, and in some instances try to 'make good' their misconduct (Maruna, 2001).

'I didn't do it for myself'

In seeking moral justification of their criminal behaviour, some offenders claimed to have committed their crimes for the sake of others. In particular, this reason was used by some offenders who had become involved with crimes which they had committed to help their families or to save their businesses from bankruptcy. Gerry, mentioned above in relation to greed, said that he had not used most of his illicit financial gains for his own benefit, but instead had given much of the money to his mother. He claimed: 'I have given a lot to my Mum who needed it … for cars, holidays etc.'

Similar comments were also put forward by Jason, who said that the money he stole was not purely for himself, claiming rather that the crime was an attempt to save his furniture-making business: 'I had a number of men working for me on a self-employed basis … they depended on that money as much as my business did … I owed it to them as well.'

Where offenders' illegal activities were said to have benefited others or 'saved' companies and jobs, they felt their actions were justified. Gareth disagreed that the illegal inter-trading between his companies was undertaken purely for selfish reasons: 'How can this be wrong? … it meant that people stayed employed and customers got their goods.' He thus sought to present his activities (in this instance providing employment and goods to the market place) as morally justified, and thus over-riding the law. Similarly, the three women mentioned in Chapter 5, claimed to have acted out of desperation, committing their crimes for the sake of their families rather than for their own benefit.

'Making it good'

A further way in which individuals sought to give themselves some moral standing was to talk about restarting their lives and paying back the money they had taken, or at least to pay back their debt to society in some other way. This is not always as selfless as it sounds, and many individuals feel bitter at being also sentenced to prison. Lord Charles Brocket, referring to fraudulent insurance claims he had submitted, said after his release from prison:

> I don't think of myself as a criminal and yet I have done technically something criminal. I put in an insurance claim that was patently dishonest and fraudulent, but at least we realised what we were

doing and we withdrew the claim. So at least we put that right (2002).

Three offenders in the sample gave similar accounts, which appeared to vary in their levels of sincerity with respect to paying back their debts to their victims or to society. Dave, an assistant management accountant claimed that he had repaid approximately a third of the £109,000 he had embezzled from the company he worked for, as a result of civil action taken out by his employers. He acknowledged that he was not entitled to any of this money, but felt that having paid back a proportion of the amount stolen (and having served time in prison as well), he could resume his life with some level of morality restored. He commented: 'I have paid back £33,000 ... I need to start again.'

In contrast to Dave, Jason, the owner of the furniture-making business mentioned above, claimed to have voluntarily paid back the full amount of £110,000 to those he had defrauded and illegally obtained finance. He said he had been able to afford this because he had sold his business and therefore had the funds to repay the money. He did not reveal in his account whether he had undertaken this in an attempt to avoid prison – treating the money simply as being 'borrowed' – or because of the adverse publicity over the victim of his fraud, an old lady (see Chapter 7). Jason did comment that the police officers who had interviewed him appeared very surprised about these repayments: 'The police queried why I had done this, but I had sold the business as a going concern, therefore I had the money to pay this.'

However, Jason said he now felt bitter that he had both repaid the money and served a prison sentence – thereby suggesting he had repaid the money to avoid a custodial sentence: 'I have paid off every-one now, therefore in a way I feel I have paid for my crime twice.'

With the exception of Debbie, the restaurant manager who openly admitted she had tried to pay back the money she had embezzled rather than face a custodial sentence, other offenders who mentioned repaying money appeared resentful about doing so and receiving a prison sentence as well. Iqbal, a Post Office owner, had been sentenced to 36 months for conspiracy with others to commit fraud, the sum involved, amounting to some £200,000. In his account, he claimed to have paid the money back, but felt bitter as he claimed that he was now actually worse off.

Rejection of injustice

The second way in which individuals tried to argue that they had accept-able reasons for committing their crimes, and thus to reclaim some moral standing, was to argue that in the circumstances surrounding their acts there was an element of injustice. Two main methods may be employed to support this assertion. First, individuals may claim, in respect of a particular criminal act on their part, that 'everyone else is doing it' (Coleman, 1987), and they therefore fail to see any moral reason why they should not engage in similar activity. Secondly, they may claim that they are justified in their actions because they feel that they have been wronged, and thus have the moral right to seek revenge (Sykes and Matza, 1957; Scott and Lyman, 1968).

Three offenders claimed to have committed their crimes as a result of feeling wronged. The first of these was Marvin, the owner of a publishing company who had been jailed for Post Office fraud, deception and forgery.

Case study – Marvin

Marvin's firm ran into financial difficulties, and he had to look for areas where costs might be cut. Because of the nature of his business, which included sending out a large volume of mail shots about his firm's publications, he regularly dealt with the Post Office. He claimed that in the past the firm had lost a considerable amount of its outgoing promotional mail; Marvin felt that this might have affected his business, and he sought revenge by avoiding postage costs – in this case by forging franking-machine labels which he was able to print on his own equipment. He admitted that he had a personal vendetta against the Post Office, and explained: 'I realised it was dishonest, but I justified this on the basis that the Post Office had messed up some letters and not refunded costs.'

Marvin's case demonstrates that although cutting costs was his primary motivation, he felt justified in his criminal actions, using the rationalisation that he had been treated unjustly when the Post Office lost his outgoing mail.

The other two offenders who claimed they had been wronged directed their anger towards their employers, who had, they felt, treated them unjustly. Sheila was an accounts assistant for a travel agency, imprisoned for embezzlement, deception and credit-card offences.

Case study – Sheila

Sheila and her husband had personal financial debts, which she tried to pay off by embezzling money, over a period of 18 months, from the travel agency where she worked. She pleaded guilty, but stated that she felt bitter at the firm's failure to help her when she was looking to re-mortgage her house. At the time she had sought a salary increase so that she would be able to meet the new repayments. However, she was refused, and she felt that she been living on false promises of monetary reward, though she did acknowledge that she had not committed her crimes primarily out of animosity towards the company.

In the same context, Sally, a management accountant for a manufacturing company who embezzled funds of £251,000 and falsified accounts from her employer, felt let down by her boss.

Case study – Sally

Although Sally cited the need to boost her self-esteem as her primary motivation for committing her crimes, she also admitted to feelings of anger towards her boss. She had originally been employed by him when the company was much smaller, in order to help him expand the business. However, the more it grew, the less her boss had to do with the day-to-day work, including the financial side, which Sally looked after. As a result, she claimed that she felt undervalued and put-upon, especially as her workload and responsibility had increased, and she also felt under-paid. Therefore, Sally said, she felt morally justified in seeking revenge on her boss, in the process abusing her position of trust and exploiting the weaknesses she had identified in the organisation's systems. She stated: 'I was not well paid, although I did a lot. I didn't feel as though I was paid what I was worth.'

At the time of her crimes this was particularly important to Sally, who also admitted to suffering from low self-esteem.

Success and fear of failure as a motive

The importance of succeeding in life, and the fear of failing, appeared to be crucial factors to some individuals when accounting for their criminality. This question of status in turn affects how people view moral victories and defeats within their own life, and demonstrates how much these can boost or deflate egos and self-esteem. It was important to many of the individuals in the sample to be seen as the 'master of' or 'being on top of' their game. Stotland (1977: 188) calls this motivation the 'ego challenge', which bring professional pride into play and generates a sense of excitement. The notion of mastering a situation is an ever-changing one, as new and potentially criminal situations present themselves to individuals – though of course fulfilment may be found in running a successful business, earning a good reputation or simply having fruitful relationships with members of their family. Steele (1988) analyses the importance of self-esteem to individuals, recognising that people need to maintain a certain level of self-worth within their daily lives. People with low levels of self-esteem, however, seem particularly vulnerable to threats, compared to those with higher levels. Individuals with higher self-esteem may be more readily able to accept some measure of failure and setbacks, without these greatly affecting their own self-worth. It therefore follows that individuals with low self-esteem may react more adversely than those with higher levels if, for example, their job, career or prospects of advancement come under threat.

Cressey (1953: 41–2) also identified the importance of threats to self-esteem during his interviews with white-collar criminals, classing such motivation as 'problems resulting from personal failure'. He found that some of his subjects were too ashamed to admit to instances of their own poor judgement or unwise behaviour. This resulted in these individuals feeling that their status as a trusted person, which was how they regarded themselves, had been compromised, thus making the problem non-shareable and leading to the pursuit of criminal solutions.

However, with the hunger to succeed comes an inherent risk of failure, and for many white-collar criminals such blows to their self-esteem may cause them to act so as to protect themselves against them. The pursuit of success and the fear of failure were indeed identified, by eight participants in the present study, as significant motives and as justifying the commission of white-collar crimes. These accounts tended to focus on success in a business context, and included those who wished to be seen as successful by their families, friends, peers and associates.

An example of an individual who was determined to achieve success in his work, and thus to boost his own self-confidence and ego, was Peter, a self-employed financial consultant convicted of money-laundering, associated with the supply of illegal drugs. He had previously owned a business that had gone bankrupt, and stated that it was very important to him to make a success of his next job at whatever cost, even if that cost included criminality. Peter's belief in himself was rooted in the fact he had always been successful in his life. He remarked: 'I have never really failed before. The buzz of the city and the Stock Exchange were just so exciting. It's a feeling you can't describe.'

Peter, and a number of other offenders when accounting for their involvement in crime, commented that the need to succeed and the fear of failure was their primary motivation, though having varying degrees of importance to each. In his account, Geoff, a 56-year-old owner of a manufacturing company, admitted that although he had encountered financial difficulties and wished to save his business, an additional factor was his feeling that he had to maintain a certain standard of living in front of his family and friends.

A similar case was that of Max, a self-employed computer consultant sentenced for conspiracy to defraud after his new business (which he had set up with associates) ran into financial difficulties. As Max had left paid, regular and stable employment to start his own business, he felt that making a success of it was very important to him. He confessed that: 'I had a great fear of failing. I needed to be good ...'

In some subjects' accounts other, more personal, reasons were also identified for needing success and minimising failure, some of these reasons relating to the offender's earlier life.

Case study – Sid

Sid, a 44-year-old habitual criminal, had been sentenced to 48 months' imprisonment for deception, involving car sales. During the course of his interview he said that from a very early age he had suffered from cerebral palsy, which back in the 1950s had been a terrible embarrassment for his family – especially his mother, who (he claimed) had as a result distanced herself from him. Sid's belief was that no-one ever expected him to make anything of himself, and that as a consequence he had left school early and gone looking for work to show people what he could do. He said: 'At the age of 14, I left home to show people I could make something of myself. People didn't credit me with a brain.'

Sid found it hard to make a living. As a result, he felt an even greater need to prove himself to his family and others, and claimed that he had no choice but to turn to crime. At the time of his interview, Sid had served a number of years in various prisons for non-white-collar offences, and really knew no other way of life. In his own eyes, he had not been able to prove his worth, proving his family's belief that he would never make anything of his life.

By contrast, Sally, a 33-year-old management accountant sentenced for embezzling from her employer and falsifying accounts, had more success in making a better life for herself, albeit in the short term.

Case study – Sally

After what she described as an oppressive childhood (due to the strictness of her parents, especially her father), Sally qualified as an accountant and helped her boss to set up a new company. Later in her employment she noticed an opportunity to embezzle funds from the business. At the time, she claimed she had recently been badly let down by a boyfriend and felt very low. Although her primary reason for committing her offences was weaknesses in the company's systems, Sally admitted that she used the money (and the knowledge that she had money to spend) to boost her ego. She claimed: 'I started taking money after two years through the BACS system. Initially it was between £100 and £600 to pay for a holiday, to boost my self-esteem.'

Although she spent the money on material goods, such as holidays, Sally claimed that she was not particularly greedy or materialistic, or even enjoyed spending a lot of money. To Sally, the planning of her purchases, and the knowledge that she had the means to do this, was in itself the most important part of the criminal act, and an ego boost which she regarded as a morally-justified reason for her crimes. She claimed: 'I didn't particularly enjoy spending the money, I enjoyed aspects of booking things … just knowing I could.'

In this way, the power of having money, which allowed her control over certain situations, was important to Sally and indeed, in her eyes, raised her self-esteem by making her the master of her game. This illustrates what Duffield and Grabosky (2001) suggest – that an individual may desire to be seen to have power over both people and situations. They also propose that in some instances this desire may for some offenders become an end in itself, as opposed to what they may obtain directly through criminal activity. Sally and Sid had both committed criminal acts to boost their own self-esteem, and there was evidence from the accounts of others in the sample that this was also a motivating factor in their own criminal behaviour.

Two separate individuals – Anne and Gerry – both pointed out in their accounts that little of the financial benefits from their criminal activities had been spent on themselves. Instead, one of their motivations appeared to be simply pleasing others. Gerry, a 30-year-old self-employed market-trader, had been sentenced to 36 months for being knowingly concerned in the evasion of duty payable. He was keen to emphasise that: 'I got people cheap goods, therefore no one disliked me ... having no enemies is very important for my self-worth.'

In this way, Gerry boosted his own ego, seeing himself as a successful person able to win the friendship and attention of others, even if this meant needing to commit criminal activities to do so. Anne, a 38-year-old supermarket garage-manager sentenced to 12 months (with six months suspended) for falsifying accounts and stealing from her employer, was unable to give any direct motives for committing her crimes. During her account, however, like Sally she stressed that she was not a materialistic person. However, in contrast to Sally – who willingly admitted that she had committed her crimes to boost her own ego – Anne did not allude to this. What she did say though was: 'I spent it [the criminal proceeds] mainly on holidays. I took eight friends to Orlando, costing about £20,000. We had a great time ... we bought Minnie Mouse ears and things. I'm embarrassed now at the amount of money we spent.'

Both Anne and Gerry thus appeared to be seeking to raise and maintain their self-esteem through their public persona, with the spending of the proceeds of their crimes being a means to that end. For, Sally however, merely having the ability to spend was what was important to her, not the spending itself.

Threats to self-esteem and blocked opportunities

The relationship between individuals and their employer may be key to understanding much white-collar criminality. Dissatisfaction towards an employer can take many forms, and is particularly relevant to white-collar criminals because of the situational nature of their crimes. Often jobs and crimes are closely associated, sometimes making it hard to identify what is criminal and what is sharp business practice. Jeyasingh studied 50 convicted white-collar criminals and stressed the importance of work issues as motivating factors in criminal behaviour. He highlighted reasons given by individuals for dissatisfaction with their working situation, including jealousy over a co-worker's promotion and progress, feeling they were paid less than they were worth, and not being warned or controlled by their supervisor when they acted illegally (1986: 21). Blocked opportunities, especially where there exists a disjuncture between individual aspirations and actual opportunities, may also cause serious dissatisfaction, and this may tempt employees to seek retribution through fraudulent activities against their employers (Sarbin, 1994: 114). Although Benson (1985) did not find employee dissatisfaction a significant issue among the offenders he interviewed, by contrast Cressey found that the issue of perceived underpayment was one which caused serious disenchantment among employees, possibly leading to criminal activities (1953: 57–66).

Within the present sample, a number of individuals gave accounts indicating disgruntlement, either at the way they were treated at work, or because the rewards they received amounted to less than they believed they were entitled to. Where individuals felt that somebody or something was standing in the way of their advancement within the organisation, they would claim that they felt their opportunities were being blocked. Individuals who perceived such a blockage tended to vent their anger and frustrations towards their current employer by criminal activity.

Dave was among the offenders who found himself in this situation. Dave was a married 31-year-old assistant management accountant, sentenced to 30 months' imprisonment for the theft of £109,000 from his employer.

Case study – Dave

In his account Dave explained how he believed that his chances of advancing within his organisation were being blocked because he lacked qualifications (although he believed he could do the job equally as well as those who had those qualifications). As a result, Dave had become disgruntled with his employers because he felt held back. He said that this had caused him to feel jealous of other staff in the office, and that his own position had become stagnant. Dave believed that his contributions were not being recognised, and his talents not being fully utilised, in the course of his work. He commented: 'I felt like I was treading water ... I admit I held a slight grudge against others.'

Dave said that he had previously been told that he would be 'rewarded' for his efforts. However, he said: 'The promotion I had been promised might never have materialised.'

When the opportunity arose, these feelings all contributed to Dave falsifying cheques over a three-year period, and he identified his dissatisfaction with his job situation as a major motivation for committing his crime.

Besides employee dissatisfaction due to blocked opportunities, crime in the workplace may also be caused by how employees view their roles and rewards. There may be certain customary practices, varying between industries or trades, which in another setting would be viewed totally differently. For instance, Mars noted how pilferage by dock workers was regarded by many as 'a morally justified addition to wages' or 'an entitlement due from exploiting employees' (1974: 222). Likewise, Zeitlin's (1971) subjects working in the retail environment felt that the store 'owed them'. In this way, employees believe that they are entitled to goods from their companies and that such pilferage is part of everyday business; they do not view it as stealing. Although these texts are quite dated now, it is interesting to note that the recent report by PricewaterhouseCoopers (PwC) (2010: 7) found that in their web-based survey of 35 countries across the globe, over two-thirds (69 per cent) of those reporting economic crime (which includes the types of white-collar crime committed against corporations, as reported in the present study) singled out asset appropriation in their responses as being one of the most prevalent types of fraud committed in their organisations.

Distancing techniques

Many of the individuals interviewed giving accounts which tried in some way to deny, rationalise or justify their behaviour attempted to 'dis-identify' (Hudson, 2005: 66) themselves from the notion of criminality. If they were unable to do this, they tried to 'dance with denial' (ibid: 66) and distance themselves in some other way to lessen or erase their self-labelling as a criminal. During their accounts, eight distancing techniques (see below) were identified, similar to those developed by Hudson (ibid).[1] The distancing techniques identified in the present study, which individuals adopted to portray themselves as 'better' and 'more acceptable' individuals in society, were as follows:

1. Distancing by normality ('it was out of character')
2. Distancing by planned activity ('it was meant to be a one-off')
3. Distancing by offender type ('I'm not a "bad" criminal')
4. Distancing by damage ('there was no victim')
5. Distancing by self control ('it could have been worse')
6. Distancing by victim type ('I did not treat everyone the same')
7. Distancing by co-operation ('I assisted the authorities')
8. Distancing by prisoner status ('I'm a "good" prisoner')

Each of these distancing techniques will now be considered in further detail.

'It was out of character'

One way for an individual to try to minimise the stigma of their offending behaviour is to account for themselves as normal and ordinary people who had acted out of character in committing their crimes. A number of accounts, stressing acceptable rather than unacceptable reasons for their criminality, and generally relating to external factors (thereby removing the responsibility from the individual), were offered by offenders during their interviews. These accounts stressed the individuals' own normality, and the atypical nature of their criminal behaviour, while at the same time not denying it. They were also keen to stress that their criminal acts were 'one-offs', sometimes drawing on past behaviour to support this and pointing to external issues to demonstrate what had influenced their decision to offend. They described themselves as ordinary people with normal family, work and social relationships, and attempted to situate their deviant acts within this framework.

Consequently, individuals who sought in this way to preserve their character as ordinary people gave accounts which attempted to stress their own normality and to situate their criminal acts as aberrant, claiming that 'I'm a good person really'. Accounts of this nature consisted of the offenders trying to emphasise the normality and respectability of their lives and aligning themselves with 'ordinary' and 'normal' non-offending individuals. For example, Kevin, the solicitor in a single-handed practice who had been sentenced for false accounting, was keen to stress that he was just an ordinary person. During his account he chose to emphasise how he had been left with little choice but to commit crime for the sake of his family. However, just because he had done so, Kevin stressed that did not mean he was not an ordinary, hard-working person with the morals to match. Attaching great importance to the nature of his job, he stressed in his account: 'I was a good person with a good job in a practice.'

One other offender presented his case in quite an interesting way, by trying to section off his criminal activities from his ordinary daily business life. Adrian, a self-employed transport owner, had been sentenced, along with others, for evasion of duty on payments amounting to over £2.5 million. In order to undertake this well-planned and sophisticated operation, he had set up a separate company solely for the purpose. Adrian's method of describing normality was to stress the legitimacy of his other company, which did not participate in the criminal activities. In this way, he did not deny that he was a criminal, but played down the criminal aspect of his life by emphasising the normal, moral and non-criminal elements of it. He said, quite proudly: 'I ran a legitimate business alongside the criminal one.'

Others who played down the criminal parts of their lives by emphasising the more normal and moral aspects included Pam, a married 50-year-old woman who had owned and run a shop with her husband, and had been sentenced to 24 months' imprisonment for conspiracy to obtain goods by deception, along with her husband and others.

Case study – Pam

In court Pam had denied her involvement in the crime, pleading not guilty. During her account, she was keen not only to stress her innocence, but also to remind me that she was indeed just an ordinary, decent, educated person who cared for her family. She emphasised: 'I have no previous. I'm educated as a secretary ... I'm a grandmother.' Pam's efforts to stress her lack of previous convictions demonstrates another way in which criminals may attempt to create a good impression and play down their criminality.

Janet, who had been convicted of housing-benefit fraud, was also keen to point out her previous lack of a criminal record. She fully acknowledged her guilt and pleaded guilty in court. Giving an open and frank account of her reasons for committing her crime, Janet was keen to stress that her criminal behaviour had been out of character, a 'one-off', committed only out of desperation because of the situation she faced at the time. She claimed: 'I've never done anything like this before, nor would I again.'

'It was meant to be a one-off'

Cressey found that business people often use the excuse of 'borrowing' to neutralise the accounts of criminal offences when they realise that they have become too deeply involved in their crime. He believes that by acting in this way these individuals were able to stay in touch with the beliefs and values of their peer groups, and thus to feel that their actions should not be seen morally as a true crime (1953: 122). Cressey also notes that many individuals he interviewed mentioned a genuine belief in their intention to repay the stolen funds, feeling that they could 'cover' the situation (ibid: 108, 118).

Offenders seeking to avoid their crime being seen as, for them, part of their normal, on-going behaviour gave reasons for treating it as a one-off offence. These ranged from greed and impatience through to complete desperation.

Case study – Geoff

Geoff, the owner of a manufacturing company, had been sentenced for fraud and false accounting. Having found himself in financial difficulty, he had decided to conspire with others to falsify invoices to factor companies, in order to gain extra money and credit. He saw this act as a one-off, short-term solution and viewed the illegal acquisition of this extra money merely as the 'borrowing' described by Cressey (1953). He commented: 'I only expected to do it for four months and trade my way out of trouble. I was just borrowing.'

Desperation was a common reason for inducing ('forcing') individuals who would normally not commit criminal behaviour to consider such a course of action. This was particularly apparent amongst those who found themselves in business difficulties, as discussed in Chapter 5. Many appeared to have got into positions where they 'had no choice' but to follow a criminal path, and were keen to stress that their offence had been a one-off, and that morally they had no intention of committing any further crimes. For example, Jason and Max both commented that they had been caught on a 'roller-coaster'. Even though they began criminal activity as a one-off solution to their financial problems, they had then become dependent on their illegal gains and had to repeat the offences to continue to finance their failing businesses.

Desperation was not the only reason which led individuals to commit crimes they previously would not have considered. Dave, a 31-year-old assistant management accountant, had been sentenced to 30 months for embezzling £109,000 from his employer. He had originally undertaken this as a one-off to help to pay his new mortgage. When he found it easy to embezzle funds to make substantial payments towards clearing this new debt, he continued to commit the crimes. In his account, Dave was keen to stress that this was out of character for him, and was initially only meant to be a 'one-off' to get together a deposit for a house more quickly. He stressed: 'It *was* a one-off at first ... I took £3500 to buy a house' (his emphasis).

'I'm not a "bad" criminal'

In wishing to be seen as relatively good, moral individuals, offenders may try to create a moral scale of offences and offenders. In doing this, they may acknowledge their own criminality, and hence their failings as individuals, but attempt to emphasise how they have been 'good' criminals, before and/or since entering the criminal-justice system. To do this, individuals in the sample attempted to position themselves morally above other types of criminal. This positioning accords with what Shover and Hochstetler say about white-collar criminals often seeking to distinguish themselves from 'real' criminals, and in so doing sometimes show an air of superiority and even arrogance (2006: 66–7, 139). They believe that the background of white-collar criminals affects how they view themselves compared to others in prison. In describing typical white-collar criminals, they remark: 'They hail from worlds where people do not do "dirty work"' (ibid: 11). A number of individuals in the present sample were keen to stress that although they might be seen as failures because they had been caught out as criminals, they were still in some way morally superior to other, non-white-collar criminals – they felt morally better people, or felt their crimes were not as serious as those of others. Thus they generally limited their social networks to those individuals who could be similarly defined, as noted by Shover and Hochstetler (2006: 139).

A second way that individuals try and show themselves to be 'good' criminals is by emphasising how they had shown restraint in their offending behaviour, which would otherwise have resulted in far more serious criminal damage. A final strategy of how to appear as 'good' criminals is to emphasise, after being caught, how they had co-operated with, and even assisted, both those investigating their offence and those responsible for them since their incarceration.

Some offenders' accounts classified their crimes as less serious compared to those of other, non-white-collar offenders, and on this basis considered themselves as less criminal than, and therefore morally superior to, other types of imprisoned offenders. For example, on arrival for his interview, Michael, a 51-year-old lawyer in a single-handed practice lawyer, was reading a broadsheet newspaper and was very eager rapidly to differentiate himself from the non-white-collar inmates. During his account he added a comment at the end of one of his sentences: '... unlike those *Sun*-reading oiks'.

Tony Parker, during his many interviews with inmates in prison, held a general antipathy towards white-collar criminals. In *Criminal Conversations* (ed. Soothill, 1999), Soothill recalls how Parker repeated what one prison governor had told him: a particularly well-behaved, white-collar inmate uncharacteristically appeared before the governor one day to complain about the nature of the offenders the prison was now accepting. All this had been prompted by the theft of the inmate's gold Schaeffer fountain-pen during 'association' the evening before. The complaint demonstrated the prisoner's desire to distance himself from other inmates, and either to deny his own criminality or to differentiate it from others', not only by his actions but in his comments to the governor: 'I regret having to make this accusation, Governor ... but the conclusion is plain. There are thieves in this prison' (ibid: 179).

Other instances of white-collar offenders positioning themselves above other types of offender were noted during the interviews in the various establishments visited. This supports the findings of Shover and Hochstetler's statement, that: 'Academic credentials are as likely to elicit a derision of respect, and self-segregation from others, who they see as "real criminals"' (2006: 139). Greg, a senior bank-manager who had been sentenced for conspiracy to lodge a £5-million bond in a Swiss bank, pleaded guilty to his crime, but did not regard himself as a criminal. As he commented during his account: 'It's not like I'm a *real* criminal, though' (his emphasis).

Greg was not alone in making statements of this nature. Geoff, the owner of a manufacturing company sentenced for conspiracy to defraud and false accounting, and Roger, the 64-year-old garage owner sentenced for trade-description infringement and conspiracy to defraud, both pleaded guilty to their crimes. However, when giving their accounts they made the following similar comments: 'I don't feel like the majority of the guys in here' (Geoff); 'I do not feel as much of a criminal as the others' (Roger).

Stuart, the managing and executive director of a number of companies, along with Gareth and Patrick (both serving their sentences in the same open prison) not only differentiated himself (because he was a white-collar criminal) from others serving time in the first (closed) prison to which he had been sent, but also added a further moral element, commenting that he was annoyed at being required to serve his time alongside sex offenders in this second prison, when he had supported a national children's charity. He complained: 'I felt punished being sent to here with sex offenders. I support the NSPCC [National Society for the Prevention of Cruelty to Children] charity.'

Besides those who differentiated themselves from others because they felt less criminal or simply different to what they saw as the more traditional, hardened criminals, some white-collar offenders defined their moral status more directly by the type of crimes they had committed. In this way, they tried to create a moral scale based not on their backgrounds, but on the crimes they had committed. As Hudson (2005: 68) points out, during the process of neutralisation by offenders, they may show contempt for other types of offenders and of offending behaviour.

Others who created a moral scale to describe their crimes compared to others included Gerry and Peter. Peter, a self-employed financial consultant, had been jailed for money-laundering associated with the supply of illegal drugs. He openly admitted his involvement in the financial aspects of the criminal operation, but disassociated himself from the drug business for which the money was being laundered. After being arrested at his father's house, and then questioned at length by the police and the US Drug Enforcement Administration (DEA), Peter still maintained his distance from the main motivation for the crime in which he was involved. He demonstrated this when he said: 'Even up to the sentencing I was totally against drugs etc. I disassociated it from the real business.'

Gerry, the 30-year-old self-employed market trader, had been sentenced for being knowingly concerned in the fraudulent evasion of duty. He claimed to have been in the retail trade all his working life, and was keen to stress that he would never get involved with drugs. However, this was not necessarily due to the moral stigma attached to such acts, but more to do with the lengthy sentences imposed for drug-related criminal activities.

Besides some of the moral distancing from other offenders in prison, a number of individuals interviewed commented that they 'felt sorry' for some of the non-white-collar offenders, whom they saw as having had little chance in life. In fact some said that they had helped some of them out by completing forms and writing and reading letters for them.

'There was no victim'

By its nature, white-collar crime is often invisible and complex, and does not always have one single, identifiable victim. Offenders therefore often feel morally justified in committing crimes where they see no victims. Peter, discussed earlier admitted that it had been easy to come to terms with what he had done because he did not see who exactly he had been hurt through his illegal money transactions: 'I could not see a victim as such.'

Offenders may think of their crimes in this way at the time of their offending, while after conviction they may consider their actions more carefully and realise the full moral implications of their behaviour. Stuart, for example, who had been sentenced to 18 months for fraudulent trading (along with Gareth and Patrick), said that since being in prison he had realised that their inter-trading of accounts and other criminal activities had actually impacted upon individual people, even though it might not have seemed that way at the time. He acknowledged this by saying: 'It's still a crime even though no-one really got hurt. Later on I realised things more clearly, though.'

A further reason offenders put forward for white-collar crimes being perceived as victimless is when these crimes are associated with the Internet, as demonstrated by Adam's account.

Case study – Adam

Adam, a 38-year-old, self-employed property broker, had embezzled a large amount of money through the electronic bank accounts and credit cards of well-known Internet banking and credit agencies. His belief was that nothing is 'safe' on the Internet and that it is easy to crack passwords. Adam's attitude was that individuals were too trusting in releasing their personal details on the Internet, and if their money was stolen, it was their own fault for being so naïve. He believed that because of the nature of cyber crimes,[2] and the anonymity of electronic fund transfers, by taking money from individuals and companies doing business online there was no identifiable victim. Adam therefore rationalised his acts as victimless.

The increasing use of the Internet for financial transactions and the rise in identity theft will only serve to give future white-collar criminals further reasons for justifying such crimes in this way.

'It could have been worse'

Yet another way in which some subjects tried to account for their behaviour in terms of being a 'moral criminal' was by trying to highlight the extent to which they had shown self-control in committing their crimes. The activities for which such individuals are convicted are often inextricably linked with their normal daily business activities (Benson, 1985: 596), and they sought to point out in their accounts how much more serious their offences could have been. Often this was related to weaknesses in controls within organisations, which they could have exploited further. Accounts of this nature therefore tried to highlight how self-controlled the individuals concerned had been in their offending. The case of Marvin demonstrates this well.

Case study – Marvin

Marvin, the publishing-company owner who believed the Post Office deserved to be defrauded because it had lost some of his outgoing mail, found a way of cutting costs by reproducing postal franking labels. He felt justified in doing this not only because of the mail losses, but also because he considered that the Post Office should have noticed the volume of postage being sent out which had not been paid for. He put a large volume of mail through the Post Office, but because he was printing his own postage labels, the franking machine only rarely needed to be topped up. Marvin acknowledged that he was guilty and that what he did was morally wrong, but he was eager to point out that the offence could have been much worse. He felt that because (at the time) the Post Office did not use non-reproduceable print on their labels, he had shown self-control in printing only a certain number of labels. '… I could have put more post through,' he said.

Likewise, two accountants, Dave and Sally, both independently stated that their bosses paid little attention to the day-to-day running of their companies' finances, thereby leaving their accountants in a position to abuse their trust and authority. Both acknowledged their guilt and the moral wrongfulness of their acts; however, both thought that their bosses should have been paying more attention to them and their work. They believed that they showed some restraint in what they had embezzled, and both stated that much larger sums of money could have been involved.

'I did not treat everyone the same'

A further way that offenders tried to stress the 'morality' of their crimes was by claiming in their accounts that they had deliberately different-iated between their victims. Three individuals were keen to stress that they were only willing to commit crimes against corporations. Adam, the self-employed property broker, who planned his crimes very ratio-nally and precisely, said that he only dealt with 'faceless' people and hence this was one reason why he had committed Internet fraud, because the victim was not identifiable. He explained further: 'I could not do anything that was to do with individual people.'

Marvin, already discussed above, not only highlighted in his account that he could have appropriated more money when defrauding the Post Office, but also admitted that when finally winding up his business, he paid off only the smaller, individual creditors and not those larger organ-isations from which he leased equipment. Marvin claimed that he did this because he felt those companies already made adequate profits.

Larger corporations were not the only organisations to which offenders did not feel so morally obligated; similar comments were noted in accounts relating to governmental organisations. Gerry, the self-employed market trader sentenced (with others) for being knowingly concerned in the evasion of duty, claimed that his criminal activity had a moral aspect in stating that he was only interested in defrauding the government or larger corporations, rather than small traders or identifiable people. He concluded his account by saying: 'I did not feel like a criminal though, fiddling the government.'

In a similar way, Sid, the 44-year-old cerebral-palsy victim sentenced to 48 months for deception relating to the sale of cars, explained how he had tried not to sell to people he knew because of the risk and the effect it would have on his standing in the community. He said: 'I did not con people I knew because of the risk of them reporting me and losing friends.' However, this appeared to be more a practical and social matter than a moral commitment towards individuals he knew.

'I assisted the authorities'

Some offenders were keen to stress how they had assisted and co-operated with the various investigatory institutions once they had been caught, to restore some element of morality to their behaviour. Iqbal, the 37-year-old Post Office owner convicted of conspiracy to defraud, originally denied his involvement and was granted bail. The next day he claimed to have talked to his solicitor, and subsequently assisted the police in the investigation of the crimes. He said: 'I gave names to my solicitor of others involved and was totally co-operative.'

Two other individuals in the sample (Anne and Janet) showed similar levels of co-operation during their investigations, but were equally keen to stress that without this co-operation they might not have been successfully convicted, or even prosecuted. Janet, a 43-year-old who had been convicted of deception relating to housing-benefit fraud, said that at the time she was being sought by the police she was in Ireland. When the police asked her to attend an interview the following day at the police station near her home, she did so willingly: 'I went to the police and told them everything, even though the police didn't know everything.'

Similarly, Anne, the supermarket garage-manager who had been sentenced for falsifying accounts and for theft from her employer, was keen to point out that her company could not accurately calculate the full monetary extent of her crimes. She had co-operated with both her company and the police, but in her account she noted: 'At this point they tried to double the figure to £200,000, but they only had accounting records going back six months, so they were reliant on me.'

Whereas these individuals to some extent believed that they had acted morally (in that they had co-operated with the authorities during the investigation and prosecution of their crimes), there were others who did not try to hide the fact that they had not been co-operative, either in an attempt to save themselves from prosecution, or to minimise the moral damage to themselves. Adrian had pleaded not guilty, relying on the possibility of there being insufficient evidence on which to convict him. Much of the evidence relating to his offence, which involved others, had been obtained from an associate who had turned Queen's Evidence against Adrian and his partners. Before the trial, this person had fled to Canada. However, during his interview Adrian suggested that he had known of this person's whereabouts, and that he had been in contact with him: 'Only two months prior to the trial at disclosure did I find out about the Queen's Evidence. Without that they would have had no case. But then he [the person who had turned Queen's Evidence] had fled to Canada. I have had some contact with him since. Customs tried 18 counts but could not use the Queen's Evidence.'

'I'm a "good" prisoner'

Benson (1990: 523) notes that many white-collar criminals are used to being in positions of power and authority in their working environments, and able to wield this power during their everyday business. But when they are incarcerated they find that their power and authority went unrecognised, and some offenders appeared to wage a 'moral crusade' throughout their sentence to prove they were not only good people, but also 'good' prisoners.

Pam had pleaded not guilty to her crime, and indeed did not believe she was guilty, claiming to have known nothing of what was going on in the shop she co-owned with her husband, where the crime was allegedly committed. She stated that she was looking after her mother-in-law at the time of the offence. However, in her account of the circumstances which led to her being imprisoned, Pam was keen to stress that she was being a good person and prisoner, even though she did not believe she should be there. She said, in a boastful manner: 'I am on enhancements[3] in prison.'

Although Pam was the only woman to stress her morality in terms of being a good prisoner, four of the men in the sample commented that being in prison was 'useless', tying this to statements that they wanted to give more back to the community in redress for their crimes. Three of these, however – Gareth, Patrick and Stuart – had run a number of companies, and been convicted, together. Furthermore, they were serving their various terms of imprisonment in the same prison at the time of their interviews. Their accounts, although to some extent varying from one to another, reflected the different roles they had each played during their crimes. There were enough similarities in their accounts, including the words and phrases they all used, to suspect that they had discussed these matters together prior to being interviewed. In fact, after seeing Gareth (which also happened to be before a lunch break), the other two made no secret of the fact that they knew some details of what Gareth had said in his interview earlier. That aside, each of them gave accounts mainly about working in the community and feeling that they should be paying for their crimes by giving something worthwhile back to society, rather than simply being incarcerated.

After a certain length of sentence has been served and when a risk-assessment has been carried out, category D prisoners are allowed to undertake work outside the prison. One of the issues regarding such work appeared to be that some of the sentences were so short that by the time the prisoners had served long enough to be eligible to work outside, their release date was very close. Adam, a 38-year-old self-employed property broker, raised this issue when he said: 'I want to work outside prison now but cannot give anything back as it is a short sentence.'

This account demonstrates that offenders who sought to use these kinds of accounts tried, in effect, to create a kind of morality by degree, even in prison. Although they acknowledged they had acted criminally, they attempted to make their type of criminality 'special' by creating a hierarchy among offenders and differentiating it, in various ways, from other crimes and criminals.

Summary

The findings in this chapter have illustrated, in the various accounts given by the offenders, that 'saving face' is important at some level to most individuals. Those whose preservation of their self appeared least important were those offenders who gave what they saw as 'unacceptable' motives, with explanations of their behaviour that mainly focused on greed (including relative greed) and addiction.

In contrast, however, accounts mainly told of acceptable reasons, with the majority of individuals keen to stress the morality of the situations surrounding their crimes, or of themselves as criminals. One common strategy was to highlight that they had committed their crimes for altruistic reasons and not for themselves, pointing out how it had benefited their families or businesses. In addition, they were keen to stress that on many occasions they had tried to 'make good' their deviant behaviour either by repaying money back or by minimising the damage they had caused.

The technique most commonly used by offenders attempting to justify their crimes and to try and restore their moral standing was to use distancing techniques. Through these they attempted to remove themselves from the reality of the crime and to lessen its impact, or to try and play down their criminality. They utilised a number of techniques to achieve this, with the most popular being to stress their normality. They undertook this in two main ways, first by stressing the ordinary nature of their lives, using business, family or social situations as examples, and secondly by claiming that their crimes were one-off, out-of-character acts which were inconsistent with the rest of their lives.

Even after entering the criminal-justice system, individuals were still keen to stress that they were not 'real' criminals, either because they did not regard themselves as having reached the same level of criminality as others, or by regarding their crimes as less serious than those that non-white-collar criminals committed. In this way offenders attempted to create new moral boundaries in the criminal-justice system, and even in prison.

Finally, what the findings of this chapter suggest is that individuals give accounts which imply that criminal behaviour can be ascribed to either acceptable or unacceptable factors. Even those individuals who morally accept their guilt, both in themselves and in the legal sense, still attempt to restore some of their moral standing by accounts which they think lessen their criminality and make their criminal behaviour more understandable and acceptable.

7
Offenders' Afterthoughts

Introduction

It may only be after prosecution and incarceration that white-collar criminals actually consider the implications of their crimes, weighing up in their afterthoughts, whether it had all been worthwhile. In taking stock of their experiences, they will undoubtedly assess the costs and benefits of committing their crimes, tallying up the losses from their behaviour against any gains they have come across during the trajectory of their offence(s). During this self-analysis, offenders considered what, if anything would have caused them to desist from their illegal activities; whether they felt jail was a deterrent and what the future may hold for them. These are all explored in this chapter. Differences were identified between male and female offenders in this context. These are explored in further detail in Chapter 8.

Losses

The issue of losses experienced by offenders is rarely addressed in the literature on white-collar crime (but see Payne, 2003, an exception to this), and very little research has been undertaken on this area. Losses do not just affect offenders – their family and friends are also deeply impacted (as well, of course, as their victims). Costs to offenders should not be considered merely in terms of financial losses, but on the basis of all the costs incurred by them as a result of their criminal behaviour, including time spent in prison. It could be argued that, given the relatively high social status of some white-collar criminals, this group – which has seemingly possessed or gained the most – has the most to lose. The costs of their criminal behaviour may be felt more acutely than in other offender groups. Figure 7.1 below demonstrates how some offenders may view their offending in terms of costs and benefits, as it were in a book-keeper's account, where costs are shown as a debit in the ledger, and benefits as a credit. These costs and benefits will be discussed in this chapter. To understand how they were viewed by the offenders themselves during and after their punishments might reveal some important issues about desisting from criminal activities.

How these losses and gains are disaggregated is also important in understanding how white-collar offenders are perceived in society, and how this perception might affect their future. Levi argues that the 'fall from grace' of white-collar offenders may be exaggerated in the media (and the literature), with many managing to retain their positions and jobs in society once released from prison (1987: 2006). Croall believes that many white-collar offenders are able to continue with their careers, or to start up new ones, more easily than other types of offenders because they have the resources and contacts to do so. She also notes that some of these offenders are able to make money from the 'stories' of their crimes, such as in memoirs, autobiographies and biographies – although it is acknowledged that these are in the minority (2001: 134). However, it

Figure 7.1 'Ledger of a criminal life' for white-collar criminals

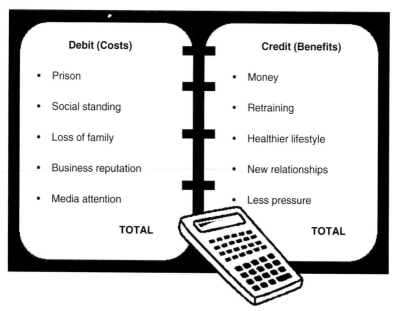

is in general the case that most white-collar criminals have better earning potential, on leaving prison, than those in other offender groups.

Typically however, the reality of incarceration for most white-collar offenders will come as a harsh shock. Yet it is still true that that such penalties '... may also have beneficial effects ... particularly if they humble the arrogant, and cause them to reassess their past conduct and make them think differently about lure they may encounter in the future' (Shover and Hochstetler, 2006: 143) – there remains the possibility that individuals may be able to turn around what is seemingly a loss into a benefit, thereby obtaining positive gains from their criminality or jail sentences. Many offenders are given the opportunity to undertake retraining or to study for new qualifications; and white-collar offenders might be more capable of taking advantage of this than less educated, lower-level offenders.

In this section, losses are considered under eight, main categories. These are:

- loss of freedom
- loss of status and reputation
- business and professional losses
- financial losses
- loss of jobs and/or professional membership
- loss of career development
- loss of close others
- losses to the family
- losses to victims

Loss of freedom

Possibly one of the worst losses an individual can experience is the loss of their freedom. It is widely considered that white-collar criminals suffer adversely in prison. For example, Payne details how such inmates find it particularly difficult to adjust to prison life – having their freedom drastically restricted, and then being told what to do and when (2003: 103). Benson and Cullen (1988), however, disagree that white-collar criminals are so sensitive to their new environment; they believe that, given such offenders' background, education and family ties, they are far more able to adjust to life in prison than criminals who have no similar such resources. Nevertheless, Payne notes that once in prison white-collar offenders may struggle to accept that their right to freedom and privacy is so limited, especially in a large group of strangers with whom they find it difficult to identify (2003: 100).

Even though at the time of the interviews 38 of the 41 offenders were being held in open or semi-open prison conditions, restrictions on their daily lives were still very much evident, even if these regimes were more lenient than they would have been in more closed institutions. Although the restrictions placed on prisoners differed remarkably between the two types of institutions visited – closed and open prisons – interestingly none of the three prisoners interviewed in a closed prison (the only one visited in the course of this study) raised the issue of loss of freedom in their accounts, whereas most of the offenders in open or semi-open prisons did.

Despite some of the prison sentences given to the white-collar criminals in the sample being relatively short compared with those imposed on other offenders, it was noted that many of the those who raised the issue of loss of freedom did so towards the beginning of their sentences. For example, Stan, aged 45, had served only two months of his 36-month sentence when he was interviewed. He was finding it difficult, even in open-prison conditions, to get used to being unable to do what he wanted, when he wanted, and to not having the contact with individuals he would normally be involved with as part of his everyday life on the outside. He admitted that 'The loss of liberty and freedom is the hardest.'

The issue of loss of freedom was not confined to middle-aged or older prisoners; the accounts of younger inmates also mentioned it in similar ways. For example, Eze, a 32-year-old offender, who had completed only five months of his 36-month sentence when he was interviewed, indicated that he was finding life in prison very difficult. His comment on the situation was strikingly similar to that of Stan's: 'I miss my freedom and doing what I want. That is the worst.'

For many of the offenders, however, their confinement in prison and resultant loss of freedom had given them a chance to reassess their lives, especially in terms of what they had taken for granted in the past. Geoff, a 56-year-old owner of a manufacturing company, had served just three months of his 12-month sentence when he was interviewed. He said: 'My biggest loss is my freedom. I do not take anything for granted any more. My only motivation is to get out.'

Yet, incarceration in prison was not the first time some offenders had felt the loss of freedom; a number commented that they had first experienced it immediately after being sentenced in court. Two of the women in the sample separately commented on the curtailment of their liberty when they were sent down to the court cells in the morning after their trials, but then had to wait until the end of the day before transportation to their respective local prisons. They complained: 'I got sent down at

11 am to the cells, and said "bye" to my sister. I had to wait the rest of the day, which was bad for a 10-minute journey to the prison, arriving at 4.45pm.' And 'I was tried in the morning and had to wait for the rest of the day under the court. Being transferred in the van was the worst ... I found it so degrading.'

Gareth, the co-owner with Patrick and Stuart of a group of companies, also referred to the indignity of being transported from court to jail: 'The worst part was the journey to prison.'

Once in prison, many offenders found that having little control over their lives – being organised, even regimented, was particularly difficult. For this group of offenders such restrictions were more difficult than for others, as they were more used to having control over their lives and sometimes being in positions where they exerted power over others, rather than themselves being subject to authority. Twenty-three offenders had previously been self-employed, and had run their own businesses; the contrast between that level of freedom and having to ask permission for mundane and trivial acts, such as making a cup of tea, was very difficult for some to come to terms with. As one offender commented: 'I am finding life hard and need to settle.'

Despite these restrictions, some offenders in the sample appeared to cope with these major changes in lifestyle and had devised different strategies to handle their new environment, such as retraining and learning new skills; a number also claimed to be working out regularly in the gymnasium. However, many offenders, as Benson (1984) noted, found it very difficult to adjust to a new life in prison, especially in their first days of incarceration. For example, Laura, a 38-year-old first-time offender said: 'I am sad in prison. HMP Town F was very scary. HMP Town G was OK, but here at HMP Town H I am more settled.'

Likewise, Alison, 50 years old, another first-time offender and facing a 42-month prison sentence, recalled her harrowing experiences when she was first detained in a local dispersal prison: 'I was on the wing at HMP Town F for four days. My body went on total shutdown.'

At the time of the interviews most prisoners appeared to have settled into their current environments, but recalled the first few days of their sentence, when they were taken to closed-regime local or dispersal prisons, as their worst. Nevertheless, there were several prisoners still failing to cope even with open conditions.

For the offenders, losing their freedom not only meant the loss of being able to decide what to do and when, but also losing access to certain people and things, especially those normally taken for granted as part of everyday life. As Anne noted: 'I miss silly little things beside my freedom, like my mobile phone, going to the shops, seeing my family.'

There is thus an opportunity for some individuals suffering loss to value what they had previously had, and become 'better' individuals in their own eyes (Payne, 2003: 103). Twenty prisoners in the sample highlighted in their accounts that they had taken their freedom for granted, and that their time in prison had made them realise how important it was. One offender (Gareth), interviewed in an open prison, summed up his experience:

> I have spent time in prison reflecting on this experience and realising the importance of people and what you miss and take for granted. Everything is now taken away. It gives you time though to think of the real issues, though the emotional scar of prison will still exist afterwards, I fear.

Loss of status and reputation

It may be argued that retaining social status and reputation is more important for white-collar criminals than for other offenders. From the accounts in the present study, it was noted that this was frequently cited as a motivation for their criminal behaviour. Because their jobs and professions are often inextricably linked with their crimes (though this can also be true of other types of offender) their criminal label tends to follow them once they have left prison (Payne, 2003: 100). Additionally, Weisburd et al (2001) suggest that imprisonment is likely to be more alien to the white-collar offender's world and that of their family and friends, and as a result the stigma associated with their imprisonment may be greater. Most white-collar criminals believe they have more to lose from imprisonment than other more typical street criminals, and this affects their behaviour in jail and how they perceive their experiences there. Their status both outside and within prison is seen as under threat; as Shover and Hochstetler note: 'White-collar offenders find intimidating both the bravado and posturing of incarcerated young, underclass men. The unpredictable physical conflict that takes place within jail is less gentlemanly than anything they have known before' (2006: 143).

One way that white-collar offenders' reputations are threatened is by sensationalist and disproportionate reporting by the media, which in some instances can become a form of entertainment for the public (Friedrichs, 1996: 21). As Levi notes, the media focus on fears and anxieties (2008: 367). Benson found that the majority of offenders he interviewed were bitter about the inaccurate media reporting of their cases, especially as they felt helpless to defend themselves against what was printed (1985: 590). Not every offender receives extensive news coverage, however, as some may be sentenced on a day when there are more newsworthy items (Benson, 1990: 523).

When examining the accounts of the offenders with respect to status issues, one of the themes that emerged was how out of place individuals felt in prison, especially when compared to the majority of their fellow-inmates. For example, Gareth, a 34-year-old co-owner and managing director of a group of companies, felt that many of the other prisoners did not come from his background and that they had little to lose in prison. Indeed, he felt they could behave in any way they wanted and the consequences of their behaviour or their prison sentence would not have such a detrimental effect on their life as they would have had on his own. He said: 'I found it hard when first in prison. As a white-collar criminal I felt very out of place. It's mainly drugs-related and violent prisoners here, who have nothing to lose.'

However, not all offenders interviewed gave negative accounts of their losses as a result of incarceration. Adam and Adrian, for example, made no comments about the loss of their freedom and liberty. In fact, Adam saw some positive aspects of being in prison (discussed later). In addition, four offenders remarked how younger prisoners tended to show them respect and even seek them out for advice on various matters.

Certainly, due to the occupational positions that most of the white-collar criminals had previously held, their reputations were of paramount importance to them, in that they had more to lose and therefore further to fall. As Shover and Hochstetler note: 'Respectability and the opinions of others hold enormously important meaning for many tempted to commit white-collar crime. They have good reason to care what others think; most have farther to fall than street offenders' (2006: 143). As Max, part-owner of a computer consultancy firm put it, as a result of his crimes: 'I have lost status and reputation in my business area.'

Because of the importance of the media's role in damaging reputations, many of the offenders raised issues in their accounts about how their portrayal as 'bad people' had affected them, contributing to the loss of their reputation and even their business. Some offenders had been fortunate not to have attracted any media coverage of their trial and conviction, and this had enabled them to hide their criminal activity, especially from families and associates. In the sample, however, most offenders commented that there had been some media coverage of their crime, either local or national, depending on the nature and severity of the offence.

Case study – Greg

Greg, a senior bank manager, who accounted for his behaviour as having been involved in a large-scale, mafia-like blackmail situation, was annoyed that his activities had been reported both locally and nationally on the front page of newspapers, with headlines claiming he had been involved in a £100 million fraud. Although he had pleaded guilty in court – a tactical move in the hope of a lower sentence – he did not believe he was guilty of any crime, and had resolved to put the record straight and salvage his reputation when he was released from jail. He claimed: 'The impact of having a criminal record is great, but I have not lost my self-respect. I intend to write a book, get it published and clear my name on release.'

Similarly, Gareth, Patrick and Stuart, the three managing and executive directors who had jointly owned a group of companies, were particularly critical in their comments about the media.

Case study – Gareth, Patrick and Stuart

These three offenders not only found the reporting of their cases had affected them, but also that the media had played a role in the failure of their companies, which is what they claimed had led them to commit their crimes. Gareth had even several times taken part in a popular national consumer-programme on television, to answer complaints against their companies, though both Patrick and Stuart stated that the number of alleged complaints was much lower than the programme claimed. When they set up further companies in the same group, in different business areas, a couple of years later, Gareth claimed they were targeted by the media, in particular by the same television programme, to which he attributed the failure of the companies' businesses.

Nevertheless, it was not simply offenders such as Greg, Gareth, Patrick and Stuart, involved in fairly high-profile cases, who commented in their accounts about the loss of reputation. Others whose cases had had a lower profile and whose activities had been reported only in their local media were equally as scathing about the effects on their reputation as higher-profile offenders were. Max, a 29-year-old self-employed co-owner of a computer-consultancy business, complained: 'There was lots of publicity ... it has been bad for my family.'

In particular, offenders were annoyed about inaccuracy and bias in the reporting of their case, feeling that balanced reports were not presented to the public. Abuu, a self-employed computer salesman convicted of deception and of conspiracy to handle stolen goods, felt that his case had been portrayed incorrectly and that the media had focused on minor details of his crimes: 'The media focused on my addiction ... alcohol and gambling etc ...'

Jason, owner of a furniture-making business, also felt reporting of his case had been selective and unreliable.

Case study – Jason

Jason had been convicted of deception and of obtaining property from a number of local companies, using many different trade names. One of these companies was owned by a single elderly woman, and Jason found that the media focused on this fact. He complained: 'I was angry when I saw the papers had headlined I had taken money off a 72-year-old lady.'

He felt bitter and angry that his crime had been depicted in a way that suggested that all the creditors he had defrauded had been as vulnerable as the woman victim. Jason claimed that she was atypical of the individuals whom he had deceived and from whom he had obtained property. He also considered that the media reporting was biased, claiming that the fact of his having repaid money to his victims went unreported.

However, not all offenders reacted with bitterness against the media for their reporting, as the case of Peter exemplifies.

Case study – Peter

Peter, convicted of money-laundering associated with the supply of controlled drugs, mentioned the involvement of the US Drugs Enforcement Agency (DEA) in his case, and that he had been arrested at his father's home during a dinner party; as his father was well known in the City, the story had made the national press. However, he stated: 'I am not bitter because I know I did it ... it has been a good lesson in reality.'

Peter fully acknowledged that he had committed a crime and that although it was embarrassing for his father and other family members at the time, he now realised that if he got involved in such high-profile cases, the media would focus on these and anyone associated with them. If they had reported anything that was untrue, he said, then he would have felt differently. But, on reflection he fully accepted what he had done and the consequences of that behaviour, including the media attention.

Whilst Peter's attitude towards the media was not typical, even more surprising was the attitude of Adam, convicted of major Internet frauds. His case had been aired on television during the national evening news, as well as being reported widely in a number of national newspapers. He was quite proud of this in his account and noted how the 'younger lads' in prison, convicted for 'minor street crimes', thought that having their cases reported in their local papers was an achievement to boast about, whereas he felt superior to them in this respect, having made the national press and television.

Business and professional losses

A further category of loss felt by offenders and outlined during their accounts was that relating to their business and professional lives. Kerley and Copes suggest that because of their economic background, their occupational positions and their educational experience, white-collar offenders can recover from prison sentences more easily than street offenders, and possibly return to jobs similar to those they held before their conviction (2004: 67). Not all researchers, however, agree with this view. Payne, for example, suggests that many white-collar crime inmates will have to think about different career aspirations and goals once they leave prison (2003: 104), and Benson found that offenders in licensed professions (in particular lawyers) and those who worked in the public sector were more likely to lose their occupational status than those from the private sector, and suffered particularly severe changes to their previous lifestyles (1984: 588). Three main areas relating to business or the professions were identified during the interviews: financial losses, loss of jobs and/or professional membership, and loss of career development. Each of these will now be explored.

Financial losses

Because many of the offenders in the sample had lost companies that they previously co-owned, or had lost their jobs, as a result of their crimes, they had felt financial losses (direct or indirect) very acutely. With the exception of two of the offenders (Adam and Adrian), none of those interviewed confessed to having made and retained any substantial, long-term financial gains from their misdemeanours, and in fact many claimed to have entered prison with little money to their name. A number had not been in work directly prior to imprisonment because of the nature of their crimes and because their cases had taken time to come to trial.[1] During this period of waiting, they had been unable to earn and by their trial, if not before, had spent any gains made through their illegal behaviour. The popular image of well-off white-collar criminals can be challenged. The case of Gareth illustrates this well.

Case study – Gareth

Gareth, managing and executive director of a group of companies, convicted with Stuart and Patrick, commented that he felt the popular image of white-collar crime, as a 'get-rich-quick scheme', was false, in that many such criminals do not make large, if any, financial gains. He observed that the amount of money listed in court, as the total which individuals are alleged to have misappropriated, is frequently misleading and does not necessarily represent money sitting in their bank accounts: 'The image of corporate fraud is all wrong. Just because it says five million, it doesn't mean that you have the money ... it usually goes on the business, not yourself.'

Gareth claimed that it was for this reason that no order was obtained,[2] which would have given the court the power to recover some or all of the money gained from his crimes. He also stated that the police had paid a leading firm of accountants £80,000 to look through his accounting records to ensure that that there were insufficient funds to enable the court to make such an order.

Sally, a management accountant who had worked for a manufacturing company, said that her boss had taken out an independent civil action to recover the money that she had stolen from him. Other offenders claimed to have taken money to fund already existing debts of one type or another and most could not, or would not, account for what had happened to their proceeds. One exception to this was Tom, sentenced for cheating Customs and Excise out of £106,000, who said: 'I made thousands from this scam and spent it all. When I entered prison I had only two pounds in my pocket. I have no money to go out to, only what I've earned in here.'

In prison he was training to be a hairdresser, and hoped to find work as such when he was released.

As well as losing their jobs as the main source of income, whether employed or self-employed, individuals had lost other benefits paid for by their employers or their companies, such as cars, private healthcare provision and contributions to pension schemes. Once they became unemployed or lost their business, they automatically lost these benefits. For those offenders who were self-employed, many had lost their business as a result of their crimes, though three businesses were continuing to trade in their owner's absence with the help of family and friends, or through business partners and associates. Roger, a 64-year-old garage owner, still had one of his businesses running while he was in prison. Jim, also a garage owner, had handed over the running of his business to his family while he was in prison. He said: 'My son and daughter have taken over the last year and they are doing well. The police have been around, but everything is OK.' And Adrian's legitimate transport business was still operating whilst he was in prison.

Loss of jobs and/or professional membership

Only one offender, Janet, who had been employed as a bar manager, had retained her job throughout her conviction and imprisonment. This was because her crime of housing-benefit fraud was unrelated to her employment, and her boss had kept in touch and even made visits to prison to see her. Debbie, the restaurant manager convicted of embezzlement, found that her company was very reasonable to her even after the crimes she had committed against it. Although, inevitably, she lost her job, two other members of her family who worked for the same company had kept theirs. She said: 'The company I worked for have been good, though there was a lot of publicity. I was suspended originally, but my husband and son still work there.'

A number of individuals had been made bankrupt, and several disqualified from holding directorships. The three managing and executive directors (Gareth, Patrick and Stuart), who had worked and committed crimes together, had all been disqualified in this way, for a term of some years. Some offenders had also lost their membership of the professional bodies to which they had previously belonged. For example, the two solicitors in the sample, Kevin and Michael, had been struck off by the Law Society. In their accounts they spoke about these losses bitterly, as though they had been cheated out of positions and memberships which they had worked hard to achieve over a number of years. Due to the prominence of their previous jobs and to some extent the status that they still held, they felt that people would think they were much better off, financially and professionally, than they actually were.

Loss of career development

While in prison individuals not only lost their job, and the financial rewards associated with it, but also lost time in which they could have gained further, vital professional experience and knowledge. The importance of 'lifelong learning' in this respect cannot be underestimated and could have a major impact on the lives of individuals when released, in terms both of continuing professional development and of the increased earning power it could bring. While the majority of the offenders had sufficient knowledge and experience to find work again, in some capacity, the younger subjects generally had more time to make a fresh start, and if necessary to retrain. Peter made an important observation shortly before being released early on parole after his exceptional 13-year sentence. He commented that his years in prison had come at a crucial period in his career, and would be very difficult to make up; his experience shows that it is not just the offenders' age that matters, but the stage in their life and career at which they are incarcerated. He pointed out: 'I have lost the best years of my life, career-wise anyway. In your twenties you establish yourself. I'm just lucky my father has contacts and will get me back into some sort of career.'

As he had been in prison during his twenties and thirties, Peter regarded this as the worst period to be 'robbed' of the time needed to establish a long and successful career. In retrospect, he wished he had simply dissolved his company, and avoided any involvement in criminal activities – he would still have been able to get a good job and establish a decent career path.

Loss of close others

When an individual is given a prison sentence tremendous pressure is also exerted on his/her family, and especially on close others such as husbands, wives and partners. At the time of interviewing, 28 offenders in the sample were married or in de facto long-term relationships. The accounts given suggest that due to the criminal behaviour itself, the sentence imposed, or the effect of imprisonment on emotional attachments, four of these relationships were in various stages of separation. Comments relating to the breakdown of these relationships included:

> My marriage is unlikely to continue now because the trust has been lost ... what does marriage mean, though? (Sally)

> I had no family commitments, but I lost the girlfriend I was going to marry. (Marvin)

> I have lost my wife after a ten-year relationship but can still see my two children, though I am still friends with my wife. I am a family man who did this for them mostly, but I am the sort of person who needs someone ... I have a new partner now. (Jason)

Frequently, offenders had shielded their family from their criminal behaviour, especially their spouse or partner, and only one subject in the sample had been convicted with her husband. Generally, family and friends had been supportive when the offending was in question. While the initial reaction of family and friends had often been one of shock, and even devastation, most offenders said that this had mutated into acceptance of what had happened, whether the individual's motives at the time of the crime were understood or not.

Jason, who was 29-years-old and divorced, commented that his parents were supporting him throughout his sentence, even though his mother had suggested to him that she believed he had always 'sailed too close to the wind'. However, none of his three brothers and two sisters, who all lived near the prison where he was interviewed, had ever made any contact or visited him. The following two comments, however, were more typical of how individuals close to an offender had reacted:

> My family and friends were devastated at first ... but everyone is fine with me now ... they all visit. (Janet)

> It was difficult for all of us, but our family all stood behind us. (Debbie)

In some instances contact with, and support from, professional associates had ceased or had seemed to 'disappear overnight', which in some cases had both surprised and hurt offenders. Gareth, the executive and managing director, with two others, of a group of companies, commented that while in prison he had found out who his true friends were.

Similarly, Greg, the 57-year-old senior bank manager sentenced for conspiracy to commit forgery, felt he had been shunned by his ex-colleagues. He said: 'I have had no contact from anyone at the bank ... they claimed to have *had* to disassociate themselves from me' (offender's emphasis).

Losses to the family

Losses as a result of an offender's criminal behaviour were not only felt by themselves but also by their families; and in their accounts offenders commented not only on their own losses but also on those which they felt others had suffered as a result of their criminality. In particular, losses which had impacted upon partners and children featured strongly in their accounts.

Many of the offenders admitted that they had only considered the impact of their behaviour on their families since entering prison. This may have been due to the fact that many had never considered they were actually committing a criminal act, or – where this was not the case – had not believed they would get caught, or that any punishment would take the form of a custodial sentence. Prison was the first time that they had fully realised the hurt their behaviour had caused their family. As Breed puts it: 'There is no better place than prison for an absence making the heart grow fonder' (1979: 63). For many, it was a painful reality check to understand the full impact of their crime on themselves and others. As one offender who had already served six months in prison recalled: 'It is painful seeing my family ... I have only accepted this in the last three to four weeks.'

As well as breakdowns in offenders' relationship with their partner, contact with other members of the family, in particular children, had also been affected. In assessing this, participants commented on how they had missed crucial times in their children's lives, such as their first words, first steps, starting school and so on. Many families also had to spend considerable time travelling to see their relative in prison, disrupting their normal routine and often having to journey to different places during the offender's sentence, as he/she was moved between institutions.

Mentioning some of these issues, Stan revealed that at the time of his interview he was receiving weekly visits from his family, including his children (two of whom were adopted). He said that it was hard for them to visit, and he believed that this pattern would not continue into the future – it was not only causing travel problems but also disrupting the children's normal weekend activities, such as football, which made him feel very guilty. He said: 'My family have suffered the most ... I do not know if I will have one to go out to, in all honesty.'

However, there were other cases where it had been decided between the parents that it was best for the children not to visit. Kevin, the single-handed solicitor, said: 'I am still with my wife; she stuck by me and we will stay together. She visits but the children don't.'

Three offenders gave accounts where there was evidence that children had been shielded from the real whereabouts of their father or other imprisoned relative. 'Working abroad' appeared to be a popular excuse, as the following comments made during interviews reveal:

> I have not seen my children since I have been in here. My wife has told them I am working in Africa. (Abuu)

> My grandchildren think I am in Germany. (Geoff)

> I agreed with my ex-wife that my 12-year-old daughter would think I was working in the States. (Adam)

In order to preserve their previous good character, it is in the interests of offenders to conceal their real whereabouts, if at all possible, while in prison, and this may not apply only to those with children, as Anne (who was being released on Boxing Day, shortly after her interview) showed, saying: 'Only my mother, sister and one friend know I am in here. Everyone else thinks I am working abroad ... even my brother. They think I am flying back here for Christmas and couldn't get an earlier flight.'

She also commented on her good fortune in that on the day of her court appearance no journalists were present, and thus there was no press reporting of her offence or sentence.

Typically, the inmates felt that because they had inflicted hurt on their family as a result of their crime, their relatives were also 'doing the sentence', which offenders generally felt very guilty about. In particular, many commented that their partners had been left a heavy burden, with the loss of a partner, their children's mother or father, their livelihood and their shared lifestyle, as well as having to handle the public shame and stigma. Many offenders interviewed, as Breed summarises it, worried about the strain they had put their families under (ibid). The following comments from offenders demonstrate their concern:

> My family was not aware of what was going on but have suffered the most. (Gareth)

> The biggest effect has been on my family, especially my wife who has had to deal with all the outside pressure whilst I'm in here shielded. (Geoff)

My family has been the ones who have been punished ... I don't take them for granted. (Stuart)

My family (I am a step-dad as well) have all lost out because I am in jail ... they have had their lifestyle cut. (Stuart)

Whereas the majority of offenders highlighted the negative effects on their relationships of their offence and time in prison, three mentioned improved relationships. This mirrors the example of Jonathan Aitken (2002), who on his release stated: 'I think that with my children, my relationship deepened in adversity'.

Peter had been convicted of money-laundering and came from a well-off, high-flying, City family. He felt that his time in prison had actually enhanced his relationship with his family, in particular with his father; this had mainly been achieved through the latter's visits. He said: 'It gave us time to talk for the first time properly ... real, quality time.' It was the first time that Peter had believed he needed to rely upon his family for support in any aspects of his life. The limited contact allowed through visits, had created an environment for them to focus on what he now regarded as the really important issues and relationships which, he had come to realise, had been neglected before his time in prison.

The second offender who saw some positive aspects of the time she spent in jail apart from her family was Sheila, who had been convicted of embezzlement, deception and credit-card offences; she claimed the money was used to cover personal debts.

Case study – Sheila

Since Sheila had been convicted, she said, her relationship with her husband had been strengthened. She felt that in the past she had shielded him from their financial difficulties and in her opinion he had done nothing to help the situation – in some instances she felt he might even have made it worse. During the period Sheila had been in prison, she felt her husband had been required to face up to the realities of their personal situation himself, especially by sorting out their finances. She stated: 'My marriage is stronger now. My husband, and parents to some extent, felt somewhat responsible for what happened and have realised the pressures they put me under.'

As Sheila noted, in addition to the lack of support from her husband, she had been put under pressure by her parents to live up to the lifestyle and achievements which her other sister had attained. Sheila claimed that her criminal behaviour resulted, at least in part, from this pressure, but her family had since been very supportive. Sheila said: 'My mother has been good, but has never visited me ... nor my father. My sister needed a few weeks to "rationalise" her feelings, but she was then very supportive and has been to see me.'

The third offender who viewed his time in prison as having bene-fitted his life and relationships took quite a different view compared with the two so far mentioned. Adam, a 38-year-old convicted of con-spiracy to defraud online banks and other credit organisations via the Internet, commented on his contact with the outside world and how visits, particularly those from his girlfriend of four years, had affected his views on his crime and incarceration. Adam said that he viewed his time in prison as a positive experience, giving him an 'escape' from the stresses of life outside. As a result, he decided that he could not be bothered to maintain the relationship with his girlfriend. With each visit, Adam said that he was reminded of the pressures from which he claimed to be free in prison, and of the additional 'burden', as he saw it, of having a girlfriend with whom he had to deal when she got upset during visits. He claimed this 'interrupted' the 'valuable' time he spent inside. He had therefore ended the relationship, and no longer had visitors, which appeared to suit him and his needs. He stated: 'I had a girlfriend of four years. But seeing her, brought the stress of outside in here ... I could not be bothered to keep the relationship going any more.'

Losses to victims

White-collar crime, by its very nature – specifically, the diffusion of responsibility and of victimisation – makes it difficult for a victim in certain (but not all) cases, difficult to identify. As Friedrichs notes, individuals are '... less likely to be conscious of this victimisation than of conventional crime victimisation' (1996: 59). Certainly, where for example the government or a large publicly-owned corporation has been defrauded, it is very difficult to identify who exactly suffered as a result of such criminal action, and correspondingly easy for the offender to claim that there has been no victim. On the other hand, where individuals or smaller, privately-owned companies are defrauded, a victim is more readily identifiable.

Although some research has been carried out on how individuals experience being made victims of white-collar crime (for example, Levi and Pithouse, 1992; 2000; Spalek, 1999; Shover et al, 1994; Levi, 1991; Moore and Mills, 1990; Button et al, 2010), very little attention has been paid to how offenders account for the losses suffered by their victims, if they acknowledge or consider them at all.

When individuals in the sample were invited to address the area of losses there was a notable absence of any consideration in their accounts about the impact on victims, or the losses that the latter might have suffered as a result of the criminal activity. As discussed above (Chapter 6), one way in which offenders tried to stress their moral characters was to point out that they had, prior to the commission of their crimes, differentiated between whom they would and would not commit crimes against. For example, Adam, who had committed a number of Internet-related frauds, stated that he would only commit crimes against corporate organisations and where any victims were 'faceless'. Gerry, in the same context, said that he would not commit crimes against identifiable people (see Chapter 6). Whether these rationalisations of differential victimisation were made before or after the event was impossible to confirm, and such accounts may have consisted merely of self-flattering comments that offenders thought sounded good but which they did not really believe.

The focus of accounts mentioning victims typically related to those whom offenders would not commit crimes against, and not how these offenders felt about the actual victims of their criminal behaviour. The absence of any mention of their victims in the accounts was surprising, considering that 21 of the 41 offenders in the sample had accepted in their inner-moral self that they had committed a crime, as detailed in the typology of legal and moral acceptance of guilt (see Chapter 4). This analysis detailed 20 acceptors and one tactical rejector, all of whom had accepted they had committed a crime.

Possibly because the interviews took place some time after the crimes (years later in some instances), there had been an opportunity for offenders to distance themselves from their crime and its victims. This distancing may have accounted for those offenders who claimed that their crimes were victimless (even those that were acceptors), such as Peter, who said he could not see a victim of his money-laundering activities and (once again) Adam, who felt that Internet fraud was essentially victimless.

Was it worth it?

Most offenders view being sentenced to a prison term as a cost to their life. Nevertheless, there are individuals who are either not so concerned about this loss, or actually plan for it before the commission of their crimes. As Stotland states: 'A little time in prison or a little fine may be a small cost to the experienced white-collar crook' (1977: 193). Rational actors, as discussed in Chapter 5, may plan for a short spell in prison and believe that this loss is worth enduring for the gains they will eventually return to once released. In addition, those who 'plan' for time in prison or reach a level of acceptance that allows them to make the most of their time inside may take full advantage of the possible benefits that a short spell in prison can offer. Certainly, as Friedrichs notes, white-collar criminals may add extra years to their life through a prison regime by ensuring that they eat a healthier, balanced diet and take more appropriate exercise than if they were living on the outside (1996: 325).

When the benefits and costs of their crimes were considered by offenders in the sample, the majority concluded on reflection that their offences had not been worth committing. The exceptions to this were Adam and Adrian, who had both committed their crimes as rationally executed and pre-planned acts. Adam was keen to stress the benefits he believed he had gained from his offending, not only in terms of the amount of money he had made (which he intended to use to fund his lifestyle when he finished his sentence, rather than unnecessarily working for a living), but also in the advantages he felt he had gained from being in jail, as opposed to working. Commenting on how he thought crime had paid for him, he said: 'Since I have been in jail I have received a tax rebate, lost weight and gained incalculable extra years on my life compared to if I had carried on working as normal.' In addition to these positive aspects, from which Adam believed he had benefitted while being in prison, he felt that life on the outside was overrated, and he did not particularly mind (at least at the time of his being interviewed) being incarcerated: 'I also realise I'm not missing a lot on the outside for now.'

Adrian, the self-employed transport owner who was sentenced to 48 months for evading tobacco duty, also found that his illicit transport business had paid off financially for him and the others involved in the scam. He commented that his wife had been arrested after paying his 'settle' (the payment of part or all of the customs duty that was owing, set by the judge at the time of sentence). He claimed the funding for this was totally legitimate, though he mentioned that the prison social worker found it hard to imagine how they could afford to pay it.

Accounts of desistance

The literature on white-collar criminals' careers, for example by Weisburd et al (2001), has highlighted a number of factors that may affect the desistance of such offenders. These include age, stability of finances, employment and commitment to satisfactory relationships. One of the important criteria for successful desistance is, as Shover and Hochstetler note, that offenders should be willing and ready to learn from past mistakes (2006: 146). Because the present study had no longitudinal dimension, and included only one interview per subject, only some elements of desisting behaviour could be identified through the accounts given.

From all the offenders interviewed, only Tom admitted having considered whether he would commit the same or a similar act again, once released from prison. There may of course have been others who were willing to take the risk again, but certainly none admitted to it at the time of the interviews.

Case study – Tom

Tom had evaded payment of taxes, to Customs and Excise, amounting to £106,000. Although he said that he had not weighed up the costs and benefits at the time of his offending (because he claimed that he had only discovered the loophole by chance), he did admit to having calculated what might happen if he repeated the offence successfully, and was more careful to preserve the money. In his opinion, even if caught, taking all costs into consideration he would still have made a net gain. But as he said: 'It would take so long to come to court and serve the sentence, I would be nearing retirement age before release, and therefore a little too old to be in here.'

Besides age as a factor contributing to desistance, potential damage to relationships was also identified as a reason for abstaining from future crime. There was also a general feeling among the majority of the offenders that they had been unprepared for the impact that their crimes would have upon their relationships with family, friends and business associates, and had concluded that their crimes had been simply not worth it.

Besides the loss of family, friends and associates, the loss of jobs, finance and reputation were considered as factors in desistance for some offenders. In particular, finding a job after being incarcerated was of great concern to many. Although only ten subjects had jobs of some kind to go to after leaving prison, 14 others had some plans for the future. However, as Anne, convicted of falsifying accounts and of theft from her employer, stated: 'It was not worth it and I would never do it again. It's hard to get a job because of the nature of the crime.'

Similarly, Max thought that at his age (29) he should not be spending vital time in prison. As he stated: 'I am only in my twenties ... therefore I'm put off completely ... it was not worth it at all.'

A number of offenders, although acknowledging that their crimes had not been worth it, did comment that they did not know what else they could have done at the time. For example, Abuu and Greg, who had been involved in separate blackmail situations, both commented that if they had not gone along with the demands made of them, they could have put both themselves and their families at risk. Greg said of his case: 'No-one could guarantee protection for me and my family 24 hours a day.'

Besides those who had felt trapped into committing their crimes through blackmail, others who had become 'desperate actors' (see Chapter 5), especially in the context of preserving their families, also commented on how they could not see what other choices they could have made in the same set of circumstances.

Sheila, who had embezzled funds from her employer, had taken the money in order to cover personal debts, both her own and of her husband's. She did not believe that her offending was worth it, nor did she have any intention of doing anything similar again – yet she had not known what else to do at the time. She commented: 'It was not worth it in terms of a custodial sentence, but obviously [the] debts needed paying off.'

A similar case was that of Janet, sentenced to 15 months for deception related to housing benefit. At the time of her crime her husband was ill, and she did not think they had enough money to manage. She commented that she would not do the same thing again, but, like Sheila, with hindsight she failed to see what else she could have done in the circumstances: 'I would not do it again. I thought I was doing the right thing and felt it was for a reason. The judge didn't see why we didn't just move [house].'

Finally, Debbie, the restaurant worker accused of embezzling from her employer, also felt that she had no choice but to intervene when the start of her daughter's NHS methadone drug-rehabilitation pro-gramme was delayed. She acknowledged: 'I could have gone to my GP etc, in hindsight, but was too distraught. I'm not sure what I would do again in the same circumstances.'

Jail as a deterrent to white-collar offenders

It is generally believed (see for example Braithwaite and Geis, 1982; Croall, 2001; Friedrichs, 1996) that white-collar crime, by its very nature, should be easier to deter than other forms of offending. Because such criminal behaviour often takes place during or even as part of the indi-vidual's work, to a white-collar offender the threat of losing employ-ment, status and income should in theory act as a strong deterrent – such people have more to lose if caught, convicted and sent to prison. Punch (1996) regards this as a powerful threat. However, as Friedrichs observes, even though such arguments sound convincing, it is difficult to know how much the threat of criminal sanctions does in fact deter white-collar criminals (1996: 344). In addition, Weisburd et al concluded, from their research with white-collar criminals, that in the case of this group of offenders a prison sentence is not necessarily the deterrent it has seemed (2001: 112–13).

All the individuals in the sample were asked whether their experi-ence in jail would deter them from future offending, but because some did not acknowledge, for various reasons, that they had committed any offence, only those who fully admitted and accepted their mis-demeanours (such as the acceptors described in Chapter 4) could give a meaningful answer. As none of the offenders had been aware of any suspicion falling on them while committing their crime, it was not a dilemma they had needed to face at the time. However, from a post hoc perspective, all the subjects said that probably nothing would have stopped them from committing their offence, apart from its being prevented by the enforcement of effective controls.

A few offenders did comment that the environment and regime of an open prison did not serve as a deterrent in itself, and that the great-est impact prison had on them was when they had been held in dis-persal or local prisons at the beginning of their sentence, before being sent to open prisons. This may have depended on where they had been held and for how long. Tom, a 50-year-old owner of a building firm convicted of tax evasion, stated: 'HMP J is not a deterrent, but the first couple of weeks in HMP K was.' Greg, a 57-year-old senior bank manager convicted of conspiracy to forge, and questioned during his interview in HMP J, said: 'I would not get involved in anything like this again. But look at these beautiful surroundings – what deterrent is this really?'

However, some prisoners (particularly women) had been put off any further criminal activity by the whole experience of jail, whether in closed or open conditions: 'Jail is a major deterrent' (Laura), and 'I've seen things in here I could not have imagined ... nor ever want to see again' (Anne).

In contrast to others' negative experience of prison, Adam said that time inside had not put him off committing crimes again. He said: 'Prison is no deterrent as a place ... especially here.'

Future occupational plans

It is often thought that white-collar criminals have a much better life to go out to after jail than most (Herlenger, 1992), and Benson (1984) notes that many such individuals manage to recover what they have lost, especially in terms of occupational status, and that unemployment is not a permanent feature of their lives after prison. Shover and Hochstetler suggest that because of the resilience of this group of offenders, many losses as a result of their conviction and imprisonment can be recovered and the status quo of their previous life can to some degree be restored (2006: 145). Hunter (2004) terms this phase in offenders' lives 'rebuilding', and is characterised by them either making a totally fresh start, or trying to regain the life they previously led, possibly through compromises.

From the sample of offenders, only Janet, a bar manager convicted of housing-benefit fraud had retained her job while in prison. The remaining 34 employed subjects had lost their jobs and/or the businesses they had previously owned, as well as their professional status and reputation. This meant they needed to start again once released. Ten offenders had got jobs to go to, or plans in place for restarting their careers. Some of the higher-level offenders (such as Greg, Peter and Stuart) appeared to have been offered gainful employment, either via their own efforts or through previous business or personal contacts. With respect to longer-term plans, 23 (56 per cent) of the 41 offenders had made plans for the future, including retraining in different professions, moving abroad and starting up their own businesses.

Summary

A number of afterthoughts were raised by offenders, relating both to themselves and to others, particularly their families, during the interviews. Although previous research reflects various experiences about how white-collar offenders adjust to prison life (see Benson and Cullen, 1988; Payne, 2003), the loss of freedom was felt as particularly harsh among the subjects in this study, especially at the beginning of their sentences. Because of the status of individuals usually (though not always) involved in white-collar crime (Shover and Hochstetler, 2006), it could be argued that this group of offenders have further to fall than other criminal types, due to what they have previously achieved. Preserving their status and respectability is very important to them, though media attention may make this difficult at times.

Whereas some researchers expect incarcerated white-collar criminals to go out to a better life than other types of offenders (Herlenger, 1992), because they are expected to be able to recover from experiences relatively easily, others disagree: Payne (2003) and Kerley and Copes (2004) suggest that many will have to seek out new careers and futures once they have been released, as jobs and career development time will have been lost, and professional recognition forfeited.

The offenders interviewed commented that relationships with their families had been affected by their imprisonment and some had lost, or feared they would lose, their partner as a result of their crime. Many of them acknowledged the impact of their offending on their family, some feeling that the burden of their sentence had fallen harder on their family than on themselves. While many relatives and friends had been supportive, some offenders found that close associates had 'disappeared'. In sharp contrast, however, there was also some evidence (from two of the offenders) that life in prison had had some positive effects on relationships, rebuilding previously broken ties.

In terms of losses to victims, offenders generally failed to recognise the damage caused to individuals and organisations, choosing instead to focus on who they would and would not commit crime against, on some kind of differential, moral scale. This was surprising given that nearly half the offenders in the sample readily accepted their guilt, either morally or legally, or both.

Ultimately, in summing up their overall experiences, the majority of offenders felt that after what they had been through their crime had simply not proved worth it, and were – as Shover and Hochstetler suggest (2006: 146) – ready to learn from past mistakes and desist from further criminal activity. Only two offenders readily admitted that their crimes had paid off, due to the substantial material gains they would enjoy when they left prison. Interestingly, however, a number of subjects commented that they had found prison itself, especially in an open establishment, no real deterrent to their criminal activity, except for the experience of the first few days in a local or dispersal institution.

8
Accounts and Gender

Introduction

To date, there has been little research in the literature on the role that women play in white-collar crime (an exception is Dodge, 2009). Where research has taken place, it has been seriously inhibited by data-collection difficulties, and when researchers have been able gain access to white-collar criminals they have predominantly focused on men; examples are Cressey's (1953) study of embezzlers, Spencer's (1959) work on white-collar criminals and Gill's (2005; 2007) studies of fraudsters. As Holtfreter points out: 'Much of the white-collar crime research failed to consider gender differences. This discrepancy was due, at least in part, to sample and data restriction issues ....' (2005: 355). So why do women feature so seldom in research into white-collar crime?

Since Sutherland first used the term 'white-collar' crime, it has tended to be masculinised. At the time he was writing, very few women participated in the workplace, but while their numbers have increased, criminologists and feminists have generally not considered women and crime in the same way as they have men. The assertion that only men commit white-collar crime, however, is too simplistic, and as Croall notes, women do indeed commit such offences (2003: 27). Davies also reminds us that Carlen et al (1985) and Carlen (1992) pointed out as far back as two decades ago that some women commit crimes for similar reasons to men, such as greed and personal gain (2003a: 290).

Nevertheless, despite these difficulties some white-collar crime research about women has taken place. However, this has tended to focus on traditional, lower-level offending, such as benefit fraud, and on motives that are needs-driven. This includes the studies, for example, by Carlen and Cook (1989) and Davies (2003a; 2003b) but these generally do not include the higher-level, white-collar crimes typically associated with men. As a result, research which includes both male and female white-collar offending has typically focused on both high- and low-level criminals (such as that by Wheeler et al, 1982; Daly, 1989; AIC and PwC, 2003), where possible gender-influenced differences may not be obvious or even identified. As Daly notes of her research within the group of offenders she studied, there were some men who were 'big fish', but most were 'little fish', not conforming to the stereotypical image of the powerful white-collar criminal (1989: 789). However, she noted that almost all of the female-instigated offences were 'petty', and in her classification would have been termed 'little fish'. Such disparities in the composition of mixed-gender samples have contributed to inconclusive findings, and results which have told us little about female white-collar offending.

Where both men and women have been considered in studies, generalisations have been made about their accounts, with greed and gain being the traditionally-cited motivations for the men's actions, and need and family commitments for the women. The problem with this is, as Davies's question reveals: 'Are there no rising white-collar crime women entrepreneurs, no "frilly-cuff" (Goldstraw, 2002) Ms Saunders or Mrs Leesons?' (2003b: 18).

Because in studies of white-collar crime women have mostly been viewed from a welfarist position, very little research has looked at women occupying positions equivalent to those of male offenders. Daly notes that where studies of women and white-collar crime have been conducted, these have tended to concentrate on statistical analyses of arrest data or on media reporting of individual cases. The literature on white-collar crime and women, as she states, is 'long on speculation and short on evidence' (Daly, 1989: 771–2). However, with increasing numbers of women in the occupational workforce, and the acknowledgement that they do indeed commit similar crimes to men, this has allowed some limited research and comparisons to be made to challenge the 'pink-collar' image of white-collar crime.

Exceptions to this include Dorothy Zietz (1981) and Kathleen Daly (1989). Zietz published her findings in 1981 from research relating to female white-collar offenders, which attempted to replicate the study that Cressey (1953) had conducted on male embezzlers, to see whether the reasons for men who 'violated positions of financial trust' applied also to women. Using the typologies which Cressey developed and expanding her sample to include further categories of white-collar crime, Zietz reviewed prison master-file cards on 100 women, and followed up her findings by interviewing a number of offenders whom she termed 'fraudulent operators'. She found that Cressey's hypothesis was generally applicable to the women in her sample. Nevertheless, the situations in which women committed their crime tended to arise from a different set of circumstances than those leading to male offending. Zietz concluded that Cressey's hypothesis would need to be modified to enable it to be applied to the women in her sample. This was particularly so where women encountered an urgent need for money, not available from their own limited resources; where they were in positions of trust and found themselves offered financial solutions to their problems; and where they were able to rationalise their actions in such a way as not to jeopardise being seen as trusted individuals (1981: 151).

Zietz identified three categories of female offenders: honest women; women who intended to steal or defraud; and women who committed crimes to support a drug habit. Within each of these categories, she described the types of women who violated financial trust, and identified a number of findings which differed from those in Cressey's study (ibid: 150–1). She found that in contrast to the men in that study, women offenders, prior to their crime, had done nothing they could not share with others in respect of their need for additional money. The only exception to this was where they had been subject to the influence of a husband or other close relative. Whereas some offenders in Cressey's study used the 'I was just borrowing' rationalisation, in Zietz's research – with the exception of one woman (in the group classified as 'honest women') – no subjects used it.

Daly (1989) also conducted research relating to both male and female white-collar crime offenders, by re-analysing the data from pre-sentence investigation (PSI) reports used in the research undertaken by Wheeler et al (1982). This included data obtained from eight federal district courts during 1976–78. Her work focused on exploring five hypotheses, which included considering the share of occupational crime committed by women, the modus operandi of male and female white-collar criminals and differences between the genders in motives over four different offence types. The five hypotheses that Daly considered were as follows (1989: 773):

- the female share of corporate (organisational) crime is very low;
- the female share of occupational crime is low;
- a woman is less likely to work in crime groups than man;
- a woman's economic gain from crime is less than a man's; and
- a man's and a woman's motives for criminal involvement differ.

On the backgrounds of the women in her sample, Daly found that they were generally younger than the men, possessed fewer educational qualifications and were more likely to have family dependants outside marriage. They also owned fewer assets, and generally held lower-level positions than the men (ibid: 778). Crimes committed by women were less likely than men to be carried out in collusion with others; however, the proportion of females working alone varied between 50 and 90 per cent, depending upon the type of offence committed (ibid: 781).

In terms of motives, Daly (ibid) found that 30–35 per cent of females gave their family's financial need as a motive (the highest category of motives), a proportion considerably lower than Zietz had found eight years earlier. This demonstrated less difference between the motivation of men and women in white-collar offences. Between 10 and 15 per cent of women gave financial gain as a motive, while 15–20 per cent gave non-financial reasons.

More up-to-date publications on gender and white-collar crime include those of Dodge and Goldstraw at al. Dodge's *Women and White-Collar Crime* (2009) is an excellent contribution to this area of the literature, though she herself acknowledges that it is based on a review and analysis of case studies and media stories. Goldstraw et al (2005) re-analyse data collected from 155 files covering 208 serious fraud offenders dealt with in Australian and New Zealand higher criminal courts during 1998 and 1999, of which 43 were women. The research attempts to replicate that of a larger study (AIC and PwC, 2003), and seeks to identify the nature, cost, offender characteristics, modus operandi and motivations of female serious fraudsters.

Goldstraw et al identify a number of differences between men and women in this research. None of the women, unlike their male counterparts, possessed post-graduate qualifications or statutory registration, and they were proportionately under-represented in professional and managerial occupations (2005: 2). Three women had committed their crimes with others, two of these being with their partner or a close relative. However, very few women claimed to have been coerced into such acts. The average cost of crime was also substantially lower for women than men (ibid).[1]

Greed was cited as the primary and most frequent motivation by both men and women (ibid: 3), with gambling as the second (for further details see ibid; AIC and PwC, 2003; Sakurai and Smith, 2003). Little difference was identified between genders for these two categories of offence. Proportionately twice as many women as men cited 'pleasing others' as a motivation, with the former giving reasons such as that they felt they could not refuse their families anything, wanted to appear a 'perfect wife' and 'mother', and wished to contribute to the household finances, thereby mirroring Zietz's 'obsessive protectors' (1981: 147).

Mitigating factors considered in this study were those circumstances offenders wished to be taken into account at the time of sentencing, and which they claimed had affected their offences (AIC and PwC, 2003: 46). Goldstraw et al (2005: 4) found that women put forward proportionally fewer mitigating factors in total than men. Female offenders also recorded no motivations or mitigating factors with regard to their future employment, whereas men were keen to point out the impact a prison sentence would have on their careers. Women raised the issue of personal hardship and highlighted factors relating to their past child-hood experiences (such as alcoholic parents, childhood sexual abuse or a generally traumatic upbringing), as well as current circumstances (poor marriages or relationships, financial difficulties or the poor health of partners). Other differences were noted relating to moral differences in accounts, in that men were keener than women to point out previous examples of good character, such as work they had previously under-taken in the community. Women, on the other hand, appeared more remorseful about their offending behaviour (ibid).

What the literature on male and female white-collar crime tells us

A review of the limited literature on gender and white-collar crime reveals two main themes. First, that men and women tend to find themselves in different situations, which affect their accounts of white-collar crime. Secondly, that they differ when they account for their offences in moral terms. However, as Davies points out, the criminal careers of female offenders in general have not been well studied (1997: 9); the nature of their roles and the circumstances leading to criminal involve-ment need further attention, as does the vocabulary used to justify their crimes.

The differences between men and women in terms of committing white-collar crime have traditionally been characterised as men offend-ing out of greed and women out of need. Men have also generally been more likely to have owned their own business, and therefore more likely to claim that they committed their crimes in order to protect it in times of economic difficulty. In contrast, women have been typified as offending not for themselves but rather for their families or for others with whom they have a close personal relationship. This would appear to accord with the groups 'obsessive protectors' and 'romantic dreamers' as identified by Zietz (1981: 147–8), and also those Daly (1989) identified as being motivated by need.

Research by Collins and Collins (2000) further supports these assertions, in that they consider the personality traits of both female white-collar offenders and non-offenders, all of whom held high-level executive positions. When comparing their findings with previous (male) white-collar crime research, they found that men were generally motivated by greed, ambition and social status, whereas women tended to commit their crimes to help others. In addition, they claim that: '... females committed frauds because they needed money for their husbands, who were in financial trouble, or for their parents who couldn't pay their medical bills. Every single woman ... committed their crime for someone else, usually their husband or boyfriend'. They note that women accounted for their crimes in a morally different way to men; unlike the latter, they readily admitted their offences and were remorseful about what they had done (ibid: 2).

However, as Goldstraw et al (2005) find, and as also to some extent does Daly (1989), women do indeed commit white-collar crimes sometimes for reasons other than simple need, and do so in similar occupational roles and circumstances as men. Coleman (1994), however, questions whether men and women, even when in these similar situations, actually have the same opportunities for committing white-collar crimes. As Box (1983) argues, female workers are more closely supervised than men in the same jobs, thereby restricting their chances for criminal activity. Croall (2003) comments that since Sutherland's defining of white-collar crime, the 'glass ceiling' – while still existing – has certainly been raised for women, so they can now more often be found in higher-level occupations. However, a full understanding of the relationship between gender, crime and work is a complex task, and to date remains to be achieved.

Considering the second of the two themes emerging from the literature review, women may give different accounts of the moral background to their involvement in crime. However, as Gonzales et al caution, the area of gender and accounts is complex and not fully understood, and it is often difficult to separate the gender issues from those of status and power (1990: 613). They cite the findings of past research, such as that of Baxter (1984) and Cupach et al (1986), to the effect that women, in response to untoward or failure events, are more likely to offer concessions and excuses, as opposed to men, who seem to resort more often to refusal.

Schönbach (1985) found men's accounts consist of more defensive tactics, such as refusals; this is in line with similar findings by Brown and Levinson (1987), who note that women are more likely to be 'polite', possibly due to their (perceived) lower status. Gonzales et al found that women tend to apologise more than men, and to rely on statements of regret such as: 'I'm so embarrassed' (1990: 618). However, they conclude that it is not clear whether this gender difference betokens genuine feelings of remorse on a woman's part, or is simply a feature of female socialisation. In addition, Gonzales et al also found gender differences in account content, with men more concerned than women with saving face and preserving status and power; they consider women may simply be providing a routine apology – 'I'm sorry' – to try and undo any damage, possibly as a precursor to a more detailed account (1992: 969). They also suggest that women may pay more attention to this type of explanation, offered at the start of a negotiation process to restore equilibrium within relationships. Besides the differences in the types of accounts given by men and women or in how they are delivered, Gonzales et al also note a difference in levels of effort – women spend a longer time on more complex explanations. In total, though, they spend no longer in conversation than men and speak at approximately the same rate (1990: 618).

As outlined earlier, most of the literature on female white-collar criminals has to date focused on their background, and on the causes of and motivations underlying their crimes, and less on their accounts. Rothman and Gandossy (1982), however, re-analysed Wheeler et al's (1982) data to examine white-collar offenders' accounts provided to federal probation officers, in order to see how these had affected decisions to impose sanctions. Although their research was not restricted to women, they did note that female accounts are more fully in accord with judicial requirements than men's, because women tended to admit guilt more often, as Wheeler et al had claimed. They also found that women provided stronger justifications in their accounts and apologised more often, exhibiting more shame and remorse than their male counterparts.

Background of the male and female offenders in the sample

In the sample of 41 offenders, there were nine women, representing 22 per cent of all the participants interviewed. At the time of the interviews the average age for both men and women was 39 years, and there was also no gender difference between the ages at which they had first begun their offending. In relation to country of origin, 25 (78 per cent) of the men and seven (also 78 per cent) of the women were from the United Kingdom. There was also virtually no difference in marital status between the genders, with 22 (69 per cent) of the men and six (67 per cent) of the women married or co-habiting.

While there was no great differences in educational attainment, Table 8.1 below shows that 11 (34 per cent) of the men had some type of tertiary qualification – either a degree or a professional qualification – whereas this applied to only two (22 per cent) of the women. These latter were Ruth, who had a degree from a UK university, and Sally, a management accountant who held professional accountancy qualifications.

Table 8.1   Educational qualifications attained by male and female offenders (highest achieved)

	Men		Women	
Primary	4	(13%)	2	(22%)
Secondary	17	(53%)	5	(56%)
Tertiary	11	(34%)	2	(22%)
Total	**32**	(100%)	**9**	(100%)

At the time of committing their offences, 35 (85 per cent) offenders had been in employment, consisting of eight (89 per cent) of the women and 27 (85 per cent) of the men, i.e. there was very little difference between the genders in this respect. Only one (11 per cent) of the female offenders was unemployed at the time of her offence. Although the proportion of men and of women in employment did not noticeably differ, the nature and level of their occupations did. Of the 35 individuals in question, 26 (96 per cent) of the men had held positions which could be described as executive-level (directors, co-owners, professionals), whereas only six (75 per cent) of the women had held similar positions. This left one (4 per cent) of the men and two (25 per cent) of the women at the level of administrative or clerical workers. Part of the difference in the sample was due to the high percentage of men who either owned or part-owned a business – 22 (81 per cent) of the 27 men, compared to only one (13 per cent) of the eight women in employment. (This was Pam, who owned a shop with her husband). Table 8.2 shows the range of jobs that male and female offenders had held prior to their conviction and sentence.

Of the 35 offenders (27 men and 8 women) who had been in employment, 25 (93 per cent) of the men had committed work-related offences. The remaining two men involved in non-work-related crimes

Table 8.2 Range of jobs for male and female white-collar offenders

Men	Women
Accountant	Accounts assistant
Assistant management accountant	Bank credit-control assistant
Building-firm owner	Bar manager
Computer consultant	Financial and administrative assistant
Electrical company owner	Management accountant
Engineering-company owner	Restaurant manager
Finance director	Shop co-owner
Financial consultant	Supermarket-garage manager
Furniture-making business owner	Unemployed
Garage owner	
Jewellery business owner	
Legal assistant	
Management accountant	
Managing/executive director	
Market trader	
Post Office manager/owner	
Property broker	
Publishing-company owner	
Senior bank manager	
Solicitor and sole partner	
Stock accountant	
Student	
Transport owner	
Unemployed	

had both been convicted of conspiracy to defraud. Seven (88 per cent) of the eight women had committed work-related crimes; the one woman guilty of a non-work-related crime was convicted of deception in relation to housing benefit. Of the seven women whose crimes were occupation-related, six (86 per cent) were employed (rather than self-employed), and all their crimes were committed against their employers. Of the 25 men whose crimes were occupation-related, only four (16 per cent) were employed (as opposed to self-employed) and two of these committed crimes against their employers. The remaining two offenders, Bharat and Matt, had offended in collusion with their employers.

Whether the modus operandi of their crimes was affected by their occupational status or the character of the women themselves, only three (33 per cent) of the nine women in the sample had involved others; these were Alison, Pam and Ruth. Alison claimed she had become involved in her illegal activities solely because of blackmail, whereas Pam claimed

Table 8.3   Offences by male and female offenders (number of instances)

Offence	Men		Women	
Conspiracy-related	15	(39%)	3	(23%)
Deception-related	6	(15%)	2	(15%)
False accounting	3	(8%)	2	(15%)
Theft from employer	1	(3%)	4	(31%)
Fraudulent trading	4	(10%)	–	(–)
Taxation-related	4	(10%)	–	(–)
Forgery	1	(3%)	1	(8%)
Credit-card offences	–	(–)	1	(8%)
Trades-description offences	1	(3%)	–	(–)
Money-laundering	1	(3%)	–	(–)
Intending to pervert the course of justice	1	(3%)	–	(–)
Perjury	1	(3%)	–	(–)
Total	**38**	**(100%)**	**13**	**(100%)**
Mean offences	**1.19**		**1.18**	

she had been wrongly convicted, since the crimes for which she had been sentenced related to her husband and an associate, not to her. Only Ruth admitted her guilt, claiming to have got involved in crime through her boyfriend and other friends, though she never claimed this as a primary reason for her actions. Of the 32 men in the sample, 23 (72 per cent) had acted with others, though none with women or with their relatives. Where male offenders had been involved with others in their crimes, this mainly consisted of business partners, co-owners, colleagues or associates, where they played equal or even leading roles in the commission of their crimes.

Table 8.3 above details the range of offences for which male and female offenders were convicted. For the 51 total offences of which the subjects in the sample were convicted, there was virtually no difference between the mean number of offences committed by men (1.19) and women (1.18). However, there were differences in the types of offences committed by men and women, the greatest difference being in conspiracy-related offences. Proportionately, just over 50 per cent more men than women committed this type of offence, possibly reflecting the greater proportion of men involved with others in their crimes. For deception-related offences there was no difference in the incidence between men and women. For the crime of false accounting, propor-

Table 8.4 Relationship of victim to male and female offenders

Victim	Men		Women	
Government	8	(25%)	2	(22%)
Employer	2	(6%)	5	(56%)
Client	1	(3%)	–	(–)
Other	21	(66%)	2	(22%)
Total	32	(100%)	9	(100%)

tionately, nearly twice as many women were convicted of this offence, and for theft from an employer, proportionately more than ten times as many women than men. This was probably reflective of the higher number of women who were employed by an organisation, rather than self-employed. Finally, fraudulent trading and tax-related offences were only committed by men, once again probably a result of the high levels of self-employment.

In analysing the victims (organisations or individuals) the crimes had been committed against, as detailed in Table 8.4 above, there was very little difference in victimisation between men and women for crimes committed against the government or clients. However, for crimes committed against employers, this included two (6 per cent) of the men (Dave and Greg) and five (56 per cent) of the women (Alison, Anne, Debbie, Ruth and Sally). This figure may be due to the higher proportion of women who were employed, rather than self-employed. For the category of 'other', there was also a substantial difference between the genders, mainly due to the men, such as Adam, Gareth, Geoff, Patrick and Stuart, committing crimes against other, external organisations.

In considering whether men and women differ in the value of the proceeds of their crime, the total amount of money taken by all 41 offenders, as accounted for in their interviews, was £239,520,500, either as lone operators or with others. This was made up of £236,403,500 for male offenders and £3,117,000 for female. This gives a mean for men of £7,387,609 and £346,333 for women. This information is represented on the graph in Figure 8.1 below. Six offenders had their amounts capped at £5 million. Because the sample consisted of offenders who had operated alone and others who had acted in collusion, it is impossible to state the exact amounts which could be apportioned to the individuals who were interviewed. However, the figures strongly suggest that the proceeds of male offenders' crime tend to be a good deal higher than for females.

Figure 8.1   Total proceeds (in £s) of offences involving males and females

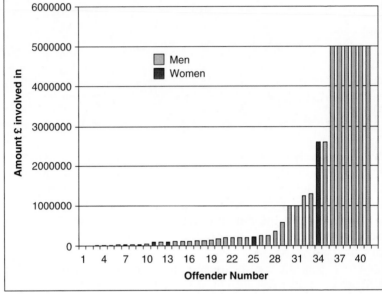

Note: Offenders at nos. 1 and 2 (one male, one female) committed crimes which involved no money.

The length of the sentence which male offenders were given ranged from 12 to 152 months, with an average of 40 months. However, the women received sentences that ranged from six months to 46 months, averaging 23 months. The amount of money that the 15 offenders who acted alone in the commission of their crimes claimed to have been sentenced for ranged from £12,500 to £250,000 for men (average £111,250), whereas amounts for women ranged from £18,000 to £251,000 (average £75,167). It is acknowledged, however, that these figures are not objective measures – since they were provided by the offenders themselves – and some may have been over- or under-estimated.

During their accounts, two female offenders raised the issue of the length of sentences they believed women received compared with men, claiming that they believed sentences were longer for women in relation to the amount of money involved. Sheila said that 'Men appear to get shorter sentences for the same offences or even worse, including large amounts of money.'

To see if this had occurred with the participants, the sample was restricted to those 15 offenders who had acted alone in the commission of their crimes (because it is impossible to allocate the proportion of proceeds involved with an individual where more than one person is involved). Taking the total amount of money offenders claimed to have been sentenced for, this was then divided by the total number of months awarded in the sentence for each individual, to produce the relation between the amount involved in the crime and the time served. If what the women claimed had been true, a lower figure would have been expected. However, as the graph in Figure 8.2 below suggests, lone women in the sample had not been disadvantaged in this way, and in fact it could be argued that men, on this basis, were proportionately more disadvantaged in the length of their sentences.[2]

Of the 41 offenders interviewed, only four (10 per cent) confessed to any prior convictions. This figure was made up of three (9 per cent) of the men and one (11 per cent) of the women. Only Ruth had previously been convicted of white-collar crimes, but had not received a custodial sentence; the three men, on the other hand, had been involved in non-white-collar crimes. No woman was identified who boasted about her crime, or about the gains she had made from it. If anything, the women tended to underestimate such gains (as opposed to the men, such as Adam and Adrian, whose accounts gave rise to the possibility

Figure 8.2 Analysis of sentence imposed on lone offenders by gender, compared with the amount of money involved in their crimes

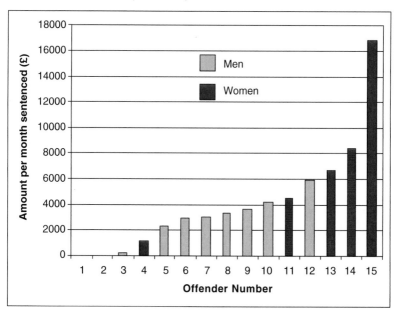

Note: Offenders 1 (male) and 2 (female) committed offences which did not involve money.

that they had exaggerated the amount in question). For example, Sheila, a 37-year-old accounts assistant in a travel agency, remarked: 'Over a period of 18 months I stole £41,000. I didn't realise it was that much … I thought it was more like £20,000.'

There was no indication that Sheila was deliberately trying to play down the amount to make it sound more acceptable; if anything, she said in her account that she had been genuinely surprised about the total amount she had taken. In contrast, however, the comments of Anne, a 38-year-old supermarket-garage manager, indicated that she disagreed with the amount for which she had been convicted: 'I was sentenced for theft and false accounting amounting to £101,000. It was more like £50,000, though.'

The differences between the characteristics of the genders appeared to be very similar to what has been noted before (for example in Zietz, 1981; Daly, 1989; Goldstraw et al, 2005). Men had more educational qualifications than women, and women tended to act as lone operators. In the sample there was a high proportion of self-employed men compared to women. However, among those men who were employees there was a relatively high percentage of work-related offences. In terms of sentencing, analysis did not show that either gender was punished more harshly than the other for their misdemeanours, certainly if related to the amounts of money involved in their crimes.

Legal and moral guilt between genders

This section will examine the differences and similarities in how men and women accounted for the legal and moral differences in their crimes, as discussed in detail in Chapter 4. Within the sample of offenders, guilty pleas varied between male and female offenders with 19 (59 per cent) of the men pleading guilty compared to seven (78 per cent) of the women, as detailed in Table 8.5 below. All four offenders who were appealing were men.

Table 8.5   Pleas in court by male and female offenders

	Men		Women	
Guilty	19	(59%)	7	(78%)
Not guilty	13	(41%)	2	(22)
Total	**32**	**(100%)**	**9**	**(100%)**

Table 8.6 below details the differences between how men and women account for legal and moral acceptance of guilt, following the categories established in Chapter 4. The largest category overall was acceptors, with 20 offenders in total. However, women were clearly over-represented in this category, with 78 per cent (n = 7) of women compared with 41 per cent (n = 13) of men. In contrast, nearly double the proportion of men (40 per cent, n = 13) than of women (22 per cent, n = 2) were found in the two rejector categories.

Considering the rejector categories first, the total number of rejectors was 12 (38 per cent) of the men and two (22 per cent) of the women. As such, they had rejected both their legal and moral status as a criminal, feeling either that there was no behaviour to answer for, or that if there was, they had not been personally involved in it.

Table 8.6   Typology of outer-legal and inner-moral selves, comparing the acceptance of guilt between male and female offenders

	Men		**Women**	
Total rejectors	12	(38%)	2	(22%)
Tactical rejectors	1	(2%)	–	(–)
Tactical acceptors	6	(19%)	–	(–)
Acceptors	13	(41%)	7	(78%)
Total	**32**	**(100%)**	**9**	**(100%)**

The two women classified as total rejectors both claimed in their accounts that they were not personally liable for the criminal activities which had taken place. Pam said that she had been looking after her sick mother-in-law at the time of the offences, and Alison claimed she had been blackmailed and coerced into her crime. These accounts are in contrast to those of the three men involved in similar situations (Abuu, Greg and Iqbal), who claimed to have been involved in blackmail situations but were not classified as total rejectors. Greg was classified as a tactical acceptor, believing himself to be innocent, and claiming he had pleaded guilty in an attempt to obtain a lower sentence. Abuu and Iqbal were both classified as acceptors, because they acknowledged some element of personal blame for the crimes despite the element of blackmail in their situation. Of the 12 men classified as total rejectors, Jack and Michael (who had been convicted of false accounting and fraudulent trading respectively) claimed that the activities which they had been involved in were not criminal. Bharat, Mazi and Okeke claimed that they were being victimised.

The other category of rejectors in the typology comprised tactical rejectors. These were offenders who had pleaded not guilty in court, while knowing that they were guilty. The wrongful plea was made on the chance that they would be found not guilty in court for reasons such as poor evidence or the complexity of the case. Analysis revealed that only one participant fitted the criterion, a male offender. Adrian was willing to 'gamble' with the system and pleaded not guilty (although he knew that he was), mainly because he believed that the complexity of his case and (in his opinion) poor evidence would give him a fair chance of being found not guilty.

Considering now the acceptor categories, tactical acceptors were defined as those pleading guilty in court, but believing they were innocent of any crime. The main reason behind this was to accept the label of being a criminal in order to reduce the length of their sentence, or even to avoid a custodial sentence altogether. No woman, compared with six (19 per cent) of the men, was found in this category. By comparison, men in this category (such as Gareth, Roger and Stuart) admitted to pleading guilty to attract a lower sentence, either because they said that their legal team had advised them to do so, or because they claimed to have made 'plea bargains' with the police. It might be interesting to examine whether defence lawyers and the police advise men and women differently in matters such as pleas, or whether the nature of their crimes is thought not to warrant such advice. Either situation could have an effect on the number of tactical acceptors among women.

The final category in the typology was acceptors. Individuals assigned to this category were those who had pleaded guilty in court and believed (at least to some extent) that they were guilty, and as such were willing to accept a criminal label. This category displayed the greatest difference between the genders, with 41 per cent (n = 13) of the men classified as acceptors, compared to seven 78 per cent (n = 7) of the women. The significant gender difference in this category suggests that women may be more willing to accept their guilt, both legally and morally, and to accept being labelled as a criminal. In terms of legal acceptance, this appears to accord with Rothman and Gandossy's finding that, legally speaking, women appear to accept guilt more readily than men (1982: 459).

From the four categories in the typology, men appeared to reject their criminality and criminal labels more than women, with 13 (40 per cent) of the men being classified as total or tactical rejectors, compared with only two (22 per cent) women. Thus it was not surprising to find that, at the time of the interviews, all the (four) offenders who were appealing were men. Besides rejecting a criminal label, the men also appeared to be more tactical players, either as rejectors or acceptors, than the women – seven (21 per cent) of the men and no women – in deciding whether or not to plead guilty in court. The men appeared to believe that such behaviour might result in a reduced custodial sentence, or a non-custodial one.

What this analysis has shown is that face-saving seemed to be less important to women than men, and that female offenders appeared more ready to accept a criminal label; this is demonstrated by the high proportion of women found to be acceptors. In addition, men were seen to be more tactical players when it came to deciding whether to plead guilty or not in court.

Differences between genders in presenting the moral self

Having considered how men and women account for themselves in legal terms, how male and female offenders did so as moral individuals will now be examined. In their accounts offenders gave what were from their perspective both acceptable and unacceptable motives. Accounts of an unacceptable nature mainly related to individuals who had committed their crimes purely for themselves, such as out of greed or because of addiction. Acceptable explanations were those involving more altruistic motives, where offenders claimed they did not commit their crimes for themselves, or where they had tried to make good their crimes since committing them.

In her interview, no woman accounted for her crime in terms of an unacceptable motive, such as greed or addiction. This is in contrast to the finding of Sakurai and Smith (2003), in their analysis of serious fraud offenders in Australia and New Zealand, that gambling was the second most frequently identified primary motivation among female offenders. Their research found that a higher proportion of women than men in their sample were motivated by gambling (Goldstraw et al, 2005: 3). Four (13 per cent) of the men in the present study admitted to unacceptable motives, mainly relating to greed and the rapid acquisition of 'easy money'.

Accounts of acceptable motives were given by both men and women, generally either by citing altruism – claiming they had committed their crimes to benefit others rather than themselves – or by stressing that they had tried to make post facto amends for their offending. Three (19 per cent) of the men (Gareth, Gerry and Jason) and three (33 per cent) of the women (Debbie, Janet and Sheila) stated directly that their criminal behaviour was undertaken to help others. In their accounts, these three women focused on how they had offended for the sake of their family. For example, Sheila, speaking of the debt she and her husband faced, said: 'My main concern was the bills and the mounting debt I needed to clear.'

Men, on the other hand, gave accounts which were not as directly related to the needs of their family. Gerry claimed to have given most of his gains to his mother, whereas Jason and Gareth focused their accounts on their business, in particular on how other people had depended on them for a living. As Jason commented: 'I had a number of men working for me on a self-employed basis ... they depended on that money as much as my business did ... I owed it to them as well.'

As mentioned in the introduction to this section, some of the offenders had tried to make good their crimes after the event. The main theme relating to this in their accounts was how they thought they did not really deserve the proceeds of their crimes. Three (9 per cent) of the men (Dave, Iqbal and Jason) recounted how they had tried to make amends for their crimes by paying back their illegal gains (either in full or in part) to their victims. However, both Dave and Jason raised the issue of feeling doubly punished by also being imprisoned, thereby casting doubt on their implicit claim to have acted in this way for uniquely moral reasons. None of the women raised the issue of making good their crimes in this way.

Another way in which subjects attempted to lessen the impact of their offending was by rejecting the notion that it had done harm, specifically by claiming that there had been no victim. In this way subjects tried to neutralise their behaviour by denying the existence of any victim, as described by Sykes and Matza (1957). No woman in the sample tried to claim that their crimes were victimless, compared with three (9 per cent) of the men (Adam, Peter and Stuart), who all claimed to be unable to see how anyone had been personally affected by their illegal behaviour. Peter had been involved in money-laundering on financial markets and Stuart in inter-trading between groups of accounts; neither could see how his offence had directly affected other people, while Adam similarly argued that his Internet crimes had no identifiable victims.

However, in seeking revenge, one (3 per cent) of the men (Marvin) and two (22 per cent) of the women (Sally and Sheila) saw their crimes as a legitimate reaction to a set of unfair circumstances. Marvin claimed to have committed his crime as revenge against the Post Office for previously losing some of his out-going promotional mail. Both Sally and

Sheila sought revenge against their employers for not getting what they thought they deserved in terms of rewards for their jobs. Sally commented: 'I didn't feel as though I was paid for my worth.'

Other motives, such as blows to self-esteem, through either blocked opportunities or fear of failure, appeared slightly more important to men than women. Six (19 per cent) of the men raised this, but only one (11 per cent) of the women (Sally). The fear of failure appeared more important to men, especially with regard to their jobs or businesses; this was demonstrated by the accounts of Geoff, Max, Peter and Sid, for example. However, Sally apparently needed to boost her self-esteem, which she claimed she did through her new-found ability to spend money and buy goods: 'I didn't particularly enjoy spending the money, I enjoyed aspects of booking things ... just knowing I could.'

Regarding blocked opportunities, men reacted negatively towards their employers particularly when chances for advancement were not made available. This was demonstrated by the accounts of Dave and Greg. Dave was a management accountant at a subsidiary office of a larger company, who said that he had been 'treading water', not given the promotion that he felt he deserved; as a result, he embezzled approximately £109,000 from his employer. Greg, a senior bank manager, had worked for his employer for 32 years, and had hoped to be made a director. When this did not materialise, he got involved with another company, members of which, he later claimed, blackmailed him into getting involved in illegal activities at his bank.

In trying to assert their morality, six (19 per cent) of the men and two (18 per cent) of the women tried in their accounts to portray their criminality as aberrant. To do this they used various strategies, including pointing out their previous normal, good behaviour and emphasising how out of character their criminal acts had been. For example, Pam was keen to point out the ordinariness of her life, such as her previous work as a secretary and being a grandmother, whereas Janet relied on emphasising that her criminal behaviour was out of character – she had never done anything like it before, nor ever would again. Kevin stated he was just a normal person, and had found himself in a position where he had no choice but to do what he did. Finally, Adrian seemed proud to stress that he had run a legitimate transport business alongside his illegitimate one.

When describing themselves as 'good criminals' both men and women emphasised in their accounts how 'controlled' they believed they had been in their illegal activities, specifically by stressing how much worse their offences could have been and how much more damage they might have caused to their victims. This was particularly notice-able where there had been a lack of monitoring procedures in control systems, and where individuals had abused their power and authority to commit crimes. Marvin claimed he could have put more unpaid post through the Post Office, and both Dave and Sally claimed they could have embezzled more money from the organisations they worked for. Six (19 per cent) of the men were also keen to point out that they were not 'real criminals' and certainly not like the majority of their fellow-prisoners, while Stuart insisted on mentioning his support for children's charities. Those offenders who claimed to be against drugs, like Peter, tried to disassociate themselves from what they saw as the 'bad' and 'immoral' elements of criminality, especially in prison. Adam, Adrian, Anne and Janet also made a point of saying that without their help and co-operation, internal and/or external authorities might not have been able to undertake successful investigation of their offending; Janet, for instance, emphasised her co-operation with the police, and Anne des-cribed her company's attempt to quantify her crime: 'At this point they tried to double the figure to £200,000, but they only had accounting records going back six months, so they were reliant on me.'

Some offenders even tried to emphasise their good character in prison. Pam was keen to stress in her interview that she was a 'good prisoner' because she was on enhancements, although most of the offenders in the sample were in the same position, and no-one else raised this issue. In addition, Adam, Gareth, Patrick and Stuart were keen to say they felt that they could have given more back to the community than they had been able to in prison. Gareth, Patrick and Stuart felt that community sen-tences would have been more worthwhile to society than incarceration. Adam felt that the rules governing working in and giving back to the community during his sentence penalised those with shorter sentences, such as white-collar criminals.

In their accounts, men and women appeared equally concerned about the fear of failure and of blows to their self-esteem. Women tended to highlight their 'normality', compared with male offenders, by pointing to their normal, everyday character and by stressing previous good behav-iour, as opposed to one-off, out-of-character actions. While this spilled over, as discussed previously, from being 'good individuals' to 'good prisoners', only men created a scale of morality once in prison, to pos-ition themselves and their crimes above other criminals. They did this by viewing other crimes and criminals (such as those associated with street crime) as 'below' and 'inferior' or even 'separate' from them, thereby attempting to disassociate themselves from the popular image of criminality.

Men and women as actors

This section details the differences in accounts presented by men and women when representing themselves as actors (rational, pressurised or seduced, as described in Chapter 5). Rational actors consisted of two main sub-categories: planning actors (those individuals who went looking for an opportunity to commit a crime) and opportunist actors (those who simply came across opportunities to do so). As for planning actors, only two individuals who fulfilled this criterion were identified in the sample; both were men (Adam and Adrian). From the accounts given, no woman purposely set out to commit her crime as part of a thought-out, rational and sophisticated plan to the extent that these two men did.

From the analysis of the research data, two main sets of circumstances were identified which appeared to attract and be conducive to opportunist actors. These were where poor systems of internal control were identified, and where individuals found themselves in positions of power and authority which they could take advantage of. Eleven offenders gave one or both of these as primary reasons for committing their crimes. Of these, six (67 per cent) were women and five (16 per cent) men. Faced with such circumstances, the women (Alison, Anne, Debbie, Ruth, Sally and Sheila) all took advantage of the opportunities presented to them in the same way as all the men (Dave, Greg, Jason, Marvin and Tom) faced with a similar situation. Therefore, moving along the scale of rationality away from planning actors, in terms of criminal expertise there was no difference identified between genders.

Although only two of the male offenders were employed by external organisations, compared with all six of the women, it could be argued that women who find themselves in a middle-management position are more able to exploit opportunities or weaknesses in systems and procedures, because they know and understand them in detail. By contrast, men, who on average tend to hold higher management positions than women (Greg, for example, a senior bank manager), could possibly inflict greater financial damage, but may be prevented from doing so because they are further removed from the day-to-day operations of the office, and thus from a 'hands-on' opportunity for criminality.

The second category of actors identified was pressurised actors. These were individuals who claimed to have committed their crimes as a result of external pressures, such as those associated with finance, their business or their family. They saw themselves as acting in response to mounting pressure from situations which could not be resolved, in their eyes, other than by crime. The amount of pressure felt varied from that brought on by offenders pursuing their own aspirations, by those in desperate situations to those individuals in threatening circumstances. Table 8.7 below details the split between male and female offenders who noted such pressures in their accounts.

Table 8.7   Men and women as pressurised actors

	Men	% of total men	Women	% of total women
Aspiring	8	(25%)	1	(11%)
Desperate	7	(22%)	3	(33%)
Threatened	3	(9%)	1	(11%)

The category of aspiring actors, who suffered from self-inflected pressure, comprised eight (25 per cent) of the men and one (11 per cent) of the women, whereas of the desperate actors, seven (22 per cent) were men and three (33 per cent) were women. Very little difference was noted in terms of numbers for threatened actors. Pressure felt by both aspiring and desperate offenders was attributed to business problems, the will to succeed or family issues.

No woman accounted for her criminality in terms of the pressure of business problems, and only one woman co-owned a business. Those men (specifically Gareth, Geoff, Jason, Marvin, Max, Patrick and Stuart) who accounted at least in part for their criminality in terms of being pressurised, described being driven by their situation either when starting up a business or through the need to keep it going. For example, Jason, the 29-year-old owner of a furniture-making business, convicted of deception and obtaining property, and Max, the 29-year-old part-owner of an IT consultancy business, convicted of conspiracy to defraud, both accounted for their involvement in crime in this way. Both had experienced pressure on setting up a new business, compared with more seasoned businessmen such as Geoff (who only became a desperate actor because of changes in his economic circumstances).

In contrast to business pressures, family pressures appeared to be felt by both men and women in the sample. The men's accounts spoke of preserving the lifestyles that their families had already achieved, as exemplified by the actions of Kevin, a single-handed solicitor who had started his own business and encountered financial difficulties, and as a result had turned to crime to maintain the level of income and standard of living his family had been used to during his previous employment. Although Jason and Max primarily accounted for their crimes in terms of business pressures, the success of their business was inextricably linked to the wealth of their family, and their comments were similar to Kevin's. However, the men in this category appeared to have turned to crime of their own free will, none claiming to have been directly put under pressure by their wife or family.

While men appeared to have suffered from pressure to maintain lifestyles, three (33 per cent) of the women – Debbie, Janet and Sheila – provided accounts identifying them as desperately needing to ensure the financial security and stability of their family, and to protect it from a threatening situation. For Janet, the pressure had been her husband's illness, while Sheila had tried to handle both her own, and her husband's spiralling personal debt, and Debbie had felt the need to intervene in her daughter's drug-addiction problem. Zietz termed women who behaved in this way 'obsessive protectors' (1981: 147) – those in positions of trust who were willing to compromise that trust when faced with the needs and responsibilities of their families.

Five offenders, of whom four were men (13 per cent) and one (11 per cent) a woman, attributed the pressure to their will (to be seen) to succeed, within their families and within society in general. This figure shows that there was little difference between the men and the women – success was therefore apparently important to both.

Turning to the final category, that of seduced actors, among the small number of offenders categorised as such more women appeared to be seduced by their partners (in terms of getting involved in criminal activities) than men, as demonstrated by Laura and Ruth. The men, by contrast, appeared to be more seduced by business associates and colleagues, as evidenced by Adrian, who claimed to have restarted his criminal activities because he was persuaded to do so by the other two financiers involved in his operation. Laura, a 38-year-old Italian, had been convicted of forgery relating to the alteration of her ex-husband's passport in order to go on holiday with her Iraqi boyfriend. While in France, she claimed to have got involved with an Iraqi family whom she attempted to smuggle back into England. She claimed that she did so in order to please her boyfriend, although he put no direct pressure on her to do this. Ruth, on the other hand, had been seduced less directly by her boyfriend and other Nigerian friends with whom she associated in City A. Ruth and others committed financial offences around the city in order to finance bringing other Nigerians into the country.

Rational actors were not purely the domain of the men, however. On a scale of rationality, they appeared to dominate the more 'planned' crimes and boast about their achievements. In contrast, the women tended to be more opportunist actors, committing crimes when circumstances allowed (and with skills equal to the men's). When considering pressure from family situations, this area was not purely the preserve of women, as previous gender research has found. The men in the study appeared to have tried to maintain the lifestyle of their families when situations struck to threaten this, whereas the women seemed to have become involved, as desperate actors, in actually trying to preserve the family when its basic needs were threatened. Although no-one in the sample had been in absolute poverty, some of the women commented that they might well have been had they not taken the action they did. The men were more affected by business pressures, mostly because they tended to be the owners and co-owners in the sample. The women, however, appeared to be more seduced by emotional partners and friends in committing their crimes, while men were more influenced by business associates and colleagues.

How losses affect male and female offenders

Loss considered in the research consisted of that undergone by the offenders themselves (such as their freedom, status and reputation), by their families and by their victims; also considered is an assessment of the costs and benefits of their crimes. It has been argued (for example, by Heidensohn, 1985; Carlen, 1998; 2002) that women's experiences in jail are different and probably worse than those of men. In their interviews loss of freedom and coping were directly brought up by three offenders, two men and one woman. In addition, two women (22 per cent) and one man (3 per cent) raised the issue of loss of freedom first being acutely felt when they had been held for a considerable time in the court cells after their trial, followed by the indignity of being transported to prison.

Because 22 of the men had owned or part-owned a business, financial losses were very important to them, while the one woman who part-owned a business (with her husband) did not mention a loss. Adam and Adrian were the only ones to admit – and to boast about – making money from their crimes, while other men, such as Tom, were keen to point out that they had made no financial gains from their illicit behaviour.

Five (16 per cent) of the men (Gareth, Kevin, Patrick, Michael and Stuart) pointed out that they had lost the right to hold directorships or had been barred from professional associations, thereby not allowing them to work again in their field of expertise after release from prison. None of the women mentioned this, though Sally had been a member of one of the professional accountancy bodies. Peter was the only person who raised the issue of losing vital career-development time, which would affect his life-long learning and earning potential.

Janet was the only woman (11 per cent) who definitely had a job to go out to, whereas nine (29 per cent) of the men were in that position. Janet's job had been kept open for her, as her crime was completely unrelated to her employment. Because of the high percentage of men who were self-employed and who allegedly committed their crimes to save their companies from bankruptcy, many of course had no business to return to. However, with regard to the longer term, five (56 per cent) of the women and 18 (56 per cent) of the men had made plans for the future.

Regarding loss of close others (including partners, family and friends), seven offenders in total raised this issue. This included four (13 per cent) of the men and three (33 per cent) of the women. Six men (19 per cent) also raised the issue of how media reporting of their crimes had further added to the harm done to their previously good reputation. No woman raised any issue about status or reputation.

Both men and women commented on how their family had been supportive, even if their relatives had sometimes found the situation difficult to accept at first. Eight (25 per cent) of the men directly raised the issue of how their families had lost out because of their criminality. They appeared to feel very guilty about this, believing that they had in effect inflicted their sentence more on their families than on themselves. Although both men and women regarded their time in prison as having a negative impact on their relationships with their family, two offenders (Peter and Sheila) both commented on how their crimes and resultant time in prison had help rebuild relationships with certain close relatives, and they were therefore able to see at least some positive aspect to their prison sentence. This appeared to have been affected by past family relationships, rather than the gender of these individuals.

Neither men nor women raised any concerns regarding the organisations and individuals who had actually suffered as a result of their crimes. With regard to jail being a deterrent, nearly all offenders generally felt their crime had not been 'worth it'. However, only men raised the fact that the prospect of an open-prison environment had little deterrent value. In weighing up the costs and benefits of their crimes, it was not surprising to find that Adam and Adrian, as rational and planning actors, were the only two in the whole sample who admitted that their crimes had been worth it, and showed no regrets about what they had done. No woman made such a remark, nor did any admit to having considered committing anything similar in the future. Of the men, only Tom admitted this, and he had dismissed the idea because of his age.

Although women were adamant that their crimes had not been worth the penalties, Debbie, Janet and Sheila all felt that given the situations they had faced (as desperate actors), they had had no choice, and would be unable to see alternatives if faced with the same set of circumstances again. Abuu and Greg also made similar comments about the blackmail to which they had been subjected, though Alison, who similarly claimed to have been blackmailed, did not. Finally, most of the men in the sample (although emphatically not having enjoyed their initial experience in closed prison conditions) raised the issue that jail, certainly in open conditions, was no major deterrent. No woman mentioned this, though half of them were interviewed while serving their sentence in a semi-open prison.

Summary

Men have traditionally been the main gender researched as white-collar crime subjects. Where women have also been considered, generalisations have been asserted about their motives, with greed and gain normally attributed to men's offending and need and family reasons cited as motivations for women. Because women in white-collar research have been mostly viewed from this welfarist position, very few studies have considered females in the equivalent, employment-level positions as their male counterparts to see if there were any gender differences in white-collar offending. However, with increasing numbers of women in the occupational workforce, coupled with the acknowledgement – given the evidence of real-life cases – that women do indeed commit similar white-collar crimes to men, some limited comparative research has been undertaken to challenge the 'pink collar' image of white-collar crime.

In the present study, one major difference emerging from the men's and the women's accounts was how they explained their involvement in crime from a moral standpoint. Preserving their previous good character appeared to be less important to the women than to the men, and the former to be more ready than the latter to accept being labelled a criminal. Additionally, a greater proportion of the women pleaded guilty in court. These findings would appear to accord with previous research on the acceptance of guilt by women, including Rothman and Gandossy (1982) and Collins and Collins (2000).

Reasons given for committing white-collar crime by women during their interviews revealed that they had generally 'drifted' into offending. No woman accounted for her crimes in terms of a rational, calculated plan, as two of the men in the sample did. The women were, however, over-represented when involved in opportunist situations, thereby showing that when in similar occupational positions to the men they were equally able and prepared to take advantage of opportunities.

In prison, both the men and the women appeared equally to feel the negative experiences of being incarcerated and losing their freedom. However, women, unlike men, did not try to create a 'scale of morality' between prisoners based on either their criminality or the crimes they had committed. However, one woman did stress in her accounts areas where she thought of herself as a 'good prisoner'. In summing up their overall experiences, most of the men and all the women appeared to agree that their crime had not been worth committing, especially in view of the problems it had already caused them and would cause them after they left prison.

Levels of research into women and white-collar offending have increased from several decades ago, though at a slower pace than in other areas of criminology. However, there is still scope for much more, in particular comparing like-for-like samples of men and women in similar occupational situations, to see if there is any genuine, replicable evidence of gender differences in white-collar criminality.

Part III
Conclusion

9
Summary

While there are a number of general texts on white-collar crime, most studies have concentrated on case studies, data analysis and theoretical debate. There are surprisingly few texts on the motivations of white-collar offenders, and even fewer which explore the accounts of their life after conviction. This book aims to make some progress towards closing these gaps, and is the result of a number of years' research involving interviews with 41 incarcerated white-collar criminals.

The analysis of the data obtained from the interviews gives a better understanding of how such offenders present their reasons for the commission of their crimes. It also provides information about the views they take of their own moral stance, and of their experience first in court, then in prison. As well as making a contribution to research in this area and to the academic body of knowledge, it is hoped that the present study will exert some influence, however small, on crime-prevention methods, particularly in the workplace, and also on methods of deterring potential white-collar criminals.

The research findings detailed throughout this book will now be considered in this final chapter under the following headings:

- How accounts are presented
- The influence of gender
- Losses
- Implications of the research

How accounts are presented

When providing accounts, individuals will generally try to present themselves as morally 'good people'. For offenders this means minimising the shame brought upon them by their public labelling as a criminal (Sykes and Matza, 1957; Benson, 1984; McBarnet, 1991). During my interviews with the offenders, some very elaborate accounts were given, especially to deny or minimise any wrong-doing. Several types of accounts were used, including refusals, excuses, justifications and concessions (Schönbach, 1980; 1990). The explanations ranged from complete denial of their criminal behaviour to a full admission of guilt, including remorse and sometimes restitution.

Offenders often gave hybrid accounts, referring to a plurality of pressures and motives. These related not simply to financial hardship or business failure, but to a wide range of circumstances contributing to the trajectory of the crimes. Some of the issues in question had existed well before the commission of any illegal act; others had surfaced suddenly, in effect triggering the offending behaviour. In giving their accounts, subjects often made comments which I interpreted as a wish, or even a need, to be 'master of their game'. They had sought to be the best, to have the best and to hold onto a certain social status, while exhibiting all the material goods which they believed were associated with this. Offenders also often felt pressured by their family, either directly or indirectly – in the latter case, particularly where much was expected of them, or where they felt they were being compared with other, successful family members. In the case of other offenders, however, pressure was exerted by themselves, through aspirations which sometimes could not be met. One of the greatest pressures most offenders had experienced was in keeping quiet about their illegal acts and avoiding discovery. Though no-one specifically raised this as an issue, several did mention the relief they felt when being caught.

Many offenders had found themselves in situations from which they could see no exit – what two of the offenders called a 'rollercoaster effect'. For some of the self-employed individuals, and even a few of those employed by others, maintenance of their family appeared to be important, and this in itself added further pressure, not only to continue with their criminal behaviour but to keep up the lifestyle they had already achieved and to which they had become accustomed. In this way, crime became economically compulsive. (However, there was no indication in the accounts that any of the male offenders had been put under any direct pressure by their partners to live up to this expectation.)

For those offenders who had previously been owners of their own business, pressure could be identified at various stages of their commercial life. It was at its greatest mainly when starting up a new company, or when some changes (personal, business-related or in the wider economy) caused financial or other difficulties. For individuals affected by this, their concerns included not only saving their business but also their own livelihood and in many cases that of their family and employees, as well as protecting their own and their company's reputation. For those who had in addition a personal fear of failure, the pressure was further increased.

Fear of failure in business, however, was not limited to those who were self-employed. Several offenders felt pressured to succeed in their chosen professional field; they were acutely aware of (what they perceived as) blocked opportunities, such as lack of promotion, or insufficient acknowledgement of the work they undertook and contribution they made to their organisation. Often, this led to anger against their bosses, and to criminality as a justified act of revenge.

Having considered the content of accounts, I will now look at how they were presented – as embodying refusals, excuses/justifications or concessions.

Refusals

In Chapter 2 we noted that refusals were defined as strategies that individuals utilised to deny responsibility for an offence or its consequences (Gonzales et al, 1990: 611). Mirroring Sykes and Matza's (1957) denial of responsibility, these strategies included both denial of the criminality of their behaviour, and denial of their own involvement. Though it could be argued that refusals should not technically be classified as accounts at all – because the individual does not recognise his/her own guilt, and thus does not accept that there is anything to be accounted for, or that they have any responsibility for the acts that have taken place. In other words, there is no face to be saved.

From the typology of the outer-legal self and inner-moral self as described in Chapter 4, 14 (34 per cent) of those who gave accounts which were effectively refusals were classified as total rejectors, rejecting both the legal guilt in committing the white-collar crime and thus the notion of themselves as criminal. All those interviewed who were placed in this category gave explanations or accounts of varying lengths and types, to detail why they were 'innocent' and wished to preserve their good character. As such, they had pleaded not guilty and did not believe they were guilty of the crime of which they had been convicted. As a consequence, they felt that their treatment was unjust, and that they had been falsely imprisoned.

Two main strategies were employed by total rejectors to defend themselves against their criminal identities. First, they refused to acknowledge that a criminal act had taken place, by describing the activities for which they had been convicted as non-criminal. For example, Michael, the solicitor, claimed that his invoices had not been inflated in cost, and therefore there was no criminal case for him to answer. Others who denied that their activities were criminal claimed that those who had convicted them did not understand the business in question, and therefore were not in a position to judge the actions of the defendant.

The second strategy utilised by total rejectors to deny their criminality was to claim that although they acknowledged that an illegal act had been committed, they had not been personally responsible for it. Usually, this refusal involved displacing blame onto others – business partners, associates, other colleagues or partners; an example of this was Pam's account, which blamed her husband for the crimes she (and he) had been convicted of. Other offenders claimed that they had been victimised, either through blackmail or being 'picked upon' by the police. Total rejectors thus attempted to reason, through their accounts, that they were not criminals.

Excuses and justifications

Located between refusals and concessions, are the wider categories of accounts known as excuses or justifications. In the study nearly all the offenders used some kind of excuse or justification to explain their criminal behaviour. These types of accounts came mainly from those individuals classified as either tactical acceptors or tactical rejectors. (However, the accounts of those individuals classified as total rejectors or acceptors also sometimes contained excuses and justifications).

Unlike refusals, excuses or justifications always recognise that a wrongful act has taken place, but individuals giving these accounts may argue that they are permissible under certain circumstances, and in some instances even necessary. Excuses tend to be more defensive in nature, whereas justifications are more positive statements, explaining the circumstances of the actions. The accounts given by the offenders in the sample consisted more of justifications than excuses, as they were keen to present their accounts in a positive way. Both excuses and justifications can be achieved by using several of the techniques of neutralisation described by Sykes and Matza (1957). These include denial of injury; denial of a victim; condemnation of condemners; and appeals to higher loyalties. They do not include denial of responsibility, as this is subsumed under accounts of refusals.

Denial of injury, as one way of excusing criminal acts, raises the question of distinguishing between crime and legitimate action. This was demonstrated for example through the account of Harry, who was appealing against his sentence because he felt that his business had been totally misunderstood by both the judge and jury. When accounts of this nature are given by white-collar criminals, it is often difficult to separate normal and genuine business activity, on the one hand, from illegal practice on the other. This is especially pertinent in the area of white-collar crime, as often the actions in question take place in the context of people's occupation – their ordinary, everyday working life. An example, highlighted in the accounts of some business-owners, was the question of whether a firm had been trading solvent or insolvent. All the individuals affected by this claimed that they were trading solvent, though the court had found otherwise. Offenders argued, though, that judge and jury had failed to understand the complexities of their business, and that they had therefore been wrongly convicted.

A further way that offenders denied injury when giving their accounts was to claim that although they accepted they had committed an illegal act, they believed that no one had been hurt by it. This was particularly noted by those who had offended against large companies or public organisations. Additionally, where the Internet had been used to defraud companies or individuals, individuals argued that as there was no identifiable victim, no one had been injured by their actions. One offender argued that those who allow their personal details to appear on such a public forum 'deserve' to be defrauded. At a less technical level, 'just borrowing', as outlined by Cressey (1953), was found as a justification where individuals took advantage of money which had been entrusted to them. In Geoff's account, he pointed out his manufacturing company had hit poor times during a recession, and therefore he used money illegally obtained from factoring companies to keep his own company going, with the intention of paying them back once he had been able to trade himself out of trouble. Unfortunately, as in many other cases where this justification was used, the situation had worsened and he was unable to repay the money taken.

Considering now those explanations in which offenders denied victimisation in their accounts, individuals using this technique challenged the very nature of the offence, claiming that under certain circumstances individuals or organisations 'had it coming', and deserved the crimes committed against them. One of the most frequently-cited reasons for this was dissatisfaction with employers, and retaliation against them – feeling put upon, as in the case of Sally, the management accountant who felt that her boss was too 'hands-off', or Janet, who felt let down by her company when she had asked for a pay rise to cover the cost of a new mortgage. Often, such justifications are linked to issues of power and authority, where individuals are able to vent their frustrations against their boss via criminality because of the senior positions they hold. For example, Dave, the management accountant who believed that he had been being unjustifiably held back in his career, said that he believed his illegal behaviour had gone unremarked not only because the accounts he prepared were correct and always completed on time, but also because of the senior position he held.

What all these examples of denying the victim have in common is that criminality was made possible by the weakness of organisational control systems and management monitoring procedures. Sally believed that her boss should have noticed that something was wrong with his company accounts, especially given that the money she purloined constituted a relatively substantial proportion of the firm's overall turnover. Repeatedly, the offenders' accounts provided examples of poor management procedures, with very little review of accountancy controls and little supervision and checking of payments and refunds, often involving signed, authorised payments being returned to the originator for posting. One interesting case was that of Marvin, whose account included the justification that the Post Office deserved to be defrauded by his avoidance of postage charges, because at a previous date they had lost some of his promotional mail, which he claimed might have adversely affected his business. What Marvin was doing in his account was what Cohen (1991) describes as a particular neutralisation technique – in turning the victim into the original wrong-doer. A situation is thus created where it easier to see any subsequent acts against the victim as legitimate and justified. Finally, several subjects were keen to point out how much worse their crimes could have been given the weaknesses of the company they had offended against; they attempted to mitigate their crime on the basis they did not take as much as they could have, at the same time trying to restore some morality to themselves by showing how 'controlled' they had been.

The next technique of neutralisation that offenders in the sample used as a means of excusing or justifying their illegal behaviour was 'condemnation of the condemners' – or what McCorkle and Korn (1954) call 'rejection of the rejectors', by which they mean that those making the original accusations are rejected by the offenders. Usually, the latter try to claim that they are no worse than their accusers. As we have seen, this was a common account used by those classified as total rejectors – particularly by garage owners against the police. In addition to the police, being the obvious agency that offenders would seek to target, are the media. For reasons different to those involved in accusing the police, individuals used techniques of neutralisation towards the media in order to salvage what little they could of their reputation and character. For example, Gareth and his business partners were very bitter towards the television programme which had first highlighted the problems in their original company, and had then, in a later programme, reported on them when they set up a new company; in effect they blamed the television company for their eventual business downfall. Offenders also complained about biased reporting by the press that had made them and their offences seem worse, or at least different to what in fact they had been. For example, Abuu felt bitter about his alcohol and gambling problems being highlighted by the media, claiming neither was related to why he had committed his crimes. Jason said that the press had picked out an elderly woman from his story, whereas she had not been typical of the people he had defrauded. He also claimed to have paid back all the money to his victims, which was not reported. Only one offender, Peter, stated that he did not feel badly towards the media, as he had admitted to what he had done and said it had been accurately reported.

Appealing to higher loyalties was the last type of neutralisation technique, also described by Sykes and Matza (1957) and displayed by offenders in their accounts. This technique is used by individuals when they believe that their needs and demands, or those of groups they belong to, overrule other loyalties to higher causes, sometimes even including the law (ibid: 669). Examples of this in the accounts given were noted when individuals claimed they had not committed their crimes for themselves. For example, Gerry commented he was not greedy himself, but had given money and goods to his mother; in the same context Geoff commented that he felt he had a duty to his employees to do what he had to, to preserve his company and thus safeguard his employees' jobs. More personal reasons were cited, in particular from Laura, who claimed she had forged her Iraqi boyfriend's passport in order to allow them to go on a holiday together, and that the trouble she got into once there, over smuggling a Iraqi family back into Britain, was to show her love for him. There were family reasons given, especially where financial problems were being encountered, such as those faced by Debbie and Sheila, both of whom commented that although they wished they had not got involved in their crimes in the first place, they were at a loss to see what else they could have done in the circumstances. That is not to say that men did not commit crimes for their family's sake – but their reasons were more focused towards saving their own business, on which the family's income depended.

Concessions

In the accounts, concessions and refusals are at opposite ends of the scale; the former are seen as the most positive type of accounts. They may also be defined as elaborate apologies, which may involve regret or embarrassment, and possibly restitution (Goffman, 1971). For example, Anne, the supermarket-garage manager, had no particular explanations for her criminal behaviour, but was embarrassed about her actions and deeply regretted the whole situation. Similarly, Debbie, the restaurant manager, wrote a letter of apology to the judge, explaining the circumstances surrounding her embezzlement from the restaurant, and offering to pay the money back instead of serving a custodial sentence. The men also sometimes apologised and expressed remorse about their behaviour, though in many cases less readily than the women.

Within the sample, a number of offenders had tried to 'make good' their crimes, at least in part, by paying back some or all of their illegal gains. For example, Jason, the furniture-maker, had voluntarily paid back £110,000 to companies he had defrauded, having sold his business as a going concern. However, it was not clear from the various accounts whether paying money back in this way had been a purely selfless act, demonstrating a real desire to change, or a gesture towards the court which might have had the effect of mitigating their criminality prior to their trial, to the point where a prison sentence might have been reduced, or even avoided altogether. Jason, for example, even though he claimed that he had willingly paid back the money involved in his crimes, did say that he felt bitter about serving time in jail as well. Additionally, Debbie not only wrote a letter to the judge explaining the circumstances surrounding her crimes, but also offered to pay the money back, instead of being sent to prison.

Some offenders also expressed a desire to change once having left prison, and to lead a normal, non-criminal life thereafter; but were unable to say what they would do if faced with the same set of circumstances. In particular, this was characteristic of those classified as desperate actors, especially when faced with family and business problems. Those who were allegedly being blackmailed also made comments along the lines of not knowing what else they could have done under the circumstances, and given the fear they lived under.

Not all the offenders, however, intended or wanted to change. Neither of the two individuals who had planned their crimes, in advance and purely as money-making schemes, made any mention of changing once they had been released, except that they would be able to work less or not at all, because of the money they had retained from their criminal activities.

The influence of gender

To date, there has been comparatively little research on female white-collar offending, and what has been published so far has revealed a mixture of findings. This is due in part to few females being included in samples, or where they have been, not being considered alongside comparable male offenders. Although the research for the present study never set out to examine this area in detail, a number of issues concerning women's accounts of their white-collar crime, as opposed to men's, were identified.

In moral terms, the women in the sample appeared more ready to admit to and accept their legal guilt and to show remorse, with 78 per cent pleading guilty, compared to 59 per cent of the men. The majority of them were classified as acceptors, suggesting that being labelled a criminal may be felt as less of a stigma by women than by men. The latter, on the other hand, were found in general to be more tactical players (mostly tactical acceptors), willing to gamble with their reputation in order to avoid or reduce a custodial sentence. However, a proportion of the men fought against being labelled criminal, even continuing this into prison, creating a moral scale where white-collar criminals were seen as superior to street criminals, and pointing out that the former were not 'real' criminals. The women, on the other hand, did not appear to be so concerned about this distinction.

Looking at the moral aspects of the accounts, no woman accounted for her crime in terms of (from the offender's perspective) 'unacceptable' motives, such as greed or addiction, though several of the men did. However, both men and women exhibited altruistic motives in their accounts, especially claiming to have committed their crimes for the sake of others, such as family members and employees. Although some of the accounts of the women tended to focus directly on the safety and security of their families, the men accounted for their altruism in a more indirect manner, with motives such as keeping their jobs, saving their employees' jobs and maintaining their family's income and lifestyle.

Only two offenders in the sample, both of whom were men, recounted that they had planned and executed their crimes as part of a sophisticated and rational plan. However, when considering the skills applied by those offenders termed here 'opportunistic', there were no marked differences between the men and the women in the identification and execution of these opportunities. The women were as skilled as the men in taking advantage of such situations, and in abusing power, authority and trust if they decided or needed to do so.

Both men and women accounted negatively for losses as a result of their criminal behaviour, loss of their freedom being one of the most commonly mentioned. In terms of professional and status losses, the men appeared more concerned about these than the women. Although women directly raised the issue of providing for their families as a reason for committing their crimes, only men raised the issue of how their families had lost out through their crimes and prison sentences. In concluding whether the crimes had been worth it overall, both men and women were equally agreed that it had not, with the exception of two men who had accepted that a jail sentence might be the price of their gains.

Losses

As many of the offenders claimed to have drifted into their criminal activities by accident, one would have thought that relief at being caught, which some offenders commented on, would have alleviated their pressures. However, once charged, convicted and sent to prison, a whole new set of pressures were felt. Payne (2003) details the general losses that white-collar criminals face when they are caught and subsequently sentenced. In this book, the losses resulting from offenders' behaviour were discussed under three heads: losses to the perpetrators themselves, to close others and to victims.

Losses experienced by the offenders themselves included loss of jobs, businesses, money and status, including loss of social and/or professional standing due to adverse media attention. However, for most individuals the greatest loss was their incarceration, and the resultant deprivation of liberty. The offenders in the sample coped to varying extents with their new lives and surroundings in prison; this was sometimes correlated with how long they had already served there. Whereas it might be assumed that many white-collar criminals would be unable to cope in prison, and feel threatened by other prisoners from different backgrounds, most (although frequently distancing themselves from these other inmates), appeared to earn a form of respect from them. This was particularly noticeable in accounts where individuals explained how they helped other prisoners to read, write, complete forms and generally to deal with problems (especially relationship breakdowns and parole refusals). It was also noted that some white-collar offenders appeared to feel sorry for other groups of prisoners, particularly when reflecting on their own crimes and realising how fortunate they were by comparison – in having the chance to start again, and access to resources to enable them to do so.

One loss which was a recurrent theme throughout the accounts of the offenders was how their families were coping, both practically and with the stigma of having a close relative in prison. A number of individuals commented on their feeling that their family, more than themselves, had been burdened with the consequences of their criminality. However, although many offenders voiced great concern over the plight of their close others, none raised directly the issue of the losses that their victims had suffered. Instead, mention of victims appeared to intimate more concern about who they would and would not consider committing crimes against.

Whether due to the nature of white-collar criminals or to the shock of being in prison – a sharp contrast with their usual external life – most of the offenders in the sample showed great potential for changing their ways, and clearly wanted to do so after the experience they had gone and were going through. Several in particular appeared to have spent considerable thought on identifying what had gone wrong, at what juncture this had occurred, and what they could do differently in the future. This post-offending analysis mainly took place after incarceration. How offenders viewed their crimes and the circumstances surrounding them also appeared to correlate with the stage their prison sentence had reached at the time of the interview. While some felt acutely remorseful and determined to change at the outset, there were others to whom, once they had spent some time in open-prison conditions and settled into a routine, life did not seem so bad, and as a result their crimes were no longer viewed as so catastrophic for them; and for some offenders, time in prison had enabled them to rebuild relationships with their families.

As a sign of their commitment to changing (or being seen as wishing to do so), a number of offenders claimed to have future plans to ensure that they did not get themselves into situations like those which had led to their crimes. For example, several individuals had trained in new areas of work, because they would find it difficult or impossible to return to their old trades and professions. Gareth planned to teach golf and thus to avoid the pressures of managing businesses, and Tom had trained as a hairdresser – a complete change from running a building firm. However, Sheila indicated that she had trained to be a hairdresser to avoid revealing to future employers that she had spent time in prison. Ruth commented how she was frightened of returning to City A, even simply for study purposes, because she was afraid of getting sucked back into her old way of life by other Nigerians living there. Debbie felt so ashamed about returning to her home town that she had decided, with her family, to move abroad and start a business there.

Final remarks

In this final chapter I have summarised how offenders will struggle, when their characters are threatened, to preserve their standing – to themselves, to others and to the community in general. I have also attempted to demonstrate a number of the techniques they use to achieve this. White-collar offenders are not a homogenous group, and although most individuals in the sample tried to give reasons for committing their crimes, many struggled to explain fully to themselves, and to me, what had happened and why. During this process, many attempted to try and present themselves as continuing to be basically good and moral individuals; they did this through various strategies, often giving multiple reasons for their behaviour. Not the least of these strategies was acceptance of guilt and responsibility at some level.

However, not all offenders sought to preserve their characters and save face, because they did not believe they had done anything illegal, and therefore fought against being labelled as criminals. There was a minority of individuals however, who readily admitted their guilt, to both themselves and others, but made little or no attempt to save face, either because it did not matter to them, or because they had no coherent explanation for their behaviour.

The white-collar criminals' accounts discussed in this book have undeniable implications for fraud prevention – in terms of both preventive methods and the way they are implemented. We have seen the importance of good internal control systems for deterring white-collar crime, and observed the need for a clear and strongly defined anti-fraud culture within organisations. White-collar offenders' claims as to what works or does not work, is an excellent resource, and we should take note of what they say. We have also seen that it is not just men whom we should profile as potential fraudsters – in comparable situations, women are as adept as men in identifying opportunities and then committing crimes; however, more research in this area is needed to flesh out the picture of women and workplace crime. However, in a climate of scarce resources available for security, we have to acknowledge that we cannot do everything, all the time. Even if we could, we have observed there are some individuals who may be willing to accept the risk of punishment and even imprisonment for what they believe will be the proceeds of their crime.

Notes

Chapter 3   Undertaking the Research

1 Personal correspondence, via email (John.Braithwaite@anu.edu.au), 27 September 2006.
2 Due to the relatively small number of subjects and to the type of material, no statistical tests were performed. However, percentages are given for each group in order to assess whether substantive differences occur between groups; also, absolute numbers within categories will be taken into account. Given the nature of the data, the interpretation of substantive differences found in terms of percentages and absolute numbers can only be qualitative.
3 These two organisations merged on 18 April 2005 to form HM Revenue and Customs (HMRC).

Chapter 4   Outer-Legal Self and Inner-Moral Self

1 Power of Attorney is the exercise of control, by agreement, over a person's financial and other assets by a solicitor or other responsible person.
2 A company 'trading solvent' is deemed able to meet any debts outstanding and to discharge any liabilities it has incurred.
3 Flotation refers to a private company deciding to list its shares for purchase and sale through a public market.
4 Doig discusses at length the suitability of courts and jurors as adjudicators in complex white-collar cases (2006: 206–9).
5 To turn Queen's Evidence is to give evidence against a co-accused. To allow this to occur, the person giving such evidence must first either plead guilty or be found guilty; this is because a defendant cannot give evidence against another defendant. Turning Queen's Evidence often results in a substantial reduction in sentence.

Chapter 5   Motivation, Opportunity and Rationality

1 A standard Euro-pallet measures 1200×1000mm, and 480 packets of (20) cigarettes would fit on each layer. Duty payable on a packet of 20 cigarettes in 1998/99 (when Adrian's operation began) was £2.56. Therefore, duty evaded per layer would equate to £1228.50. If pallets were stacked 1000mm high, 55 layers could be fitted onto each. This would equate to duty evaded of £67,584 per palette. If Adrian was importing eight palettes a week at the start of his activities, this would mean duty evaded of over half a million pounds a week (£540,672).
2 'Teeming and lading' describes a process whereby income received by an organisation is not banked immediately, nor assigned against the correct debtor's account. The debtor may, however, receive a receipt, thereby leaving someone

in the organisation to bank the money and misappropriate the income against other accounts, usually their own.

3 BACS is an acronym for the Bankers Automated Clearing Services system, which is designed for making regular automated payments to the same people or customers and is widely adopted by many companies.

Chapter 6   The Self as a Moral Person

1 Hudson (2005), in her analysis of interviews with sex offenders, identified nine techniques. These were: distancing by category; degree of physical contact; consent; premeditation; the age of the victim; relationship to the victim; repeat offending; temporary aberration; and shame.

2 For further discussion on the impact of cyber-crime, see for example Newman and Clarke, 2003; Jewkes, 2003; Smith, Grabosky and Urbas, 2004; Grabosky, 2006; Wall, 2007; 2009.

3 Prisoners have three levels of status – basic, standard and enhanced. Prisoners on the enhanced level are awarded additional privileges, such as extra visits and additional money. All prisoners start on the standard level, and according to their behaviour can be moved up or down, gaining or losing privileges.

Chapter 7   Offenders' Afterthoughts

1 Smith (2003: 5) in a conference paper to the Evaluation in Crime and Justice: Trends and Methods, entitled *Methodological impediments to researching serious fraud in Australia and New Zealand* analysed cases that had resulted in a judicial determination during 1998 and 1999 and found that the most lengthy proceedings by jurisdictions varied from 3 years 11 months to 15 years 6 months.

2 A confiscation order is made after conviction to deprive the defendant of the benefit that he has obtained from crime (Source: Crown Prosecution Service (2009)).

Chapter 8   Accounts and Gender

1 A$165,505 and A$1,340,532 for women and men respectively.

2 It is acknowledged that the length of sentence imposed on individuals is not based purely on the proceeds of their crime(s), but is influenced by a series of mitigating or aggravating factors, including the complexity of the case, any previous convictions and what plea the offender enters in court.

Bibliography

Aitken, J. Interview in *Toffs Behind Bars*. Channel 5 TV: 2002, October 11.

Alalehto, T. (2003) 'Economic Crime: Does Personality Matter?' *International Journal of Offender Therapy and Comparative Criminology* 47(3): 335–55.

Arksey, H. and Knight, P. (1999) *Interviewing for Social Scientists: An Introductory Resource with Examples*. London: Sage.

Australian Institute of Criminology and PricewaterhouseCoopers (2003) 'Serious Fraud in Australia and New Zealand'. *Research and Public Policy Series*, No. 48. Canberra: Australian Institute of Criminology.

Bamfield, J. (2006) 'Management', in M. Gill (ed.) *The Handbook of Security*. Basingstoke: Palgrave.

Baumeister, R. and Newman, L. (1994) 'How Stories Make Sense of Personal Experiences: Motives That Shape Autobiographical Narratives'. *Personality and Social Psychology Bulletin* 20(6): 676–90.

Baxter, L.A. (1984) 'An Investigation of Compliance-Gaining as Politeness'. *Human Communication Research* 10: 427–56.

Becker, G. (1974) 'Crime and Punishment: An Economic Approach', in G. Becker and W. Landes (eds) *Essays on the Economics of Crime and Punishment*. New York: Columbia University Press.

Becker, H. and Geer, B. (2004) 'Participant Observation Interviewing', in C. Seale (ed.) *Social Research Methods*. London: Routledge.

Benson, M.L. (1984) 'The Fall From Grace: Loss of Occupational Status as a Consequence of Conviction for a White-Collar Crime'. *Criminology* 22(4): 573–93.

Benson, M.L. (1985) 'Denying the Guilty Mind: Accounting for Involvement in a White-Collar Crime'. *Criminology* 23(4): 583–608.

Benson, M.L. (1990) 'Emotions and Adjudications: Status Degradation Among White-Collar Criminals'. *Justice Quarterly* 7(3): 515–28.

Benson, M.L. and Cullen, F.T. (1988) 'The Special Sensitivity of White-Collar Offenders to Prison: A Critique and Research Agenda'. *Journal of Criminal Justice* 16: 213–21.

Benson, M.L. and Simpson, S. (2009) *White-Collar Crime: An Opportunity Perspective*. New York: Routledge.

Bernasco, W. (2010) *Offenders on Offending: Learning about Crime from Criminals*. Cullompton: Willan Publishing.

Billig, M., Condor, S., Edward, D., Gane, M., Middleton, D. and Radley, A. (1988) *Ideological Dilemmas: A Social Psychology of Everyday Thinking*. London: Sage.

Blickle, G., Schlegel, A., Fassbender, P. and Klein, U. (2006) 'Some Personality Correlates of Business White-Collar Crime'. *Applied Psychology: An International Review* 55(2): 220–33.

Bloch, H.A. and Geis, G. (1962) *Men, Crime and Society*. New York: Random House.

Blum, R.H. (1972) *Deceivers and Deceived*. Springfield, IL: Charles Thomas.

Blumberg, P. (1989) *The Predatory Society: Deception in the American Market Place*. New York: Oxford University Press.

Box, S. (1983) *Power, Crime and Mystification*. London: Tavistock.

Braithwaite, J. (1985) 'White-Collar Crime'. *Annual Review of Sociology* 11: 1–25.

Braithwaite, J. (1989) *Crime, Shame and Reintegration*. New York: Cambridge University Press.

Braithwaite, J. (1992) 'Poverty, Power and White-Collar Crime', in K. Schlegel and D. Weisburd (eds) *White-Collar Crime Reconsidered*. Boston, MA: Northeastern University Press.

Braithwaite, J. (2006) Personal email correspondence with J. Braithwaite, [John.Braithwaite@anu.edu.au] 27 September 2006 'Reference Query'.

Braithwaite, J. and Geis, G. (1982) 'On Theory and Action for Corporate Crime Control'. *Crime and Delinquency* 28: 292–314.

Braithwaite, J. and Makkai, T. (1991) 'Testing an Expected Utility Model of Corporate Deterrence'. *Law and Society Review* 25: 7–39.

Breed, B. (1979) *White Collar Bird*. London: John Clarke Books.

Brocket, C. Interview in *Toffs Behind Bars*. Channel 5 TV: 2002, October 11.

Brown and Levinson (1987) *Politeness: Some Universals in Language Usage*. Cambridge: Cambridge University Press.

Button, M., Lewis, C. and Tapley, J. (2010) *Fraud Typologies and Victims of Fraud*. London: NFA Literature Review.

Carlen, P. (1992) 'Criminal Women and Criminal Justice: The Limits to, and Potential of, Feminist and Left Realist Perspectives', in R. Matthews and J. Young (eds) *Issues in Realist Criminology*. London: Sage.

Carlen, P. (1998) *Sledgehammer: Women's Imprisonment at the Millennium*. London: Macmillan.

Carlen, P. (2002) 'Introduction: Women and Punishment', in P. Carlen (ed.) *Women and Punishment: The Struggle for Justice*. Cullompton: William Publishing.

Carlen, P. and Cook, D. (1989) (eds) *Paying for Crime*. Milton Keynes: Open University Press.

Carlen, P., Hicks, J., O'Dwyer, J., Christina, D. and Tchaikovsky, C. (1985) *Criminal Women*. Cambridge: Polity Press.

Chambliss, W. (1964) 'The Negative Self: An Empirical Assessment of a Theoretical Assumption'. *Sociological Inquiry* 35: 108–12.

Chapple, C. and Nofziger, S. (2000) 'Bingo! Hints of Deviance in the Accounts of Sociability and Profit of Bingo Players'. *Deviant Behaviour* 21: 489–517.

Clinard, M.B. and Quinney, R. (1973) *Criminal Behaviour Systems: A Typology*. New York: Holt, Rinehart and Winston.

Clinard, M.B. and Yeager, P.C. (1980) *Corporate Crime*. New York: Free Press.

Cohen, S. (2001) *States of Denial: Knowing about Atrocities and Suffering*. Cambridge: Polity Press.

Coleman, J.W. (1987) 'Toward an Integrated Theory of White-Collar Crime'. *American Journal of Sociology* 93(2): 406–39.

Coleman, J.W. (1994) *The Criminal Elite: The Sociology of White-Collar Crime (3rd ed.)*. New York: St. Martin's Press.

Collins, J.M. and Collins, M.D. (April 6, 2000) *White-Collar Women Steal For Love* [On-line]. URL: http://www.apbnews.com Accessed June 15, 2002.

Copes, H. and Hochstetler, A. (2006) 'Why I'll Talk: Offenders' Motives for Participating in Qualitative Research', in P. Cromwell (ed.) *In Their Own Words: Criminals on Crime* (4th edn). Los Angeles: Roxbury.

Copes, H. and Hochstetler, A. (2010) 'Interviewing the Incarcerated: Pitfalls and Promises', in W. Bernasco (ed.) (2010) *Offenders on Offending: Learning about Crime from Criminals*. Cullompton: Willan Publishing.

Cornish, D. and Clarke R. (1986) 'Preface', in D. Cornish and R. Clarke (eds) *The Reasoning Criminal*. New York: Springer Kerlap.

Cornish, D. and Clarke, R. (2005) 'Opportunities, Precipitators and Criminal Decisions', in *Theory for Practice in Situational Crime Prevention. Crime Prevention Studies*, Vol. 16. Monsey: Criminal Justice Press.

Cressey, D.R. (1953) *Other People's Money: A Study in the Social Psychology of Embezzlement*. New York: Free Press.

Croall, H. (1992) *White-Collar Crime*. Buckingham: Open University Press.

Croall, H. (2001) *Understanding White Collar Crime*. Buckingham: Open University Press.

Croall, H. (2003) 'Men's Business? Some Gender Questions About White Collar Crime'. *Criminal Justice Matters* 53: 26–7.

Croall, H. (2010) 'Middle-range Business Crime: Rogue and Respectable Businesses, Family Firms and Entrepreneurs', in F. Brookman, M. Maguire, H. Pierpoint and T.H. Bennett (eds) *Handbook of Crime*. Cullompton: Willan Publishing.

Crown Prosecution Service (2009) *Proceeds of Crime Guidance: Confiscation and Ancillary Orders – Post POCA 2002*. London: Crown Prosecution Service.

Cullen, F.T., Maakestad, W.J. and Cavender, G. (1987) *Corporate Crime Under Attack: The Ford Pinto Case and Beyond*. Cincinnati, Ohio: Anderson Publishing.

Cupach, W.R. and Metts, R. (1994) *Facework*. California: Thousand Oaks.

Cupach, W.R., Metts, R. and Hazelton, V. (1986) 'Coping with Embarrassing Predicaments: Remedial Strategies and Their Perceived Utility'. *Journal of Language and Social Psychology* 5: 181–200.

Daly, K. (1989) 'Gender and Varieties of White-Collar Crime'. *Criminology* 27: 769–94.

Davies, P.A. (1997) 'Women, Crime and an Informal Economy: Female Offending and Crime for Gain'. *The British Criminology Conferences: Selected Proceedings Vol. 2*. Papers from the British Society of Criminology Conference, Belfast, 1997. M. Brogden (ed.), British Society of Criminology.

Davies, P.A. (2003a) 'Is Economic Crime a Man's Game?' *Feminist Theory* 4(3): 283–303.

Davies, P.A. (2003b) 'Women, Crime and Work: Gender and the Labour Market'. *Criminal Justice Matters* 53: 18–19.

Denzin, N.K. (1970) *Sociological Methods: A Sourcebook*. New York: McGraw-Hill.

Dexter, L.A. (1970) *Elite and Specialized Interviewing*. Evanston: Northwestern University Press.

Dilulio, J. (1987) *Governing Prisons*. New York: Free Press.

Dodge, M. (2009) *Women and White-Collar Crime*. Englewood Cliffs, NJ: Prentice Hall.

Doig, A. (2006) *Fraud*. Cullompton: Willan Publishing.

Duffield, G. and Grabosky, P. (2001) 'The Psychology of Fraud'. *Trends and Issues in Crime and Criminal Justice*, No. 199. Canberra: Australian Institute of Criminology.

Edelhertz, H. (1970) *The Nature, Impact and Prosecution of White-Collar Crime*. Washington DC: National Institute of Law Enforcement and Criminal Justice.

Ernst & Young (2003) *Fraud the Unmanaged Risk: Eight Global Survey*. Johannesburg: Ernst and Young.

Finch, J. (1984) '"It's Great to Have Someone to Talk to": Ethics and Politics of Interviewing Women', in C. Bell and H. Roberts (eds) *Social Researching: Politics, Problems, Practice*. London: Routledge.

Fox, J.A. and Tracy, P.E. (1989) 'A Field Experiment on Insurance Fraud in Auto Body Repair'. *Criminology* 27(3): 589–603.

Fraud Act 2006 (c35) London: Office of Public Sector Information.

Friedrichs, D.O. (1996) *Trusted Criminals: White Collar Crime in Contemporary Society* (1st edn). Belmont: Wadsworth.

Fritsche, I. (2002) 'Account Strategies for the Violation of Social Norms: Integration and Extension of Sociological and Social Psychological Typologies'. *Journal for the Theory of Social Behaviour* 32(4): 371–94.

Geis, G. (1967) 'White Collar Crime: The Heavy Electrical Equipment Antitrust Cases of 1961', in M. Clinnard and R. Quinney (eds) *Criminal Behaviour Systems: A Typology*. New York: Holt, Rinehart and Winston.

Ghiselli, R. and Ismail, J. (1998) 'Employee Theft and Efficacy of Certain Control Procedures in Commercial Food Service Operations'. *Journal of Hospitality & Tourism Research*, 22(2): 174–87.

Gibbons, D. (1994) *Talking about Crime and Criminals: Problems and Issues in Theory Development in Criminology*. Englewood Cliffs, NJ: Prentice Hall.

Gill, M. (ed.) (1994) *Crime at Work – Studies in Security and Crime Prevention*. Leicester: Perpetuity Press.

Gill, M. (2005) *Learning From Fraudsters*. Protiviti.

Gill, M. (2007) *Learning from Fraudsters: Reinforcing the Message*. Protiviti.

Gill, M. and Goldstraw-White, J.E. (2010) 'Theft and Fraud by Employees', in F. Brookman, M. Maguire, H. Pierpoint and T.H. Bennett (eds) *Handbook of Crime*. Cullompton: Willan Publishing.

Gill, M. and Goldstraw-White, J.E. (forthcoming) 'Motives', in A. Doig and S. Greenhalgh (eds) *The Handbook of Fraud Investigation and Prevention*. Aldershot: Gower.

Goffman, E. (1959) *The Presentation of Self in Everyday Life*. New York: Doubleday.

Goffman, E. (1971) *Relations in Public: Microstudies of the Public Order*. New York: Basic Books.

Goldstraw, J.E. (2002) 'White-Collar–Frilly-Cuff: Gender Difference in White-Collar Crime'. Paper presented at the *British Society of Criminology Conference*. Keele University, 2002, July 18–21.

Goldstraw, J.E. (2003) 'They Had It Coming: White-Collar Offenders Talk About the "Justification" of Their Crimes'. Paper presented at the *ANZSOC Conference*, Sydney, 2003, October 1–3.

Goldstraw, J.E., Smith, R.G. and Sakurai, Y. (2005) 'Gender and Serious Fraud in Australia and New Zealand'. *Trends and Issues in Crime and Criminal Justice*, No. 292. Canberra: Australian Institute of Criminology.

Gonzales, M.H., Pederson, J.H., Manning, D.J. and Wetter, D.W. et al (1990) 'Pardon My Gaffe: Effects of Sex, Status, and Consequence Severity on Accounts'. *Journal of Personality and Social Psychology* 58(4): 610–21.

Gonzales, M.H., Manning, D.J. and Haugen, J. (1992) 'Explaining Our Sins: Factors Influencing Offender Accounts and Anticipated Victim Responses'. *Journal of Personality and Social Psychology* 62(6): 958–71.

Gottfredson, M.R. and Hirschi, T. (1990) *A General Theory of Crime*. Stanford, CA: Stanford University Press.

Grabosky, P.N. (2006) *Electronic Crime*. New York: Prentice Hall.

Grabosky, P.N. and Duffield, G. (2001) 'Red Flags of Fraud'. *Trends and Issues in Crime and Criminal Justice*, No. 200. Canberra: Australian Institute of Criminology.

Grabosky, P.N. and Smith, R.G. (1998) *Crime in the Digital Age: Controlling Telecommunications and Cyberspace Illegalities*. New Brunswick, NJ: Transaction Publishers.

Greenwald, A.G. and Breckler, S.J. (1985) 'To Whom is the Self Presented?' in B.R. Schlenker (ed.) *The Self and Social Life*. New York: McGraw-Hill.

Hayes, R. (2007) *Retail Security and Loss Prevention* (2nd edn). Basingstoke: Palgrave.

Hayes, R. (2008) 'Strategies to Detect and Prevent Work-place Dishonesty'. *CRISP Report*, ASIS Foundation. Online at: http://www.asisonline.org/foundation/noframe/research/crisp.html.

Heath, J. (2008) 'Business Ethics and Moral Motivation: A Criminological Perspective'. *Journal of Business Ethics* 83: 595–614.

Heatherton, T. and Nichols, P. (1994) 'Personal Accounts of Successful Versus Failed Attempts at Life Change'. *Personality and Social Psychology Bulletin* 20(6): 664–75.

Heidensohn, F. (1985) *Women and Crime*. Basingstoke: Macmillan.

Heltsley, M. and Calhoun, T.C. (2003) 'The Good Mother: Neutralisation Techniques Used by Pageant Mothers'. *Deviant Behaviour* 24: 81–100.

Herlenger, C. (1992) 'Country Club Criminals'. *Scholastic Update* 125(1): 11–12.

Hilton, D. (1990) 'Conversational Processes and Causal Explanation'. *Psychological Bulletin* 107(1): 65–81.

Hindelang, M.J. (1970) 'The Commitment of Delinquents to Their Misdeeds: Do Delinquents Drift?' *Social Problems* 21: 370–85.

Hirschi, T. (1969) *Causes of Delinquency*. Berkeley: University of California Press.

Hobbs, D. (2000) 'Researching Serious Crime', in R.D. King and E. Wincup (eds) *Doing Research on Crime and Justice*. Oxford: Oxford University Press.

Holtfreter, K. (2005) 'Is Occupational Fraud "Typical" White-Collar Crime? A Comparison of Individual and Organizational Characteristics'. *Journal of Criminal Justice* 33: 353–65.

Hudson, K. (2005) *Offending Identities: Sex Offenders' Perspectives on Their Treatment and Management*. Cullompton: Willan Publishing.

Hunter, B. (2004) *Desistance and White-Collar Crime*. Unpublished master's dissertation: Keele University.

Jackall, R. (1988) *Moral Maze: The World of Corporate Managers*. Oxford: Oxford University Press.

Jewkes, Y. (2003) *Dot.cons: Crime, Deviance and Identity on the Internet*. Cullompton: Willan Publishing.

Jeyasingh, J.V. (1986) 'Inside White Collar Crime'. *Social Defence* 21(82): 17–24.

Jones, S. (2004) 'Depth Interviewing', in C. Seale (ed.) *Social Research Methods*. London: Routledge.

Kerley, K. and Copes, H. (2004) 'The Effects of Criminal Justice on Employment Stability for White-Collar and Street Level Offenders'. *International Journal of Offender Therapy and Comparative Criminology* 48: 65–84.

King, K.M. (1990) 'Neutralizing Marginally Deviant Behaviour: Bingo Players and Superstition'. *Journal of Gambling Studies* 6(1): 43–61.

King, R.D. (2000) 'Doing Research in Prisons', in R.D. King and E. Wincup (eds) *Doing Research on Crime and Justice*. Oxford: Oxford University Press.

Klockars, C. (1974) *The Professional Fence*. New York: Free Press.

KPMG (2010) *Unfinished Business: Is Fraud Risk Management Used to Its Full Potential?* London: KPMG. Download at: http://www.kpmg.co.uk/pubs/beforepdf.cfm?PubID=3321

Krambia-Kapardis, M. (2001) *Enhancing the Auditor's Fraud Detection Ability: An Interdisciplinary Approach*. Peter Lang: Frankfurt am Main.

Leeson, N. (1996) *Rogue Trader*. London: Little, Brown and Company.

Levi, M. (1987) *Regulating Fraud: White-Collar Crime and the Criminal Process*. London: Tavistock.

Levi, M. (1991) 'Credit and Cheque Card Fraud: Some Victim Survey Data and Their Implications'. *Research Bulletin* 31: 3–8. Home Office Research and Statistics Department.

Levi, M. (2002) 'Suite Justice or Sweet Charity? Some Explorations of Shaming and Incapacitating Business Fraudsters'. *Punishment and Society* 4(2): 147–63.

Levi, M. (2008) *The Phantom Capitalists: The Organisation and Control of Long-Firm Fraud*, 2nd edn. Andover: Ashgate.

Levi, M. and Pithouse, A. (1992) 'The Victims of Fraud', in D. Downes (ed.) *Unravelling Criminal Justice*. London: Macmillan.

Levi, M. and Pithouse, A. (2000) *White Collar Crime and its Victims*. Oxford: Clarendon Press.

Levi, M., Burrows, J., Fleming, M.H. and Hopkins, M. (with the assistance of Matthews, K.) (2007) *The Nature, Extent and Economic Impact of Fraud in the UK*. London: Association of Chief Police Officers.

Lewis, R.V. (2002) *White Collar Crime and Offenders: A 20-Year Longitudinal Cohort Study*. New York: Writers Club Press.

Liebling, A. (1999) 'Doing Research in Prison: Breaking the Silence?' *Theoretical Criminology* 3(2): 147–73.

Lofland, J. (2004) 'Field Notes', in C. Seale (ed.) *Social Research Methods*. London: Routledge.

Mars, G. (1974) 'Dock Pilferage', in P. Rock and M. McIntosh (eds) *Deviance and Social Control*. London: Tavistock.

Martin, C. (2000) 'Doing Research in a Prison Setting', in V. Jupp, P. Davies and P. Francis (eds) *Doing Criminological Research*. London: Sage.

Maruna, S. (1997) 'Going Straight: Desistance from Crime and Life Narratives of Reform', in A. Lieblich and R. Josselson (eds) *The Narrative Study of Lives*. London: Sage.

Maruna, S. (2001) *Making Good: How Ex-Convicts Reform and Rebuild Their Lives*. Washington DC: American Psychological Association Books.

Maruna, S. and Copes, H. (2004) 'Excuses, Excuses: What Have We Learned in Five Decades of Neutralization Research?' *Crime and Justice: A Review of Research* 32: 221–320.

Matza, D. (1964) *Delinquency and Drift*. New York: Wiley.

McBarnet, D. (1991) 'Whiter than White Collar Crime: Tax, Fraud Insurance and the Management of Stigma'. *British Journal of Sociology* 42: 323–44.

McCorkle, L. and Korn, R. (1954) 'Resocialization within Walls'. *The Annals of the American Academy of Political and Social Sciences* 293: 88–98.

McLaughlin, M.L., Cody, M.J. and O'Hair, H.D. (1983) 'The Management of Failure Events: Some Contextual Determinants of Accounting Behavior'. *Human Communication Research* 9: 208–24.

Measor, L. (1985) 'Interviewing: A Strategy in Qualitative Research', in R. Burgess (ed.) *Strategies of Educational Research: Qualitative Methods*. Lewes: Falmer Press.

Milgram, S. (1963) 'Behavioral Study of Obedience'. *Journal of Abnormal Psychology* 67(4): 371–8.

Mills, C.W. (1940) 'Situated Action and the Vocabulary of Motives'. *American Sociological Review* 5: 904–13.

Minor, W.W. (1981) 'Techniques of Neutralisation: A Reconceptualization and Empirical Examination'. *Journal of Research in Crime and Delinquency* 18: 295–318.

Moore, E. and Mills, M. (1990) 'The Neglected Victims and Unexamined Costs of White Collar Crime'. *Crime & Delinquency* 36: 408–18.

National Fraud Authority (2010) *Annual Fraud Indicator*. London: Attorney General Office. http://www.attorneygeneral.gov.uk/nfa/GuidetoInformation/Documents/NFA_fraud_indicator.pdf

Nelken, D. (1994) *The Futures of Criminology*. London: Sage.

Nettler, G. (1982a) *Lying, Cheating, Stealing*. Cincinnati, Ohio: Anderson Publishing.

Nettler, G. (1982b) 'Embezzlement Without Problems'. *British Journal of Criminology* 14: 70–7.

Newman, G.R. and Clarke, R.V. (2003) *Superhighway Robbery: Preventing E-Commerce Crime*. Cullompton: Willan Publishing.

Oakley, A. (1981) 'Interviewing Women: A Contradiction in Terms', in H. Roberts (ed.) *Doing Feminist Research*. London: Routledge and Kegan Paul.

Ogren, R.W. (1973) 'The Ineffectiveness of the Criminal Sanction in Fraud and Corruption Cases: Losing the Battle against White-Collar Crime'. *American Criminal law Review* 11: 959–88.

Passas, N. (1990) 'Anomie and Corporate Deviance'. *Contemporary Crisis* 4: 157–78.

Paternoster, R. and Simpson, S.S. (1993) 'A Rational Choice Theory of Corporate Crime', in R.V. Clarke and M. Felson (eds) *Routine Activities and Rational Choice*. New Brunswick NJ: Transaction.

Payne, B.K. (2003) *Incarcerating White-Collar Offenders*. Springfield Illinois: Thomas.

Pearce, F. (1976) *Crimes of the Powerful*. London: Pluto Press.

Potter, J. and Wetherell, M. (1987) *Discourse and Social Psychology*. London: Sage.

PricewaterhouseCoopers (PwC) (2010) *Fraud in the Public Sector*. London: PwC. Download at: http://www.pwc.co.uk/eng/publications/fraud_in_the_public_sector.html

Proceeds of Crime Act 2002 (c.29) London: HMSO.

Punch, M. (1996) *Dirty Business: Exploring Corporate Misconduct*. London: Sage.

Ribbens, J. (1989) 'Interviewing: An "Unnatural Situation?"' in *Women Studies International Forum* 12: 579–92.

Rosenmerkel, S. (2001) 'Wrongfulness and Harmfulness as Components of White Collar Offences'. *Journal of Contemporary Criminal Justice* 17: 308–27.

Ross, M. (1989) 'Relation of Implicit Theories to the Construction of Personal Histories'. *Psychology Review* 96(2): 341–57.

Rothman, M.L. and Gandossy, R.P. (1982) 'Sad Tales: The Accounts of White-Collar Defendants and the Decision to Sanction'. *Pacific Sociological Review* 25(4): 449–73.

Rubin, H.J. and Rubin, I.S. (1995) *Qualitative Interviewing: The Art of Hearing Data*. Newbury, CA: Sage.

Sakurai, Y. and Smith, R.G. (2003) 'Gambling as a motivation for the commission of financial crime'. *Trends and Issues in Crime and Criminal Justice*, No. 256. Canberra: Australian Institute of Criminology.

Sarbin, T.R. (1994) 'A Criminological Approach to Security Violations', in T. Sarbin, R. Carney and C. Eoyang (eds) *Citizen Espionage: Studies in Trust and Betrayal*. Westport, Connecticut: Praegar.

Scher, S.J. (1989) *The Effects of Apologies and Apology Structure on Social Perception and Social Action*. Unpublished doctoral dissertation: Princeton University.

Schlenker, B.R. (1980) *Impression Management: The Self-Concept, Social Identity, and Interpersonal Relations*. Monterey, CA: Brooks/Cole Publishing.

Schönbach, P. (1980) 'A Category System for Account Phases'. *European Journal of Social Psychology* 10: 195–200.

Schönbach, P. (1985) 'A Taxonomy of Account Phases: Revised, Explained, and Applied'. *Berichte aus der Arbeitseinheit-Soczialpsychologie* [Report from the working unit in social psychology]. Bochum, West Germany: Ruhr-Universität.

Schönbach, P. (1990) *Account Episodes: The Management or Escalation of Conflict*. Cambridge: Cambridge University Press.

Schwartz, R.D. and Scholnick, J.H. (1964) 'Two Studies of Legal Stigma', in H.S. Becker (ed.) *The Other Side*. New York: Free Press.

Scott, D.W. (1989) 'Policing Corporate Collusion'. *Criminology* 27: 559–87.

Scott, M.B. and Lyman, S.M. (1968) 'Accounts'. *American Sociological Review* 33: 46–62.

Shapiro, S.P. (1980) *Thinking About White-Collar Crime: Matters of Conceptualization and Research*. Washington DC: US. Government Printing Office.

Shapiro, S.P. (1990) 'Collaring the Crime, Not the Criminal: Re-Considering the Concept of White-Collar Crime'. *American Sociological Review* 55: 346–65.

Shover, N., Coffey, G.S. and Sanders, C. (2004) 'Dialing for Dollars: Opportunities, Justifications, and Telemarketing Fraud'. *Qualitative Sociology* 27: 55–75.

Shover, N., Fox, G.L. and Mills, M. (1994) 'Long-term Consequences of Victimization by White-Collar Crime'. *Justice Quarterly* 11(1): 75–98.

Shover, N. and Hochstetler, A. (2006) *Choosing White-Collar Crime*. Cambridge: Cambridge University Press.

Sifakis, C. (2001) *Frauds, Deceptions and Swindles*. New York: Checkmark Books.

Silverman, D. (1993) *Interpreting Qualitative Data: Methods for Analysing Talk, Text and Interaction*. London: Sage.

Slapper, G. and Tombs, S. (1999) *Corporate Crime*. London: Longman.

Smith, R.G. (2003) 'Methodological Impediments to Researching Serious Fraud in Australia and New Zealand'. Paper presented at the *Evaluation in Crime and Justice: Trends and Methods Conference* convened by the Australian Institute of Criminology in conjunction with the Australian Bureau of Statistics Canberra 2003 March 24–5.

Smith, R.G., Grabosky, P.N. and Urbas, G. (2004) *Cyber Criminals on Trial*. Cambridge: Cambridge University Press.

Snyder, C. and Higgins, R. (1988) 'Excuses: Their Effective Role in the Negotiation of Reality'. *Psychological Bulletin* 104(1): 23–35.

Soothill, K. (ed.) (1999) *Criminal Conversations: An Anthology of the Work of Tony Parker*. London: Routledge.

Spalek, B. (1999) 'Exploring Victimisation: A Study Looking at the Impact of the Maxwell Scandal Upon the Maxwell Pensioners'. *International Review of Victimology* 6(3): 213–30.

Spalek, B. (2001a) 'Regulation, White-Collar Crime and the Bank of Credit and Commerce International'. *The Howard Journal of Criminal Justice* 40: 166–79.

Spalek, B. (2001b) 'White-Collar Crime Victims and the Issue of Trust'. *The British Criminology Conference: Selected Proceedings Vol. 4*. Papers from the British Society of Criminology Conference, Leicester, July 2000. R. Tarling (ed.), British Society of Criminology.

Spencer, J.C. (1959) 'A Study of Incarcerated White-Collar Offenders', in G. Geis (ed.) *White Collar Criminal*. New York: Atherton Press.

Spradley, J. (2003) 'Asking Descriptive Questions', in M.R. Pogrebin (ed.) *Qualitative Approaches to Criminal Justice: Perspectives from the Field*. Thousand Oaks, CA: Sage.

Steele, C.M. (1988) 'The Psychology of Self-Affirmation: Sustaining the Integrity of the Self', in L. Berkowitz (ed.) *Advances in Experimental Social Psychology* 21: 261–302.

Steffensmeier, D. and Allan, E. (1996) 'Gender and Crime: Towards a Gendered Theory of Female Offending'. *Annual Review of Sociology* 22: 459–87.

Stotland, E. (1977) 'White Collar Criminals'. *Journal of Social Issues* 33: 179–96.

Sutherland, E.H. (1947) *Criminology* (4th edn). Philadelphia: Lippincott.

Sykes, G.M. and Matza, D. (1957) 'Techniques of Neutralisation: A Theory of Delinquency'. *American Sociological Review* 22(6): 664–70.

Tappan, P. (1947) 'Who is the Criminal?' *American Sociology Review* 12: 96–102.

Thurman, Q.C. (1984) 'Deviance and the Neutralization of Moral Commitment: An Empirical Analysis'. *Deviant Behaviour* 5: 291–304.

Tilley, N. (1993) 'The Prevention of Crime Against Small Businesses: The Safer Cities Experience'. *Crime Prevention Unit Series Paper 45*. London: Home Office.

Ting-Toomey, S. (1994) *The Challenge of Facework, Cross-cultural and Interpersonal Issues*. Albany: State University of New York Press.

Vaughan, D. (1983) *Controlling Unlawful Corporate Behaviour*. Chicago: University of Chicago Press.

Vaughan, D. and Carlo, G. (1975) 'The Appliance Repairman: A Study of Victim-Responsiveness and Fraud'. *Journal of Research in Crime and Delinquency* 12: 153–61.

Wall, D.S. (1999) 'Cybercrimes: New Wine, No Bottles?' in P. Davies, P. Francis and V. Jupp (eds) *Invisible Crimes*. London: Macmillan.

Wall, D.S. (2007) *Cybercrime: The Transformation of Crime in the Information Age*. Cambridge: Polity.

Wall, D.S. (2009) *Crime and Deviance in Cyberspace*. Aldershot: Ashgate.

Weisburd, D., Waring, E. with Chayet, E.F. (2001) *White-Collar Crime and Criminal Careers*. Cambridge: Cambridge University Press.

Weisburd, D., Wheeler, S., Waring, E. and Bode, N. (1991) *Crimes of the Middle Classes: White-collar Offenders in the Federal Courts*. New Haven, CT: Yale University Press.

Wheeler, S., Weisburd, D. and Bode, N. (1982) 'Sentencing the White Collar Offender: Rhetoric And Reality'. *The American Sociological Review* 47: 641–59.

Wikstrom, P.H. (2006) 'Individuals, Settings, and Acts of Crime: Situational Mechanisms and the Explanation of Crime', in P.H. Wikstrom and R. Sampson (eds) *The Explanation of Crime*. Cambridge: Cambridge University Press.

Willott, S., Griffin, C. and Torrance, M. (2001) 'Snakes and Ladders: Upper-Middle Class Male Offenders Talk About Economic Crime'. *Criminology* 39(2): 441–66.

Wolfe, D.T. and Hermanson, D.R. (2004) 'The Fraud Diamond: Considering the Four Elements of Fraud'. *The CPA Journal* 74(12): 38–42.

Wortman, C. (1976) 'Casual Attributes and Personal Control'. *New Directions in Attribution Research*, Vol. 1.

Zeitlin, L.R. (1971) 'A Little Larceny Can Do a Lot for Employee Morale'. *Psychology Today* 5: 22, 24, 26, 64.

Zietz, D. (1981) *Women Who Embezzle or Defraud: A Study of Convicted Felons*. New York: Praeger.

Index